Global Business Leadership

Global Business Leadership

E.S. Wibbeke
A Book in the *Managing Cultural Differences Series*

AMSTERDAM • BOSTON • HEIDELBERG • LONDON • NEW YORK • OXFORD
PARIS • SAN DIEGO • SAN FRANCISCO • SINGAPORE • SYDNEY • TOKYO
Butterworth-Heinemann is an imprint of Elsevier

Butterworth-Heinemann is an imprint of Elsevier
Linacre House, Jordan Hill, Oxford OX2 8DP, UK
30 Corporate Drive, Suite 400, Burlington, MA 01803, USA

First edition 2009

British Library Cataloguing in Publication Data
A catalogue record for this book is available from the British Library

Library of Congress Cataloging-in-Publication Data
A catalog record for this book is available from the Library of Congress

ISBN: 978-0-7506-8408-8

For information on all Butterworth-Heinemann publications
visit our website at www.elsevierdirect.com

Typeset by Charon Tec Ltd., A Macmillan Company. (www.macmillansolutions.com)

Printed and bound in United States of America
09 10 11 12   10 9 8 7 6 5 4 3 2 1

Global Business Leadership is dedicated to my mother, Rose. She was the best example of leadership I have ever seen.
If given half the chance, she could have ruled the world. She always did what was right with what was left.

I also dedicate this book to the steadfast commitment of Michael, a person of unparalleled patience.

Contents

1

Failure to Survive 1. New Challenges for Leaders 2. New Challenges for Organizations 5. Paradigm Shift 7. How Interdependent Are We As a Global Village? 7. Why is Culture Such a Big Deal? 9. Leadership Evolving 11. New Roles for Leaders 11. What are the Implications of All This Change for Global Business Leaders? 14. Seven Key Principles of a New Leadership Paradigm 17. Framing Context 17. The Journey to New Leadership Frontiers 20. The Bottom Line 21.

2

Defining the Indefinable 23. Dimensions and Patterns of Culture 26. The Effect of Culture on Leadership and Organizations 30. A Briefing on Western Leadership Theory 31. The Essentialist Perspective 35. The Contextualist Perspective 39. The Culture–Leadership Link and Intercultural Leadership Competency 42. Prior Research on Intercultural Leadership Competency 44. The Bottom Line 45.

3

Taking the High Ground 55. Ethics of Purpose (Teleology) 56. Ethics of Principle (Deontology) 56. Ethics of Consequence (Utilitarianism) 57.

4

The Principle of "Communication" 81

5

The Principle of "Consciousness" 99

6

The Principle of "Contrasts" 113

7

The Principle of "Context" 141

Acknowledgement

Throughout my journey in the global business world, I have encountered countless individuals who continue to inspire me with their generosity and knowledge. These include: Dr. George Simons, Dr. Robert Moran, Dr. Geert Hofstede, Dr. Geert Jan Hofstede, and Dr. Paul Pedersen. I have also been incredibly lucky to have worked with many outstanding individuals who include: Wes Kashiwagi, Alison Tanaka, David Wisz, Jane Dodge, Aram Ordubegian, Ashley Houk, Alan Richter, Garry Shirts, Alexandra Fenzl, Rich Kuslan, Gary Robinson, Mary Connerley, LuEllen Schafer, John Sheridan, Karina Jensen, and Jennifer Woo. My editor, Ailsa Marks at Elsevier, has been most helpful. I have also been blessed with the invaluable mentorship of Dr. Philip Harris. Most of all, it is with the continued support of John Sheridan, James Sheridan, and Dr. Cynthia Loubier with which this book has come to fruition.

Foreword

One might question whether, following more than a dozen volumes in this *Managing Cultural Differences Series* edited by Drs. Philip R. Harris and Robert T. Moran, there remains fertile ground to be ploughed regarding cultural differences and their impact on the effectiveness of "global leaders." The answer, as this book illustrates, is "Yes." Dr. Wibbeke clearly has advanced the discussion in both theoretical and practical areas.

It is not difficult to discern patterns of change in the content of "leadership" and "management" studies over the past 40 years. It would be helpful if there were conveniently universal definitions for these two terms. In my mind, "management" focuses more on task definition, resource allocation, and organizational design. "Leadership" is involved more with vision, motivation, and trust. Both call for competence in core skills, commitment to desired organizational outcomes, high levels of personal energy, and considerable emotional resilience. Both require some degree of empathy for colleagues and strangers. For sustained success, both demand adherence to an ethical code whose implementation precludes the erosion of trust and confidence within a team or across cultures. In reality, managing and leading are inseparable components of practice.

The existence of this series of books confirms a basic trend in approaching leader development. That is the notion that productive, healthy adults who have earned positions of responsibility require continuing education to facilitate career success. Today, in response to this notion, there are not dozens but hundreds of seminars and workshops dedicated to "cross-cultural leadership," available from Fontainebleau to Minneapolis to Shanghai.

If one change in focus and content of leader development efforts over the years is the notably increased attention to continuous learning in the executive and middle manager ranks, a second and closely related issue—also mentioned in a variety of discussions by Dr. Wibbeke—is the recognition of the power of awareness, both self and contextual, as foundations for leader competence and growth. Recognition of the role of self-knowledge is surely not new. From Socrates to Shakespeare and beyond, it was there. However, serious attention to the issue remains erratic. The idea of spending time and money developing "awareness" in the already "successful," busy people who are candidates for cross-cultural adventures are not always well received. "Self-awareness," a cousin to "self-reflection," is the unique ingredient leading to personal growth and change—the lubricant for learning. Unaware of our proclivities, biases, strengths, or shortcomings, it is difficult to improve as leaders. The most highly regarded leader development programs—understanding that measuring "effectiveness" in any educational program is problematic—are those with a strong component of individually tailored behavioral feedback.

Excursions into the need for cross-cultural sensitivity, with deference to the particular role of empathy, are rightly predicated on the reality that the internal needs and drives of "global leaders" are critical to the discussion. The degree of challenge involved in enhancing cross-cultural effectiveness is related to the prevailing gap between the environmental complexity and the operable level of individual competencies. Whether or not the hard-wired narcissists can escape from their impediments through any kind of educational intervention is debatable. Modifying the adult personality to increase the probability for success in diverse settings generally requires an emotionally healthy person to begin with. The odds of renovating a self-centered adult bully seem low.

The second part of "awareness," also specifically addressed in this tour through which Dr. Wibbeke's new book, *Global Business Leadership*, leads us is the capability of individuals to sense the nuances of context. Such recognition of social and interpersonal circumstance depends on a deeper understanding of the local climate than that which might be gained by a course on social protocol. While a training course in local customs might suffice to permit a talented American lobbyist to function for a few weeks in Beijing, the necessary capacity of a true "global leader" to build sturdy relationships, create teams, and establish trust demands a more sophisticated intellectual and emotional intervention. Such topics include comparative ethics; the impact of local and regional governments; the constraints of family, religion, and clan; and the translated pressures of international politics on regional business practices. It is, however, the crucial self-awareness attribute that permits these topics to penetrate our personal armor and craft deeper understanding of the external environment. Such understanding of course is the catalyst for cross-cultural success. As we discuss requirements for cross-cultural effectiveness, it becomes clear that the basic elements of awareness are also cornerstones for solid leadership and management at home. The reality is that not all of our leaders and managers working exclusively in the domestic environment have acquired the skills for routine success on their home field. Perhaps their working on the fresher, more tangible and fashionable challenges of cross-cultural business will stimulate interest in good leadership in general.

We might note also that much of today's global setting is significantly "Anglicized." It is sometimes difficult to conduct business in a local non-English mode. Native competence in English seems commonly superior to American efforts to master another dialect. Many cross-cultural workshops in Europe and Asia are conducted in English. There are more Chinese studying English than there are Americans and British learning English. In venues from the air traffic control system to the World Bank, English is prevalent. American business people have succeeded in many areas of international commerce, including membership on the boards of major corporations headquartered outside the United States. The stereotype of American executives as typically fumbling among foreign compatriots seems increasingly inaccurate, even as any level of gouache behavior appears to be less tolerable. In other words, we are not starting from a zero base in enhancing cross-cultural effectiveness. However, the issue demands continuing attention as cultural and international diversity touch increasingly more lives, and international expectations for empathetic competence rise.

As we deal with issues of individual effectiveness in the global marketplace, Dr. Wibbeke and others have explored the notion of a common set of principles and behaviors ("behaviors" are more important!) that could facilitate leader success regardless of context. Both Dr. Bernard Bass and Dr. David Campbell, for example, have found in their research certain behaviors, such as those resulting in inspirational leadership and intellectual stimulation, to be, with modest local adaptation, quite universal in their positive impact in a wide variety of settings. From a weak anecdotal base, my own conclusion would be also that some basic assumptions of Western approaches to leading find traction in foreign settings. I noted, for example, the reaction of Vietnamese soldiers to various styles of leadership. They seemed to respond positively to four classic leader attributes that we have taught in American military schools for decades: (1) Be competent in core skills. (In that environment it was my providing and directing rotary-wing and fixed-wing aviation support at the right place and time.) (2) Be willing to share risk and hardship. (We all slung our hammocks between trees, ate the same cold rice balls, and went out on the exposed landing zone to welcome helicopters.) (3) Keep people informed; and avoid surprises whenever possible. (We told them in as much detail as possible—noting certain linguistic obstacles—what the plans were for tomorrow, including what we thought the weather and the enemy might have in mind.) (4) Listen to what others have to say. (Indigenous soldiers on the march don't pretend to be strategists. But they may know a lot about the local enemy, and which bugs will crawl inside the eyelets of your boots. Further, most seem to appreciate an opportunity to be heard—which may at times differ from the local hierarchical culture!) I don't find it difficult to believe that the essence of those four behaviors is relevant for the "global leader."

It is possible to overdose on local culture, to imbibe too deeply of customs and practices that can compromise personal or corporate values. Here again we can confront the issue of short- versus long-term orientation. When a customary "gift" to inspecting officials could provide immediate business reward, the savvy manager weighs very seriously the potential for strategic embarrassment later on. There are times to respond promptly to ambient expectations of form and protocol. Indiscriminate deference to local norms, however, can be a recipe for future disaster. Most responsible business people worldwide understand this. Codes of ethics are, ultimately, pragmatic pathways to accomplishment.

This book is replete with vital information supporting success in both personal growth and business productivity. Naturally, the definition and measurement of "success" itself remains a germinal issue. A reading of Dr. Wibbeke's thoughtful work should stimulate, reflection on the meaning of "success" at home and in the global marketplace.

Walter F. Ulmer, Jr.
Lieutenant General, U.S. Army (Retired)
Former Commandant of Cadets at West Point
Former President and CEO, Center for Creative Leadership
Moneta, Virginia, U.S.A.

Prologue

"I think I can work with any of them."
—Carlos Slim Helu, World's Wealthiest Individual

The greatest challenge facing leaders in this era of globalization is working effectively through cultural barriers to achieve business goals and objectives. Although U.S. corporations have been expanding across international boundaries for decades, the rapid global advance of technology, especially the Internet, as well as changes in investment processes and trade relationships, has eliminated previous barriers, thus opening markets and necessitating an even greater level of competence. The risk of not possessing the appropriate organizational capability, specifically in leadership, is great. This book seeks to provide U.S. business leaders with a cultural roadmap to navigate these vast oceans of cultural differences through leadership styles. I hope its content and strategies will prove useful to leaders in all business professions as well as students of international commerce. Finally, may this volume further the leadership competencies of leaders in business-related fields who seek to understand how cultural understanding is key to uncovering new global opportunities.

Global Business Leadership examines the dynamic role of leadership from an intercultural perspective. Learning about how other cultures both define and exert leadership is crucial in gaining and maintaining market share. Intercultural knowledge in this sense denotes how other cultures approach concepts such as ambiguity and change—the means to the unspoken side of business. Today's leaders are confronted with a plethora of published data about both their colleagues and competitors, however such information does not begin to cover the ways others form opinions or make decisions. Such intangible concepts can only be grasped through stepping back and examining the cultural underpinnings of another's background and development. The latter is done by making the connections between what a culture values and how it views leadership. Only through the committed exchange of ideas with diverse constituencies will U.S. leaders begin to cross the cultural divide growing in the global business arena.

In addition, past research pointed to specific competency variables without detailed explanations and input from intercultural participating experts. This author's doctoral dissertation presented such intercultural feedback. Pedersen and Connerley determined that most leadership literature focused on data obtained from study participants and researchers from the United States, whereas this dissertation encompassed feedback from intercultural researchers from Africa, the Americas, Asia, Europe, and the Middle East. Further, in this book, there is a unique perspective on the new global workforce. This book is aimed at undergraduate and graduate business students, as well as career professionals, and current and future leaders of commerce.

Knowledge leaders of today are operating in a flat world. Physical borders have been dropped across trading zones, such as the European Union and Mercosur, and leaders deal daily with multiple groups in numerous countries, both online and offline. The Internet has become the great equalizer where small firms can appear large and where the attainment of knowledge becomes currency. Competent global leaders become great assets to their organizations when they can improve their global shrewdness consistently through interaction with their diverse business counterparts around the world.

What consultants in global business have failed to thus far is to connect effectively culture to leadership in the U.S. definitively. Further, they have not sufficiently linked leadership development to cross-cultural understanding, especially as it relates to globalization. This text attempts to address these issues and inadequacies within the present framework of a globally competent leader. This matter will be discussed in this volume because it helps to improve communications, increase effectiveness, and enable leaders to be both more understanding and more understood across boundaries.

The GLOBE project delved into the connection between culture and leadership and its work is ongoing. The work by the GLOBE project on international management research features contributions from many middle managers from numerous organizations in over a multitude of countries. The project's publications present a collection of global research addressing the culture of particular countries, and recommendations on how managers should conduct business in these countries. All of the work done by GLOBE is being facilitated by means of various publications, through print and electronic media. By creating sustainable prosperity worldwide, the informed leader who competently operates across cultures can always be at home, despite the business destination.

Global Business Leadership is organized into 10 chapters. The first chapter discusses the challenges facing both leaders and organizations and the paradigm of a changing global landscape. The seven key principles of this new leadership paradigm entitled the Geoleadership Model follows. The second chapter provides in-depth definitions of both culture and leadership and how competency in both realms is inextricably linked. The third chapter focuses on the first concept of the Geoleadership Model: care; and introduces the first case study of the book. The fourth chapter highlights the principle of communication and looks at how an organization such as Wal-Mart delivers its message globally. The fifth chapter discusses the variable of consciousness and how self-reflection by a leader can lead to greater cultural adaptability. The sixth chapter investigates the idea of contrasting worldviews and how such meaning is interpreted differently in other cultures. The seventh chapter hones in on the leading within context of a given situation. The eighth chapter describes how leaders must retain an adaptive global mindset and remain flexible when confronted with the increasing speed of organizational change. The ninth chapter concentrates on the importance of a leader's learning agility in remaining capable of thriving in a global space.

The epilogue summarizes and updates the book's principal messages. It underscores our belief that culturally competent leaders are essential globalists and change agents in the global marketplace. In the conclusion, we propose that leaders in the era of globalization combine the seven principles of the Geoleadership Model to increase their competence: care, communication, consciousness, contrasts, context, change, and capability. The rationale of this work is that the globally competent leader embodies all seven of these principles and practices them consistently while leading an organization with global reach.

The following definitions serve to delineate the intended meanings of certain concepts presented in this book:

- *American and North American*: For the purposes of this book, the term *American* refers strictly to the United States.
- *Competence/Competency/Competencies*: The term *competence* reflects a specific range of skill, knowledge, or ability.
- *Cross-cultural*: The terms *cross-cultural, global, intercultural,* and *international* will appear interchangeably to describe variables relevant to many cultures around the world.
- *Culture*: The term *Culture* reflects the learned and shared knowledge, beliefs, and rules of social groups that influence behavior.
- *Global Leadership*: The term *Global leadership* reflected the act and art of creating shared meaning and action that led to achieving desired results across global boundaries.

Intercultural: Please see *cross-cultural* above

- *Leadership*: How an individual influences others to act for certain goals that represent the values and the motivations of both leaders and followers.
- *Situational Leadership*: It reflects how the external environment and situation exerted influence on a leader's behavior.

When global leaders or would-be leaders appreciate the concepts and interdependence of the seven Geoleadership principles, then the transformation of mindsets and organizations can occur. Essentially this book on Geoleadership is a further discussion on the topic of organizational leadership, which stemmed from my doctoral dissertation entitled *Intercultural Leadership Competencies for U.S. Business Leaders in the New Millennium*. A select panel of intercultural experts provided consensus on what exact global leadership competencies were necessary for U.S. business leaders in the globalized marketplace. This dissertation appears to be the first research on intercultural leadership competencies solely on the World Wide Web. This showed that this research does not require participating experts to interact in face-to-face communications, which made the method useful in conducting surveys with qualified participants in a global arena.

In conclusion, the doctoral research and subsequent work for this book, *Global Business Leadership*, stems from my professional experience as a cross-cultural consultant and my desire to continue writing on the fusion of culture and leadership. In addition, as a child of immigrants to the United States, I have always been keenly aware of "living between cultures" and trying to take one mindset and adapt it to be effective with others of different mindsets. As a confirmed globalist, I am optimistic that this book will demonstrate the incredible value of seeing the cultural foundation of decision-making and how leaders committed to learning this will only thrive in this time of global change. As an educator, I am convinced that my message is relevant across borders.

E.S. Wibbeke
La Jolla, California, U.S.

1

Geoleadership Challenges

This is the most important time in human history. Other times thought they were it. They were wrong. This is it.

—Jean Houston

Failure to Survive

It may be a small world, but are we worlds apart? Increasing globalization has created greater complexity for those leading and managing organizations.[1] More accurately, globalization has created an awareness of the complexity that was always there but not recognized. Now, there is no choice. Leaders at all levels of organizations, and especially those at higher levels, must work across national and cultural boundaries to achieve goals and objectives. Corporations have been expanding for decades across international boundaries, and the rapid advance of technology worldwide as well as the growing complexity of investment processes and trade relationships have eliminated barriers. Opening markets requires an even greater level of competence. The risk of not possessing the appropriate organizational competence, specifically in leadership, is enormous.[2] How big is the problem?

The conservative estimate is that fully 70% of global business ventures worldwide fail due to the mismanagement of intercultural differences.[3]

While business opportunities are increasing with globalization, so is the demand for leaders who possess new competencies.[4] In order to remain competitive, global business leaders need to be able to adapt to diverse national, organizational, and professional cultures.[5] What is more, leaders must be aware of the pitfalls of working in global contexts and the potential risk of lost opportunities.

New Challenges for Leaders

Leaders of today face new challenges including communicating and interacting across regional, national, ethnic, cultural, language, and legal boundaries; dealing with and implementing continual change; coping with increased ambiguity; negotiating and resolving conflict; motivating a multicultural workforce; and in some cases managing a foreign assignment and living as an expatriate.[6] The challenge is how to manage multiple, simultaneous cultural identities. A leader who can accommodate and master these challenges practices what we refer to as Geoleadership.

Interpersonal communication and interactions pose several leadership challenges for intercultural leaders and managers. Differences in language, and in cultural preferences for pace, social penetration, intonation, spatial distance, implicit versus explicit styles, and more all play a role in the success or failure of any intercultural communication.

Communication technology presents challenges for leaders working in intercultural contexts. Instant communication technology connects the globe, providing businesspersons with unprecedented opportunities. Consultants can log on and instantly connect with clients in London, Paris, or Istanbul. Managers can instantly videoconference with their counterparts in South Africa and can transfer documents around the world in seconds. Workers know that when they send a PowerPoint presentation to Saudi Arabia, their counterparts will be able to open it with a click. The seemingly worldwide acceptance and use of "common" technologies, both hardware and software, creates an illusion of familiarity.

However, although a significant portion of the world uses Microsoft Windows, it is not safe to assume that all people have the same values or face the same issues. In reality, our computer operating systems may be one of the few things that humanity has in common. There is a risk in our overreliance on technology to solve all of our problems. After all, more plumbing does not increase the quality of our water. Rather, it should be noted, the most effective flow results from the proper development and adjustment of the entire system.

Reflect for a minute about the variety of cultures there are just within the United States, sometimes within the same city. Los Angeles has a different feel about it than New York. In San Francisco, the Italian-American neighborhood of North Beach is quite different from that same city's Chinatown district. Suburbs and urban centers certainly have noticeable differences.

These settings are different because they make up what is referred to as sub-cultures: cultures within cultures with perhaps small but distinctive differences. Some of these subcultures are based on ethnicity, while others vary more because of profession or economic status. Ethnographic, demographic (age, gender, residence), status (educational, social, economic), and affiliation (formal and informal) all are combined in cultural identity.

Yet the issue is much broader than just the diversity encountered in today's domestic workforce. In organizations today, workforce diversity means working across national and geographic boundaries, with employees from various countries reporting to a manager in yet another country. The business leader of today is dealing with the world. The tendency of American business leaders to emphasize getting to "back end" results quickly while most of the world's cultures emphasize "front end" loading has proved costly.

Someone once quipped that the "only good *change*, is the change rattling in your pocket.[7]" Amusing as that statement is, the implicit message is that change is okay when it belongs to you as an individual, when it is your idea; however, when change happens to you, it is not as easy a proposition. The cliché of the early nineties that "change is constant" is now passé.

In this global business marketplace gone is the illusion of certainty. Organizational life for leaders and managers is fraught with *ambiguity*. There is no cradle-to-tomb employment agreements. Technologies replace and obsolete each other minute by minute rather than decade by decade, or year by year. Industries that were once considered stable industries are no longer. The entire life cycle of a single economy can elapse before your child reaches preschool. Leaders do not have the luxury of taking for granted anything once thought of as material.

A Little Straight Talk from the Managerial Trenches

You understand that our concept of time has changed if you manage a global team of workers; with reports in Rio de Janeiro, Toronto, Sydney, Grenoble, Milan, Dusseldorf, Punjab, Singapore, and Istanbul, who interact with a business partner in Taiwan. You have a weekly teleconference on Monday morning; but, when is Monday morning?

You are past "change as a constant" when you have been hired by one mega-corporation, survived a company split, a merger (which was really an acquisition), led a divisional downsizing, were spun-off, then became an allied business, were promoted 4 times, reported to 12 different executives, had your office relocated 5 times, lived on two continents simultaneously, all within 30 months and while sitting at the same desk. You are also past the old "change management" models.

Learning how to interact in other cultures takes effort beyond just learning another culture's language. For the American business leader operating in another culture, interaction requires a deeper cultural understanding about how things are done. Additionally, there are certain leader roles that, by themselves, require a high level of skill. One such skill is *negotiating*. The fact is cultures vary in perceptions about negotiating; some frown of it, especially in certain situations, while other cultures rely on it as an integral aspect of any business exchange. Mismatches commonly occur between culturally different individuals due to misunderstandings about discretionary power, about what is and is not negotiable. Another issue frequently blocking negotiations between culturally different individuals is approach. For example, cultures that adopt "positive face" will display sociability and solidarity in their interaction style, often using informality, friendliness, and use of first names to show "inclusiveness" or lack of distance. This approach may create a sense of uneasiness for members of a culture whose approach is to adopt a position of "negative face," showing deference and distance to other parties for fear of offending them or threatening their face. The concept of "face" refers to a person's public self-image, that which they desire to present to others. Positive face comes from a desire for appreciation and approval from others. Negative face is the desire to not be imposed on or to impose upon others.[8] The concept of "face" as a projected public image can be found across most cultures.

When people do not have a common frame of reference—as is found within a culture—misunderstandings, *conflict*, and productivity problems tend to arise. A manager described a situation within his team: individual members tend to support members from their own culture and consistently clash with team members from other cultures. An atmosphere of tension and hostility pervaded the team and without intervention resulted in business loss. Conflict resolution is yet another aspect of intercultural business relationships, as with negotiating, that requires a high level of knowledge. The majority of intercultural conflicts are caused by misunderstandings about differing norms, styles, communication rhythms, values, and approach.

Motivation presents a dual challenge for intercultural business leaders. On one level, *motive*, which is directly linked with values, possesses a test of a leader's ability to understand what causes someone to do what they do. On a related level, providing a motivational work environment for employees who are different in their needs and expectations requires that a leader accurately interpret situations and respond in a culturally acceptable manner. What worked well in one culture does not guarantee success in another culture.

The strategy of sending American corporate leaders and managers abroad for *foreign assignments* is not new. Increasingly, however, corporations recruit leaders and managers to take foreign assignments to solve dicey business problems in their overseas locations. An entire consulting industry has sprung up in the United States to serve organizations that need to maximize the success of these personnel decisions because the success rate in the recent past has been poor. The chief reason for the lack of success is due to culture clash–managers are sent to foreign cultures with a mandate to "fix the problem" only to encounter a culture with a different mind-set.[9] If you can experience culture shock, as an American, traveling two states over, or from one telephone interaction to another, imagine what you would feel, as a unilingual American manager with no previous travel outside the United States, when your corporation transfers you to an overseas assignment in Taiwan. For example, when American Field Service (AFS) selects high school students to go abroad they "select students who have (1) proven ability to fail (2) a sense of humor, and (3) a low goal-task orientation." Task-oriented people tend to have more difficulty adjusting in an unfamiliar culture.

New Challenges for Organizations

In an increasingly competitive global marketplace, companies are under pressure to develop competitive market strategies, develop products in increasingly short development timeframes, reduce operating expenses, and, at the same time, increase market share. With traditional market differentiation limited, many companies strive to increase their competitive advantage in extraordinary ways. New companies are entering the global market seeking to understand what competitive advantage means in a crowded quixotic economy.[10] Most companies realize that the ability to create or acquire human capital or talent assets can provide a singular competitive advantage. Leadership talent may be *the critical driver* of corporate performance and a company's ability to maintain competitive advantage far into the future.[11]

Read any respected business magazine, business journal, or website sponsored by a respected business school producing MBA graduates, and what you will find is a phenomenal level of agreement on two things related to global business. "Specifically, one, that such leaders are in short supply, and, two that intercultural leaders require an entirely new and broader set of skills".

Competent leaders are in short supply chiefly because of demographic trends and because the job demands and requirements have expanded.[12] Currently, the United States is producing too few leaders with comprehensive international perspectives and experiences to meet the demands.[13] With current demographic trends, including the upcoming retirements of many "baby boomers" (i.e. people born between 1946 and 1964), the U.S. leadership talent shortage is projected to continue into the next several decades.[14] However, as Exhibit 1.1 illustrates, the talent shortage has gone global.

Exhibit 1.1

___

The World is Our Oyster

The outsourcing boom shows no sign of slowing. Gartner, a research firm estimates that global spending on IT outsourcing will rise from $193 billion in 2004 to $260 billion in 2009. However, there are caveats. The most important is that Indian-based companies themselves are encountering severe skills shortages. Wage inflation in India's IT sector is about 16% a year, and turnover is 40%. NASSCOM predicts that India's IT sector will face a shortfall of 500,000 professionals by 2010. GE Capital has posted signs in its Indian offices saying, "Trespassers will be recruited." Skills shortages are at their most acute among managers. Several Indian companies have had to bring in Western CEOs: the Tata Group, for example, has put Raymond Bickson, a Hawaiian, in charge of its hotel business. Good middle managers are rare: annual wage increases for project managers in IT have averaged 23% a year over the past 4 years.

The looming skills shortage and the drive upmarket have made companies obsessive about finding and holding on to the right people. They are investing heavily in education and training, partly to attract the best talent and partly to keep their existing workers up to speed. "We're investing in training like the Dickens," says Nandan Nilekani, Infosys's CEO. The company has increased its training budget from $100 million to $125 million. It has also moved one of its board members, T. V. Mohandas Pai, from chief financial officer to director of human resources to show that it is serious. In the year to March 2006 Infosys screened 1.4 million applications, tested 164,000 applicants, and interviewed 48,700 to make 21,000 appointments. Companies are also getting much more imaginative about identifying new sources of talent. Wipro has different training programs for different talent pools including one to help people get a university degree while working for the company. Mr. Pai describes Infosys as a "human-capital supply-chain company." But to keep the supply chain going, India must improve its universities.

Excerpted from and permission granted: Talent Survey, October 7, 2006, The Economist print edition.

___

Currently, scarcely one-third of U.S. graduate level business schools offers international degree specialization and only 39 American graduate business institutions provide leadership degree programs. Yet, leadership roles demand a profound understanding of particular languages and cultures, including those from where danger might arise.[15]

It is no longer enough to possess leadership skills learned from a domestic education or experience.[16] Corporate boards and stockholders increasingly rely on their executives and managers to navigate the tangled jungle of global business. American employees outfitted with only their professionally oriented degrees and experience rely on their leaders and managers to guide them through the complexity of intercultural contexts.[17] Companies must not only equip their leaders with additional skills, they must prepare leaders to navigate varied ethnic, religious, national, and cultural contexts to meet worldwide business demands.[18]

Paradigm Shift

In a recent survey of 130 fortune 500 firm executives across Europe, North America (United States and Canada), and Asia, 85% did not feel that they had an adequate number of intercultural leaders and 67% thought that their existing leaders needed additional skills and knowledge before they could even meet needed capabilities.[19] So what exactly is going on here?

The reality is that the leadership approach of the 20th century is as obsolete as the word processor. In an interview, former GE CEO Jack Welch had this to say:

> "The Jack Welch of the future cannot be like me. I spent my entire career in the United States. The next head of General Electric will be somebody who spent time in Bombay, in Hong Kong, in Buenos Aires. We have to send our best and brightest overseas and make sure that they have the training that will allow them to be the intercultural leaders who will make GE flourish in the future."
>
> —Jack Welch[20]

Perhaps Mr. Welch, who is known as a visionary, is on to something. Implicit in his statement is that American companies cannot expect to operate their businesses from within foreign markets without intimately "knowing" those markets. In the past, international companies did business with foreign markets (i.e. sold goods abroad), but that is a different proposition than opening or moving business segment operations to foreign soil. Global business is more complex than simply marketing goods in overseas markets.

How Interdependent Are We As a Global Village?

If you think that you are untouched by globalization, think again. Today, roughly two-thirds of all companies, worldwide, all companies worldwide compete globally. As is clear from the global expansion maps included in Figure 1.1, an extraordinary amount of expansion has occurred during the last 30 years.

Not only are North American companies expanding abroad, but also foreign interests have bought into North American companies, and foreign companies are expanding operations in the United States and Canada.[21] For example, French tire maker, Michelin, earns 37% of its revenue from the United States and has operations within North America. However,

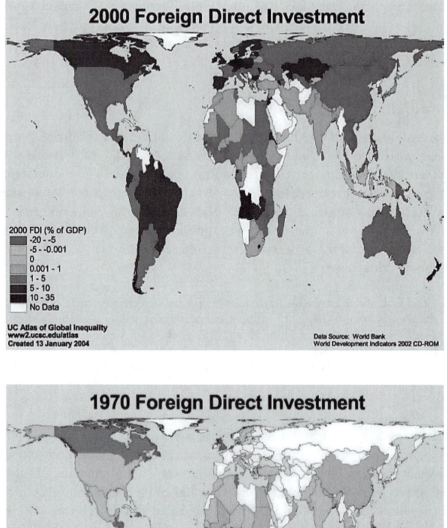

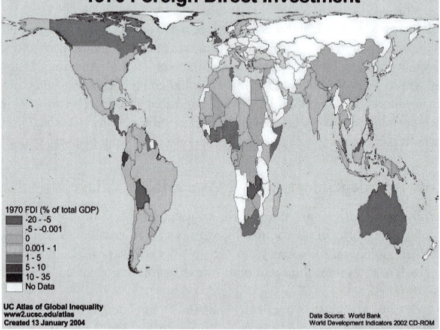

Figure 1.1 2000 Foreign Direct Investment; 1970 Foreign Direct Investment
Source: Excerpted from and Permission granted. UCSC Atlas of Global, Inequality, January 13, 2004, www.ucsc.edu/atlas.

globalization works both ways. Consider that Microsoft makes 52% of its revenue from overseas markets and has operations on foreign soil. Moreover, we have a tendency to forget that organizations like Burger King are now foreign owned. We are truly living in the age of *globalization* with ever-expanding networks of competition and increasing levels of interdependence on resource supplies and products all of which transcend national boundaries. *Global organizations*, then, are those that produce and sell goods or services in more than one country, have operations in foreign markets and have established interdependencies, such as suppliers, who are foreign-based.[22]

The problem is that American companies needing to solve costly business problems abroad find themselves in a quandary, namely, how to entice U.S. managers (men and women) to leave their home country, uprooting their families, to relocate half a world away to some culture they previously had only read about in magazines or seen glamorized in a Hollywood movie. Enticements generally consist of bonuses and the promise of promotion. However, research shows that only 10% are promoted, while 60% receive demotions, with another 25% leaving the company.[23] What we do not know is whether the manager ever rated a promotion; what we do know is that companies have transferred the countless of managers with little or no preparation.[24] What we are just beginning to deal with is determining the right preparation.

In addition to extraordinary business leadership skills, a leader now needs cultural intelligence. Cultural intelligence requires transcending one's own cultural background to interact with diverse and unknown intelligences.[25] People with high cultural intelligence are able to discern what true behaviors represent for individuals and groups compared to which behaviors are not universal or aberrational.[26] The gap between the universal and the aberrational is what we call culture.[27] Having this level of competence requires a comprehensive understanding of intercultural distinctions. Moreover, intercultural competence requires a highly developed sense of awareness to discern the global as well as the local similarities and distinctions within each context and within truly intercultural contexts.

Why is Culture Such a Big Deal?

When we operate from an ethnocentric worldview, we develop perspectives and beliefs that we hold to be true. This is only natural. However, it can quickly feel unnatural when you encounter the customs, values, and laws of people from other cultures, who also hold their perspectives and beliefs to be true. Therein lays the dilemma. Nobody is right; nobody is wrong, just different! The simple truth is, culture is important because culture controls our life with or without our permission.

Leading across national boundaries is no small task. We know from Geert Hofstede's cultural research[28] and E. T. Hall's research on language[29] people differ across cultures along certain dimensions, such as individualism versus collectivism, power distance, short- versus long-term orientation, time orientation, and patterns and pace of speech to name a few. Moreover, research has demonstrated that differences occur within cultures, too. Even within a national culture, there are regional variations between individuals relative to the culture as a whole. This can be due to many things including immigration, and regional, ethnic, and political differences.

The world is a very different place beyond your country's borders. In 2004, there were more than 200 nations and 5000 ethnic groups.[30] Two-thirds of these countries possess at least one significant minority—an ethnic or religious group that comprises at least 10% of the population. The key to being successful in international business is recognizing how different things are and doing the homework necessary to understand with whom you are doing business.[31] Exhibit 1.2 presents a recent situation that serves as a good example: Google Goes to China.

Exhibit 1.2

When in China, Do as Google Did?

Google is a staple of most everyone's computer environment. Google is popular because the company's technology works and it gives web surfers what they want. The company is the epitome of "dot.com" success. They are the company that stood up to the U.S. government to protect privacy and their motto is "Don't do Evil."

Recently, Google leadership decided to widen its reach by entering the Chinese Internet market. In their negotiations with the Chinese government, Google faced the challenge of censorship. Simply put, the Chinese government made it clear that doing Internet business in China meant complying with Chinese policies.

The Chinese government has been blocking websites for years and Google decided to comply with the government's standards to make searching easier. It is anticipated that sites discussing Tiananmen Square, freedom for Tibet, or other politically sensitive subjects will be blocked from Chinese users. Long time Google enthusiasts were angry, some even calling for a boycott. How vehement was the criticism in the United States?

Google's launch of a new, self-censored search engine in China is a "black day" for freedom of expression—*Reporters without Borders*[32]
  Adapted from: http://news.bbc.co.uk/1/hi/technology/4647398.stm

Arguably, censorship is against what the American culture stands for; so how can one of the newly crowned U.S. business icons bend to the Communist government's command?

(Continued)

Exhibit 1.2   (Continued)

From Google's standpoint the question is: "How could they not?"
With over 1 billion people, China is not a market to be ignored by any global organization. To do so would simply be shortsighted. Google felt that it had to make this compromise in order to stay in the (Chinese) market. Company leadership argues that their staying in China is keeping the Chinese population connected to the outside world.

> "While removing search results is inconsistent with Google's mission, providing no information is more inconsistent with our mission."
> —Google press release[33]

With U.S. businesses collectively raising their eyebrows, only time will tell if the company made the right business decision. The answer is probably in the eyes of the beholder.

Does Google's decision demonstrate cultural intelligence and sensitivity? Yes. Does Goggle's decision compromise the company's own moral standards? Arguably, the answer is no. Why? When a business decides to go global, it must decide to accept a simple paradoxical principle: all people are created equal as human "beings" and all cultures have, by birthright, the right to express difference.

The Google case illustrates the types of decisions that leaders must make when they are differentiating beyond just their familiar territory. It is not a question of eliminating judgment of "right" from "wrong"; it is a question of first, understanding other cultures, and then, making judgments about what is "right" and "wrong." The danger comes when people judge behaviors outside the context where those behaviors are learned and demonstrated. As a global business leader, you deal with different governments, different laws, and different ways of life.[34] The intercultural leader has to be prepared.

Leadership Evolving

New Roles for Leaders

It has been widely observed that the global economy is in yet another stage of *transition* to newer economies. The emergence of the "knowledge economy" in the 1990s was compared in strength and scope with the emergence of the manufacturing economy of the 1890s and the mass-production economy of the 1940s and 1950s. Yet, despite the United States having been touted as the *de facto* leader of that burgeoning economy because of our supposed educational and other advantages, we witnessed a different scenario unfold as the wholesale off-shoring of jobs emptied the corporate parking lots of economic centers such as in the Silicon Valley of California. This sea change, to the knowledge economy, brought about widespread changes to how people in organizations worked.[35]

With all the talk about new economies, though, it is first important to understand what is meant by "new economy" before we discuss the implications of the various new economies themselves.

What people mean when they talk about new economies is the creation of a new basis for an economy. In the last case, the wellspring is the flow of information and the creation of "knowledge." Economists and management writers have been talking for some years now about the differences between older economies that are/were valuated on physical assets, such as facilities and equipment and the new economy that is measured on the less tangible assets such as intellectual capital and patents. Thus, in the new economy growth occurs through innovation rather than mass production. However, while there is widespread agreement that a defining aspect of the new economy is the increased importance of knowledge. Defining what we mean by *knowledge* as it pertains to the concept of *economy* may be the most important issue. *Knowledge* is an intellectual product. *Intellectual capital* has been defined as "intellectual material—knowledge, information, intellectual property, and experience—that can be put to use in the creation of wealth." Within the knowledge economy, there have been two types of knowledge industries identified. The first are those industries whose major product is knowledge itself. The second are those industries that manage or convey information.[36]

The first group includes industries such as software, biotechnology, and information technology hardware. These industries employ occupations such as engineers, scientists, programmers, and designers, whose major output is research and development that translates into new products and services. These industries are driven not by machinery, skilled shop workers, or even capital—although these continue to play a role— individuals engaged in research, design, and development drive theses industries. While these industries purportedly constitute less than 7% of the general economy's total output they play significant roles in driving the *new* knowledge economy. Just as traditional industries like automobile manufacturers and steel producers drove growth in the 1950s and 1960s, knowledge production and information processing firms are now the growth leaders of the new economy.[37]

The second group of industries is involved in managing, processing, and distributing information. These industries include telecommunications, banking, insurance, advertising, law, medicine, and much of government and education; and professions such as managers, lawyers, bankers, sales reps, accountants, and teachers. In these industries, effective handling and managing of information—rather than breakthrough knowledge generation—are the keys to growth.[38]

As it turns out, factors such as tax codes which drove U.S. corporations to relocate jobs overseas and the ready availability of educated, cheap, and willing workers in other countries, along with the migration of manufacturing to Asian countries, diminished the strength of the so-called "knowledge economy" in the United States.

However, we now see the emergence of yet another economy, referred to as the "creativity economy." Again, American companies perceive an advantage and are banking on the perceived American business prowess in innovation; arguably, the competition is, and will be, tough.[39]

There are more similarities between the knowledge and creativity economies than between those (two) and older industrial economies. Unlike older economies that are/were based on scarcity, or the depletion of resources, the knowledge economy's fundamental unit of measure is information (knowledge, intelligence, etc.) which can be used, reused, and can actually grow through its utilization. The creativity economy's unit of measure is concepts. Because of mediating technologies such as the Internet and mobile computing, the effect of location is reduced significantly. Virtual marketplaces and virtual organizations are created offering speed and agility. Both of these new economies require that organizations recognize "intellectual capital" (the brainpower of employees) as their chief asset. These characteristics among others create some interesting implications for organizations.[40]

The lessons from recent global business history, if learned, are that North Americans are not the only talented players on the field, and globalization is not a phenomenon driven by Americans exclusively. Hoovers estimates that there are well over 25 million global businesses and they do not all originate in the United States.[41] Exhibit 1.3 presents the 2007 A. T. Kearney Foreign Policy Globalization Index, which shows the world's most integrated

Exhibit 1.3

The Global Top 20

Singapore	Denmark	Sweden	New Zealand
Hong Kong	United States	United Kingdom	Norway
Netherlands	Canada	Australia	Finland
Switzerland	Jordan	Austria	Czech Republic
Ireland	Estonia	Belgium	Slovenia

Adapted from and permission granted: The Global Top 20, November| October 2007, The Economist print edition.

countries in terms of political engagement, technological connectivity, personal contact, and economic integration.

What are the Implications of All This Change for Global Business Leaders?

The managerial responsibility of leadership is undergoing the most significant change since the Industrial Revolution. We are not alone in this observation. Rather, we find a convergence of opinion that the current transition is extraordinary; from CEOs of global corporations[42] to major publications[43] and premiere professional organizations and scholars.[44]

Economies based on knowledge and creativity require that organizations possess a level of management sophistication far above anything previously seen. Outdated concepts, like "supervision" and "training," will be transformed into concepts like "design muse" and "learning guide." Leaders and managers now need to be competent in their "technical" profession, possess keen business acumen, understand how to stimulate creativity and in addition, they must become "intercultural ambassadors."[45]

Organizations now cannot afford to have work cultures burdened with politics and power conflicts where creativity is obstructed and where managers have no cultural awareness. Since intelligence, creativity, knowledge, and expertise resides within the personage of individuals, it is incumbent upon leaders to accept that their primary role is to cultivate a socially harmonious work environment in which interaction is optimized and where diverse people flourish—whether that work environment is virtual or actual.[46]

However, perhaps the greatest change in leadership perspective is that leaders must understand that the very concept of leadership, and therefore its practice, varies between cultures. This understanding is an essential factor in possessing intercultural leadership competence.[47] In Exhibit 1.4, German Bayer Biotech executive Elizabeth Zamora describes her experience learning to speak Chinese because of China's increasing expansion into South American countries.

In order to acquire or develop new competencies though, all business leaders must first know what specific competencies to develop and how to acquire them. A number of recent studies demonstrate a remarkable convergence in perspective as to what constitutes the skills, experience, characteristics, and knowledge necessary for intercultural leaders to possess.[48] All agree that the trend toward globalization is likely irreversible, that truly intercultural leaders are in short supply, and that the "new intercultural leader" is and will be operating at a much higher level of capability than ever before. The question is what those capabilities are and how leaders can acquire them.

Exhibit 1.4

Across Latin America, Mandarin Is in the Air

By Juan Forero

Elizabeth Zamora is a busy mother and executive. Still, for 3 hours every Saturday, she slides into a battered wooden desk at Bogota's National University and follows along as Yuan Juhua, a language instructor sent here by China's government, teaches the intricacies of Mandarin.

Zamora already speaks German and English, but she struggles to learn written Chinese characters and mimic tones unknown in Spanish. She persists for a simple reason: China is voraciously scouring Latin America for everything from oil to lumber, and there is money to be made. That prospect has not only Zamora but business people in much of Latin America flocking to learn the Chinese language, increasingly heard in boardrooms and on executive junkets.

"It's fundamental to communicate in their language when you go there or they come here," said Zamora, 40, a sales executive for the German drugmaker Bayer, which is growing dramatically in China. "If you don't know their language, you're lost."

Latin America, with its vast farmlands and ample oil reserves and mineral deposits, has become a prime destination for investors and others from China, whose economy has been growing at 9% annually. The total value of trade between China and Latin America rose from just over $10 billion in 2000 to $50 billion last year, according to Chinese trade data.

"Latin American countries want to diversify their markets, and they see a huge opportunity, not just in the present but in the potential for growth," said Chris Sabatini, a senior director of policy for the New York-based Council of the Americas, a business association that encourages trade in the Americas. "Latin Americans, as people in any country, should be opportunistic, and they see opportunity with China."

Chinese companies are investing in farmland and energy installations in Brazil. Beijing has signed a free-trade agreement with Chile, its first with a Latin American country, while announcing investments in the Chilean copper industry and gas and oil fields in Ecuador, Argentina, and Bolivia. Beijing has also cemented a $5 billion oil deal with President Hugo Chávez of Venezuela, which is seeking to diversify exports to other countries beyond the United States.

The arrival of China in a largely Spanish-speaking region half a world away might seem unusual. But Beijing is in a relentless quest for oil, coal, iron ore and copper for its factories, soybean and poultry to feed its 1.3 billion people, lumber for housing, and fish meal for its livestock. President Hu Jintao's government, which 2 years ago pledged $100 billion in investments for several South American countries, said it also wants to bankroll road, port and railroad developments that would help bring exports more quickly to China.

Veering toward China, though, is far from easy for entrepreneurs and students from a region that has long been intertwined with the giant to the north. The United States remains the biggest investor in Latin America, its trade with the region eight times that of China's. English prevails as a second language.

(Continued)

Exhibit 1.4   (Continued)

Mandarin, on the other hand, is considered far harder to learn, with dialects and a tenor significantly different from the phonetic cadences of Spanish and Portuguese. Yet the Chinese language is making gains, as is the revolutionary idea of looking west across the Pacific for business opportunities.

"The world is divided into east and west, and the culture is completely different," said Miguel Angel Poveda, president of the Colombo-China Chamber of Commerce in Bogota. "The only way to get around it is to understand the culture and learn to do business with them, but in their language."

Many of those taking up the challenge are young, like Leidy Catalina Ortega, 17, who recently dropped an English-language class in favor of Mandarin. Her parents want to import clothing from China to sell in Bogota. If she learns the language, she will help manage the business. "If you're interested and work hard, you can learn and talk almost like they do," she said. "You are afraid at first. Later you get it and move on."

Universities across Latin America, from Mexico to Buenos Aires, are founding Asian studies programs and teaching Chinese. Institutions of all kinds—some are expensive one-on-one tutorials and others are fly-by-night language academies staffed by illegal Chinese immigrants—are being inundated with new students.

The University of Buenos Aires started its Chinese-language department in 2004 after Hu led a high-level delegation to Argentina, Brazil, and other countries. "It generated so much interest, and people started to say, 'Where is there a place to learn Chinese?'" Maria Chao, the coordinator of the department, said by phone from Buenos Aires. "They see the language as a way to communicate and cut some distance between the two countries."

But in her wildest dreams, Chao said, she could not have foreseen how intense the interest would be. Instead of 20 students, as she expected, more than 600 signed up for classes. Now there are more than 1000 students studying Chinese at the university, she said, in nearly 70 classes. Chao, who was born in China and immigrated to Argentina at age 5, said she has been astounded by the interest people have in China. She recently asked a policeman for directions and, without missing a beat, he responded: " Ni hao ma," Mandarin for "How are you?"

In Peru, which has a dynamic Chinese immigrant community and an economy that is growing at 5% annually, business people are looking for classes that can quickly give them an advantage as the country's trade with China grows. Joseph Cruz, 46 years, who has been teaching Chinese for 23 years, will soon launch a course for executives costing $2200 a year, a hefty sum in Peru.

The course, to be taught at Lima's Catholic University, will not just deal with grammar and vocabulary, but with the trappings of Chinese culture and history, from Confucian philosophy to the importance of tea. "The idea is to use these courses to teach people how Chinese thinking is reflected in modern China," Cruz said. "We're not going to waste their money."

China, too, sees great opportunity in Latin America, said Zhao Xingtian, cultural counselor at the Chinese Embassy in Bogota. He spoke on a recent night as a Colombian–Chinese salsa band—singing in both Mandarin and

(Continued)

Exhibit 1.4   (Continued)

Spanish—prepared to play at a cocktail party given by the Colombo-Chinese Chamber of Commerce.

"Many Chinese would like to come to this country, know its people, drink its coffee," said Zhao, speaking a fluid Spanish. "It makes us very happy that many Colombians want to learn Chinese. It's a good beginning. It's a good cultural exchange between Latin America and China."

China is dispatching teachers abroad, sending people like Yuan Juhua to countries that just a few years ago gave short shrift to the idea of strengthening ties with Beijing. Yuan arrived here just 2 years ago to help launch the National University's Mandarin program. Now, her 12-year-old daughter speaks fluent Spanish, and Yuan divides her time between teaching university students during the day and business people on weekends.

The university "didn't have any resources for the Chinese program, so after I came here, everything was a challenge for me," Yuan said. She also found teaching Spanish speakers a challenge. "These two languages are very different, and because of that, it's difficult for Chinese people to study Spanish and people here to study Chinese," Yuan said. Many drop out after level one, the first of four offered. "If they don't have patience and enthusiasm, it's hard to get to level two," she said.

In a break from Yuan's class, Miguel Aroca, a petroleum engineer for France's Total oil company, recounted the difficulties of reaching level two. Aroca, 33 years and fluent in English and French, said he wanted to study Mandarin as a hobby. Now he realizes it is a career tool. Mastering it will not be easy. "It went from being a hobby to being real work," he said. "The last exam, I was really stressed out."

Excerpted from and permission granted: Washington Post, September 22, 2006, Washington Post print edition, p. A01.

Seven Key Principles of a New Leadership Paradigm

Framing Context

It is quite challenging, even with the best of intentions, to think about anything without your thoughts being steeped deeply in cultural meaning—that includes the well-intended and well-researched book you are reading now. We simply do not exist outside of a cultural and social context. The following little colloquial story will illustrate this point. Say you were born on the beach of an uninhabited island in the middle of some ocean, and orphaned immediately at birth because your poor mother and father were washed out to sea before you laid eyes on them, and you were "raised" by native orangutans. You would still be a creature of your culture. In this case, your culture would be those native primates.

The problem with even the best-intentioned recommendations for leadership competence in intercultural contexts is that they still have a cultural bias. In other words, the very concept of leadership is culturally bound. Leadership is not what *you* think of as leadership everywhere else on this planet.

Here are some examples to illustrate the point

In French, leadership, "conduite," means to guide one's own behavior, to guide others, or command action.[49] In France, although the French are famous for protesting, authority holds deference and respect.

In German, leadership, "Führung," means guidance, and in organizations, it is construed to consist of uncertainty reduction. The leader guides action. Further, leaders guide by the rules in such a way as to motivate.[50]

In Chinese, leadership, 领导, means the leader and the led. The leader is one who "walks in front" and guides the group through teaching "the way." Here, the implication is that leadership can only be a relational activity.[51]

In Arabic, there is a word "Sheikh" that has different meanings according to the regional culture within the Middle East. Literally, "Sheikh" means a man over 40 years. However, in the Gulf and Saudi Arabia "Sheikh" means a person from the Royal Family. In Egypt, "Sheikh" means a scholar of religion. In Lebanon, "Sheikh" means a religious leader even among Christians. The socio-economic and political culture of the Middle East plays a role in influencing the definition of leadership. In general, it is agreeable among people from the Middle East that leadership is tied to seniority before any other qualification.

During the period when Egypt was a monarchy, it was improper presenting King Farook as the leader of Egypt. However, they used the term leadership to describe heads of the opposition parties. During the 1950s, many Arab countries were ruled by military officers. Since then "leadership" has become a descriptive term of presidency. There have been great business innovators who were recognized as leaders for their role in starting new industries. However, that was before the 1952 revolution. Now, in the Middle East the term leadership is a political term, nothing else, with the exception that in Iran, leadership is a religious term more than a political one. As far as organizational or business leaders, they cannot share the term no matter how great their contribution.[52]

Is there one best way to lead, or is leadership, at best, contextually dependent?

In a landmark study on intercultural leadership competence, leading intercultural experts from around the world participated in a consensus building effort to determine the critical competencies for intercultural leadership and in how leaders can acquire them.[53] While the study's inquiry questions directed to the panelists focused on U.S. business leaders to delimit the research properly, panelists concluded that their recommendations held for all leaders engaged in global enterprise. The researcher's investigation yielded both surprising and anticipated results.

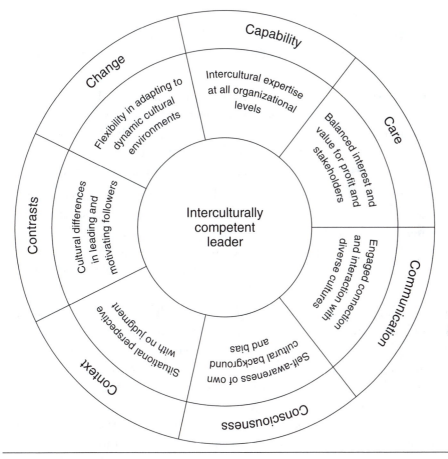

Figure 1.2 Geoleadership Model
Source: Sheridan 2005

From the analysis, the research results revealed seven critical factors considered necessary for intercultural leadership competence. These seven critical factors were integrated and form the foundation for, Geoleadership, a fresh Intercultural Leadership Model.[54] In the section following, we present and briefly describe the seven factors considered necessary for intercultural leadership competence. Figure 1.2 provides a graphic representation of the Geoleadership Model.

Care: Global business leaders should hold and maintain equal concern for the bottom line and for stakeholder groups. One of the clearest and starkest criticisms of American leaders, and businesses, is perceived to be that their focus on profit, seemingly above all other considerations. While we can agree that one objective of business is profit creation, we also believe that a longer (term) and broader (social systems) serves business, ultimately.[55]

Communication: In order for business leaders to lead effectively in intercultural situations, such leaders necessarily must engage and interact with those cultures in whose countries they work, if not with many cultures.

Closely related to context is that leaders must reach out to people in other cultures with a desire to understand and appreciate that culture and its people.[56] Leaders must learner communication skills that promote listening and open respectful dialog.

Consciousness: In today's global economy, a person filling the role of leader and manager needs to develop self-awareness. A leader's awareness must be expandable as contexts shift around them, such that the leader becomes clear of a personal cultural background and bias relative to that of other people. Building consciousness means being able to expand your awareness.[57]

Contrasts: Leaders must be able to work comfortably and effectively with ambiguity. Developing a tolerance for working with contrasting perspectives, methods, and with differing value systems is critical. Working in ambiguous contexts requires patience and consciousness. Working at such a high level of consciousness means that leaders must be able to perceive multiple levels of meaning simultaneously.[58]

Context: Global business leaders must develop the ability to perceive, discern, and adapt to the situations within which they work, and to suspend judgment. As trite as it may seem the old expression "when in Rome, do as the Romans do" seems to apply. We want to be careful here, not to suggest that leaders patronize the people with who they interact in intercultural contexts. In truth, we submit that American business leaders have some work to do, in authentically interacting with other cultures. What all of this means, is that all global business leaders must attend to the situation in which they find themselves. Leaders need to understand each culturally learned behavior in the context of where that behavior originates and appears.[59]

Change: Postmodern organizations require adaptive leaders, leaders who demonstrate flexibility in adapting to dynamic cultural environments. Intercultural leaders must shift from the old mechanistic mindsets of the industrial era to the flexible adaptive perspective of organizational life as what it is, a complex socio-cultural system.

Capability: In order for a leader to be effective in intercultural situations, there must be development of sufficient personal and organization capability. Intercultural competence requires that leaders are able to assess their own and others' capability and build it where there is deficit.[60] Most important is the leader's influence in facilitating an organizational culture capable of intercultural learning agility.

The Journey to New Leadership Frontiers

Chapter 2 provides an overview of culture theory, leadership theory and a discussion about the interaction of culture and leadership. In Chapters 3–9, we detail each of the model competencies and then we present case studies of business leaders who are trying to expand their markets and reach their company's potential. Through the case studies, we demonstrate the use of the Geoleadership Model[61] so that you can see how to employ it in different situations.

A competent intercultural leader has vision, yet is not rigid; is intentioned, yet not self-serving; is engaging, yet not political; is decisive, yet consensual; above all, s/he is cosmopolitan.

To be a true Geoleader you must recognize that cultures are always evolving and that your own intercultural education will never end.

The Bottom Line

Globally, societies are changing and so are organizations. Globalization and other changes create a new business climate, which requires different competencies from leaders. The risk of not becoming competent at leading global organizations and businesses is a costly failure. It has always been important for leaders to be competent at interpersonal relations, communicating, decision-making, visioning, problem solving, negotiating, influencing, and inspiring. However, in a constantly evolving global environment, where there are multiple and varying environments, leaders need new skills that enable them to traverse new territory. The role of leader has shifted at the same time that the expectations of leaders is less clear because cultural differences, economic changes, generational shifts, political and social upheaval.

One of the primary reasons why so many global businesses have failed is due to unresolved cultural differences. Cultures vary widely in how they view business including how to lead and how to follow. Even with the minimal understanding of cultural differences that can be learned through distant study, the going can be tough and frustrating.

The combination of globalization, complex societal changes, demographic changes, and the lack of skilled business leaders being graduated from business schools has created a global talent crisis. Juxtaposed to this phenomenon is a postmodern perspective of leadership as being something that can emerge anywhere in an organization when it is needed.

We closed the chapter with a preview of a new intercultural leadership model. The new Geoleadership Model can provide a roadmap for leaders to gain the competencies necessary for intercultural leadership and is explored throughout the remainder of this book.

2

Leader Does as Culture Is?

I believe that the capacity that any organization needs is for leadership to appear anywhere it is needed, when it is needed.

—Margaret J. Wheatley

Globalization presents unique intercultural challenges for business leaders.[62] Leading any social milieu requires that you possess, and act from, a set of values and principles (standards of behavior) and it is especially helpful when your values support rather than thwart your endeavors. The problem for intercultural leaders is that what is valued highly in one culture may be objectionable in another. Even worse, culture provides people with both the lenses with which to make sense of the world and the blinders that hinder perceiving someone else's reality.[63] What is culture and how does it affect leadership and organizations?

Defining the Indefinable

Culture remains one of the most misunderstood constructs within organizations.[64] Culture may appear specifically related to ethnicity, nationality, demography, or status. As the classic definition states, culture is "the collective programming of the mind that distinguishes the members of one human group from another."[65] The term itself is derived from a Latin root *colere*, (Oxford Concise Dictionary, 2005) which means to prepare and develop. Thus, in this definition we can see the other form of the original word, which is (to) cultivate, meaning to grow. We accept the definition of culture proposed by Harris, Moran & Moran: "Culture is a distinctly human means of adapting to circumstances and transmitting this coping skill and knowledge to subsequent generations."[66]

A general theory that explains culture has only been in the Western lexicon since the mid-20th century and essentially holds that culture is an interpretive and adaptive mechanism used by humans to understand and deal with their own nature and the environment around them. Human interest in culture surely is not new. One can speculate that being able to understand people beyond one's own tribe has been at least a secondary pursuit for as long as humankind has wandered from home terrain. The systematic examination of culture as social phenomenon began in earnest with early folklorists and anthropologists.

A number of early groundbreaking studies and writings about culture began appearing in the 1880s with such classics as Fraser's *The Golden Bough*, Radcliffe-Brown's *The Andaman Islanders*, van Gennep's *Rites of Passage*, Benedict's *Patterns of Culture*, and others such as Margaret Mead, a pioneering American anthropologist. However, the majority of these works concerned cultures not of the so-called modern world. It was not until late 1950s that studies of culture began to concern themselves with contemporary Western culture. In 1959, Hall published his now famous, *The Silent Language*, in which he postulated the idea that cultures can be typed according to certain characteristic dimensions of behavior. Although Hall did not conduct empirical investigation, working in the U.S. Foreign Service provided suitable opportunity for participant-observation.

Hall posited that all cultures could be categorized along two dimensions: as being either high or low context and as being either polychronic or monochronic in their time orientation. The central premise undergirding high versus low context is that communication constitutes a transaction of information. In high-context cultures, information is passed with most of the information in the physical location or internalized by the person, and very little is coded within the explicit transmission. In contrast, a low-context communication contains as part of the explicit message the bulk of the information. Distilled, this means low-context cultures are more explicit and high-context cultures are more implicit in their communication style.

In high-context societies, people have close connections, long history, and many aspects of culturally sanctioned behavior which are implicit because most members know what to do and what to think from years of interaction with each other. Societies such as China, Japan, India, and France are considered high context. Conversely, in low-context societies, such as the United States and United Kingdom, people tend to have many connections but of shorter duration or for some specific reason. In these societies, cultural behavior and beliefs tend to be explicit so that those coming into the cultural environment know how to behave.

In Chinese culture, communication tends to be very efficient. In business, people tend to discuss issues during the time they work, sometimes over a meal. When it comes to meetings, Chinese have a tendency to discuss things in advance and consider meetings ceremonial where the already commonly agreed decision will be announced. This is important in the way of "giving and keeping face." Conversely, the American and German way of conducting business meetings is to inform the attendees of a meeting about the hard and necessary facts during the actual meeting. For Chinese, issues, circumstances, and relationships are as important as work so they would comment only in a more private or appropriate occasion.

People from India or China, when hired by a North American company, tend to ask many questions, and can be perceived by their Western counterparts to be overly inquisitive before they commit to something. Americans might sometimes find that behaviors intrusive and unnecessary. They place great importance on ambience, decorum, the relative status of the participants in a communication, and the manner of the messages' delivery. Conversely, American employees keep work and friendship away from each other as much as possible. Discussions at work in a professional environment would be to the point and concise. High-context cultures are often misunderstood as being too relationship oriented. The fact is that these cultures tend to value relationships more than the task. These differences in cultural ways of life create misunderstandings and miscommunication.

Hall's second postulate concerns cultures' orientation to time, that is, how each culture perceives and structures time. Table 2.1 illustrates Hall's monochronic and polychronic cultures.

Culture has been described as a mental exercise in its systematic sending, sorting, and processing of information.[67] It has been suggested that culture is an abstract idea, rather than something concrete.[68] Arguably, culture is not simply an abstraction, because it can be known in terms of behavioral patterns and shared experiences.[69] This shared experience is the cumulative deposit of knowledge and patterns of shared psychological properties acquired by a group of people, which are passed onto subsequent generations.[70] These psychological properties include assumptions, beliefs, and values.

In practice, culture can be perceived as artifacts and practices that facilitate meaning-making.[71] When shared collectively, such properties become acculturated norms and accepted behaviors. Visit most organizations and these properties can be observed as artifacts, behaviors, underlying assumptions, and espoused values through vision and mission statements, organizational logos and other company propaganda.[72] In a sense then, culture is the container, or context, in which all behaviors are learned.[73] Since culture provides context and differs among social situations and environments, what are some of these differences?

Table 2.1 Monochronic and Polychronic Cultures

	Monochronic culture	Polychronic culture
Interpersonal relations	Interpersonal relations are subordinate to present schedule	Present schedule is subordinate to Interpersonal relations
Activity co-ordination	Schedule co-ordinates activity; appointment time is rigid	Interpersonal relations co-ordinate activity; appointment time is flexible
Task handling	One task at a time	Many tasks are handled simultaneously
Breaks and personal time	Breaks and personal time are sacrosanct regardless of personal ties.	Breaks and personal time are subordinate to personal ties
Temporal structure	Time is inflexible; time is tangible	Time is flexible; time is fluid
Work/personal time separability	Work time is clearly separable from personal time	Work time is not clearly separable from personal time
Organizational perception	Activities are isolated from organization as a whole; tasks are measured by output in time (activity per hour or minute)	Activities are integrated into organization as a whole; tasks are measured as part of overall organizational goal

Source: Adapted from Victor, D. A. (1992). International business communication. Harper-Collins, New York.

Dimensions and Patterns of Culture

Many models exist to help sort out the differences among national cultural values.[74] The germinal work of Hofstede provides one of the more convenient models highlighting the differences between cultures.[75] Hofstede determined that five universal categories of culture describe basically the problems of humanity with which every society must cope. Hofstede determined the five dimensions by studying International Business Machines (IBM) workers in different countries.[76] The benefit of studying one company across countries was that it allowed for the control of many variables in the workplace, where nationality stands out as the major difference across samples. The five dimensions that emerged were power distance, individualism versus collectivism, masculinity versus femininity, uncertainty avoidance, and long-term versus short-term orientation.

Power distance refers to "the extent to which the less powerful members of institutions and organizations within a country expect and accept that power is distributed unequally."[77] Hofstede defined *institutions* as the basic elements of society. Such institutions include the family or school. People work within organizations. Power distance appears relative to other variables such as social class, education level, and occupation. The United States ranks low on power distance, which signals greater equality between social levels.

The second dimension, individualism versus collectivism, refers to the extent to which ties between individuals are loose or integrated. More individualistic societies, such as the United States, stress the importance of the individual in work and society, whereas collectivist societies stress the importance of the group over an individual's needs. In the IBM study, individualism was associated with a work orientation concerned with personal time, freedom, and challenge.[78] The collectivistic group focused more upon the interdependence between the employee and the organization. Confrontation is more likely in individualistic countries such as the United States.[79]

The third dimension is masculinity versus femininity.[80] A masculine culture values people and organizations that are aggressive and competitive, such as the United States. Masculinity stands for a preference for heroism, assertiveness, and material success; femininity stands for a preference for relationships and modesty. Masculine societies focus more on achievement in the workplace, as opposed to the more feminine countries that might focus on quality of life.[81] Overall, masculine countries strive for a performance society, while feminine countries strive for a well-being society.

The fourth dimension is uncertainty avoidance, the "extent to which the members of a culture feel threatened by uncertain or unknown situations."[82] Uncertainty avoidance measures the amount of ambiguity a society will tolerate. The countries high in uncertainty avoidance prefer rules, regulations, and structure. In contrast, countries with low uncertainty avoidance prefer few laws or rules. The United States reflects a lower uncertainty avoidance score and focuses on a greater level of tolerance for a variety of ideas, thoughts, and beliefs.

The fifth dimension describes a culture's "long-term versus short-term orientation." Short-term orientation focuses on personal steadiness and stability. The short-term orientation tends to be more past and present oriented. Long-term orientations are associated with persistence and preserving status and order. The United States reflects a more short-term orientation in its business environment.[83]

Hofstede's five universal categories of culture provide a brief overview of some differences in national culture that must be resolved in the global environment. It is important to gain a more complete understanding of the intercultural leadership criterion for its communication and maximization by leaders for business success. American business organizations and leaders must transcend their traditional ethnocentric framework and learn to adapt in a world of cultural differences. The first step for business leaders is to learn to understand how cultural differences affect leadership and life within and across organizations.[84] Table 2.2 illustrates the components of Hofstede's model.

Table 2.2 Hofstede's Model

Power distance index					
1–20	21–40	41–60	61–80	81–100	101–120
Individuality					
1–20	21–40	41–60	61–80	81–100	101–120
Masculinity					
1–20	21–40	41–60	61–80	81–100	101–120
Uncertainty avoidance index					
1–20	21–40	41–60	61–80	81–100	101–120
Long-term avoidance					
1–20	21–40	41–60	61–80	81–100	101–120

Country	PDI	IDV	MAS	UAI	LTO
Malaysia	104	26	50	36	
Guatemala	95	6	37	101	
Panama	95	11	44	86	
Philippines	94	32	64	44	19
Mexico	81	30	69	82	
Venezuela	81	12	73	76	
China	80	20	66	40	118
Egypt	80	38	52	68	
Iraq	80	38	52	68	
Kuwait	80	38	52	68	
Lebanon	80	38	52	68	
Libya	80	38	52	68	
Saudi Arabia	80	38	52	68	
United Arab Emirates	80	38	52	68	
Ecuador	78	8	63	67	
Indonesia	78	14	46	48	
Ghana	77	20	46	54	16
India	77	48	56	40	61
Nigeria	77	20	46	54	16
Sierra Leone	77	20	46	54	16
Singapore	74	20	48	8	48

(Continued)

Table 2.2 (Continued)

Brazil	69	38	49	76	65
France	68	71	43	86	
Hong Kong	68	25	57	29	96
Poland	68	60	64	93	
Colombia	67	13	64	80	
El Salvador	66	19	40	94	
Turkey	66	37	45	85	
Belgium	65	75	54	94	
Ethiopia	64	27	41	52	25
Kenya	64	27	41	52	25
Peru	64	16	42	87	
Tanzania	64	27	41	52	25
Thailand	64	20	34	64	56
Zambia	64	27	41	52	25
Chile	63	23	28	86	
Portugal	63	27	31	104	
Uruguay	61	36	38	100	
Greece	60	35	57	112	
South Korea	60	18	39	85	75
Iran	58	41	43	59	
Taiwan	58	17	45	69	87
Czech Republic	57	58	57	74	
Spain	57	51	42	86	
Pakistan	55	14	50	70	
Japan	54	46	95	92	80
Italy	50	76	70	75	
Argentina	49	46	56	86	
South Africa	49	65	63	49	
Hungary	46	55	88	82	
Jamaica	45	39	68	13	
United States	40	91	62	46	29
Netherlands	38	80	14	53	44
Australia	36	90	61	51	31
Costa Rica	35	15	21	86	
Germany	35	67	66	65	31
United Kingdom	35	89	66	35	25
Switzerland	34	68	70	58	
Finland	33	63	26	59	
Norway	31	69	8	50	20
Sweden	31	71	5	29	33
Ireland	28	70	68	35	
New Zealand	22	79	58	49	30
Denmark	18	74	16	23	
Israel	13	54	47	81	
Austria	11	55	79	70	

Source: Adapted from and permission granted: Geert Hofstede, 2007; Geert Hofstede website: http://feweb.uvt.nl/center/hofstede/index.htm

The Effect of Culture on Leadership and Organizations

For people interacting within organizations, culture assumes a multi-focal role that combines personal, national, ethnic, professional, religious, and corporate characteristics.[85] Since cultural influences derive from individual cultural values, people often experience difficulty defining their cultural influences.[86] Not only is culture manifested externally, but also resides within the person; it is not separate from other learned experiences.[87]

There are several ways to identify how culture influences leadership. Primarily, culture shapes the image of the ideal of a particular nation or organization.[88] Cultural groups vary in their conceptions of what is important for effective leadership.[89] Culture influences the personality traits and work values of leaders and followers in a country or organization. Personality appears as the outcome of a lifelong process of interaction between individuals and their environment, resulting in systematic differences in the person–typical behavior of people who grow up in different cultures.[90]

To a significant extent, culture determines the actual pattern of leadership behaviors in a country or organization. Cultural values and norms likely influence the attitudes and behaviors of leaders in ways unconscious to them.[91] In addition, cultural values reflect societal norms in the relationships between individuals. These norms specify acceptable forms of leadership behaviors. For example, the norms appear as societal laws limiting the use of power to influence the decisions and actions of others.[92]

Intercultural leaders must balance commercial and cultural concerns.[93] Commercial imperatives focus on the salient leadership capabilities that corporations must possess to respond successfully to customer needs and competitive threats. Globalization increases the need to understand the impact of diverse backgrounds and philosophies. Leaders in the early 21st century need to look at the world with a local–global perspective and develop products and strategies that work within as well as across borders. The current reality is that the forces of globalization are drawing all cultures into a virtual and time-independent global business zone.[94]

Corporate executives in the early 21st century need to develop business and leadership characteristics that are effective outside of their own national boundaries. In the multinational, indeed global, environment, American traditions are not the only force. National differences in mental programming have become increasingly important because an increasing number of activities in the world demand the cooperation of people from different nations. As previously mentioned, cultural difference is one of the most significant and troublesome variables for multinational businesses to solve.[95]

As the business world becomes more global, it is necessary to understand that each culture views the world differently and that managerial practices that are effective in one culture may be ineffective in another. Leadership theories previously focused on firms, perspectives, and objectives most relevant to American managers and leaders. Typically, ethnocentrism has been the dominant tendency for U.S. business leaders operating abroad, as if language, values, and behaviors were standardized and homogenized throughout the world.[96]

A Briefing on Western Leadership Theory

Interest in leadership as a concept and a practice is not new. All of the world's major religions discuss the topic of leadership from Confucianism, to Islam, to Hinduism, to Judeo-Christian texts going back thousands of years. While addressing leadership from these vantage points now is not the point, it is important, nevertheless to understand that for as long as human beings have been recording their histories; leadership has been a topic of interest across all cultures. Examining definitions across cultural perspective reveals that there is both consensus and dissonance among the meanings attributed to leadership.

Viewed through a philosophical lens, Western leadership theories fall into two major categories, those promoting essentialism (something having an ideal nature) and those promoting contextualism (what is known is relative).[97] From the essentialist perspective, leadership consists of a core set of traits, behaviors, skills, or characteristics that cuts across situations, cultures, philosophies, and moral systems.[98] From the contextualistic viewpoint, leadership can be understood only as complex irreducible system that is highly influenced by social, cultural, psychological, processual, circumstantial, and historical factors.[99] Table 2.3 depicts the various leadership theories and in which category they fall.

The Western leadership literature generally deals with the essentialist and contextualist perspectives as though they are incompatible theories. In the following section, we discuss these two perspectives from the view that they are not necessarily contrary, but rather complimentary. We briefly introduce their origins and describe the major tenets and assumptions of each perspective. However, we avoid the tendency to try to define leadership because, in our experience as interculturalists and social and management scientists, while leadership is learnable, knowable, and practicable, it is also emergent and evolving. What it is not is definable without consideration of propinquity. In other words, while leadership is definable in this moment, in this place, and while some of its components may endure

Table 2.3

Essentialist					Contextualist
TRAIT (1500–1990s)	**BEHAVIOR** (1940–2001)	**SITUATIONAL & CONTINGENCY** (1960–Current)	**POWER** (1500–Present)	**CHARISMA TRANSFORMATIONAL/ TRANSACTIONAL** (1800–Present)	**COGNITIVE** (1980–Present)
Machiavelli (1513)	Lewin et al. (1943)	Sartre (1956)	Machiavelli Will to Power (1513)	CHARISMA	EMERGENT
Great Man Stogdill (1948)	Autocratic Democratic & Laissez-faire Katz et al. (1950)	Temporality Theory Fiedler (1964)	Weber (1947) Feudal	Weber (1947) Charisma	Gronn (2002)
Desired Traits Flanagan (1951)	Michigan Flanagan (1951)	Contingency Model Hersey & Blanchard (1969)	Bureaucratic French & Raven (1959)	House (1977) Impression Management	Distributed
Critical Incidents Katz (1955)	Behavior Fleishman et al. (1953)	Situation Model Evans et al. (1970)	Sources Social Exchange Graen et al. (1975)	Bass (1985)	Pearce & Conger (2003)
Skill Taxonomy McGregor (1960)	Ohio State Merton (1957)	Path Goal Vroom & Yetton (1973)	Vertical	Conger & Kanungo (1987)	Shared
Theory Xs,Y McClelland (1965)	Role Theory Yukl (1971)	Normative Decision Model Graen et al. (1975)	Dyad		Linsky & Heifetz (2002) Adaptive
Stories Boyatzis (1982)	Participative Leadership Mintzberg (1973)	Leader, Member Exchange Kerr & Jermier (1978)			Hazy (2004)
					Co-existent
					Uhl-Bien (2006) Relational
					Lichtenstein et al. (2007)
					Complexity

Traits & Competencies Yukl (1989) / Trait Correlates	Managerial Roles	Group Maintenance Boje (1980, 2001) / Problem, Solve, Learn Model	Process Yukl (1989) / Behavioral Determinant Howell & Costley (2001) / Adaptive Behavior

UNIVERSAL PRINCIPLES	TRANSFORMATIONAL TRANSACTIONAL	CONTEXT	COGNITIVE
Greenleaf (1970)	Weber (1947) Transformational	Birnbaum (1992)	Bensimon, Neumann, & Birnbaum (1989)
Servant Covey (1990) Principle-Centered	Burns (1978) Transformation and Transactional		Bolman & Deal (1991)
Spiritual (1992) Bullis & Glaser	Bass (1985) Transformational		Martinko (1995)
Mayer, Davis, & Shoorman (1995) Trust	Bennis & Nanus (1985) Transformational		Attribution McCormick (2002)
	Schein (1985) Culture Change		Self-efficacy

(Continued)

Table 2.3 *(Continued)*

Essentialist	Contextualist
	CULTURAL
	Ferguson (1984) Anti-bureaucratic Feminist Leadership
	Rosener (1990) Genderization of Leadership
	Helegesen (1990) Gender Barriers
	Calais & Smircich (1991)
	Feminist Leadership Astin & Leland (1991) Social Change
	Cantor & Bemay (1993) Metaphors
	Tierney (1993) Pluralistic Leadership
	CROSS-CULTURAL
	House, Wright, & Aditya (1997)
	Globe Dickson, Den Hartog, & Mitchelson (2003) Ethical Leadership

Source: Adapted from Boje (2005): http://business.nmsu.edu/~dboje/

the next human evolution, in the next decade today's definition may not be entirely suitable. Moreover, while we may accurately define leadership presently for the American business culture, our definition, derived from our own culturally biased understanding of leadership and may not at all be representative of leadership conceptualized in other cultures. Viewed with an intercultural lens, leadership may be understood as consisting of elemental characteristics that may exhibit continuity and/or mutability. One organization though that continually presents recommended research on leadership study is the Center for Creative Leadership (www.ccl.org).

The Essentialist Perspective

The majority of essentialist leadership theories originated in the United States or other Western-perspective countries. Arguably, many essentialist leadership theories are characteristically ethnocentric. To the North American reader, an example of how ethnocentric perspectives color our world is the annual event in sports of the World Series of Baseball.

While the sport of baseball is now played in a few countries more than just in the United States, at the time of its inception, baseball was strictly an American sport. Imagine the surprise of foreign visitors to the United States, in the fall of 1952, at the notion that the New York Yankees were the "World Champions of Baseball" given that no team outside the United States played in the World Series. To some Americans, "World Series" literally meant that "the world" consisted of the United States. To other Americans, it meant that baseball was exclusive to the United States and therefore could be viewed as "the world" of baseball. Even now, with baseball flourishing in other countries, American baseball teams still play in the "World Series of Baseball" each year. Of course, people from the United States are not the only people who operate with an ethnocentric perspective of the world. The point is that cultural bias influences our perspective of life; therefore, cultural bias influences our theories about everything.

In reviewing the leadership literature, it is striking how Western, particularly American, theory dominates. Arguably, one reason why essentialist leadership theories dominate the body of literature on leadership globally is that North American and some European countries, as centers of capitalism, led the spread of globalization. Although, it is important, however, to understand that even within the essentialist school of thought, there are cultural variations.

The worldview of essentialism is deeply rooted in the philosophies of Plato and Aristotle who posited that there are two realities of the universe: one that is the essence and the second that is perceived. The essential universe is that which is perfect and ideal, and the perceived universe is that which is in a constant state of flux. In this view, the goal of scientific observations is to identify that which is ideal. From this, it is easy to see the leap to conceptualizing leadership as consisting of essential attributes that must be common across all of creation, since these ideals are in fact at the essence of leadership.

Essentialists believe that the fundamental laws of nature hinge on the essential properties of the material effects on which they operate. These laws are not forced upon the world by God or nature, but rather are inherent properties.[100] To the essentialist, natural objects operate the way they do because to operate otherwise would be contrary to their natures. Therefore, natural laws are metaphysically necessary, and consequently, there are necessary connections between events and material effects.

How Does the Essentialist View Leadership?

The answer is that, to essentialists, because leadership is a natural effect, it is subject to the laws of nature and has a fundamental character that governs its operation. What this means to leadership theorists of this philosophical bent, is that social scientists must search for leadership's ideal character. An essentialist, then, seeks to establish a general theory of leadership that permeates all human experience. Simply stated, essentialists seek to identify and prove pure leadership irrespective of human variability.

Within the essentialist leadership perspective, the major theories include trait, behavioral, power, exchange, and situational. These five groupings of leadership theory are probably the most recognizable theories to North American business leaders and managers. To say that essentialist leadership theory has shaped the American business culture is a gross understatement. Countless American MBA graduates have been minted from the essentialists' mold. Dozens of "how-to" books, innumerable management development programs and a myriad of corporate leadership cultures have been cast from the "ideal leader" paradigm.

Early *trait* theorists sought to determine what makes some leaders great, and what characteristics distinguish leaders from followers. The trait approach assumes that certain physical, social, and personal characteristics are inherent in leaders. The objective of this exercise was to identify the right sets of traits and characteristics in order to select the right people to become leaders. The problem is that trait research has not been able to identify a set of traits that can consistently distinguish leaders from followers. In an important review of the leadership literature published in 1948, Ralph Stogdill concluded that the existing research had not demonstrated the utility of the trait approach. It turns out that in some studies many followers exhibited the same traits, and more so, than some so-identified good leaders. Because of the lack of consistent findings linking individual traits to leadership effectiveness, researchers abandoned empirical studies of leader traits in the 1950s.

Behavioral leadership theories approach leadership from the perspective that leadership is a learned skill rather than inborn in particular people as trait theory postulated. However, behavioral theories approach the concept of leadership again from the viewpoint there is a specific set of behaviors demonstrated by leaders that distinguishes them from other people.

The most well-known behavioral leadership studies took place at Ohio State University[101] and the University of Michigan in the late 1940s and 1950s. Interest in the Ohio and Michigan studies provoked countless other leadership studies and both studies continue to be widely cited. The Michigan study[102] undertook to determine the principles and methods of leadership that led to productivity and job satisfaction.

The study identified two factors that consistently appeared in the study of leaders. Initiating structure, sometimes called task-oriented behavior, involves planning, organizing, and co-ordinating the work of subordinates. Consideration involves showing concern for subordinates, being supportive, recognizing subordinates' accomplishments, and providing for subordinates' welfare. From the study, two general leadership orientations were identified: an employee orientation and a production orientation. Leaders with an employee orientation showed genuine concern for interpersonal relations. Those with a production orientation focused on the task or technical aspects of the job.

The conclusion of the Michigan study was that an employee orientation and general supervision rather than close supervision yielded better results. The study's author, Rensis Likert, eventually developed four "systems" of management based on these studies; he advocated System 4 (the participative-group system, which was the most participatory set of leader behaviors) as resulting in the most positive outcomes.

One concept based largely on the behavioral approach to leadership effectiveness was the Managerial (or Leadership) Grid, developed by Blake and Mouton.[103] The grid combines "concern for production" with "concern for people" and presents five alternative behavioral styles of leadership. A leader who emphasized neither was practicing "impoverished management" according to the grid. When a leader emphasized concern for people and placed little emphasis on production, he was considered a "country-club" manager. The leader emphasizing a concern for production, but who paid little attention to the concerns of subordinates, was deemed a "task" manager. A leader who tried to balance concern for production and concern for people was termed a "middle-of-the-road" manager. In the last quadrant, leaders who were able to exhibit simultaneous high concern for production and high concern for people were practicing what Likert referred to as, "team management." According to the prescriptions of the grid, team management was the "ideal" leadership approach. The Managerial Grid became a major consulting tool and the basis for countless American corporate leadership development programs.

The assumption of the leader behavior approach is that there are certain behaviors that are universally effective for leaders. Unfortunately, empirical research has not demonstrated consistent relationships between task- or person-oriented leader behaviors and leader effectiveness.

The situational approach to leadership presumes that the best way to manage is to tailor leadership direction to the particular circumstances faced within an employee group. The situational approach to management assumes that the right thing to do depends on a complex variety of critical internal environment contingencies. However, it is important to understand that situational theory does have essentialist roots.

Essentialists document idealized and universal personality traits and situations, and match the leader's orientation with certain organizational situations. Fiedler is one of the early writers on situational theory, examining how a leader's personality or behavior affects leadership performance focusing on aspects of the organization.[104] The "essential" leader's personality traits are task-oriented versus relationship-oriented. The "essential" leadership environment feature is situational control marked by: (1) the leader being or feeling accepted and supported by group members; (2) the task is clear-cut and structured; and (3) the leader has the ability to reward and punish, and thus obtain compliance. The task-motivated leader performs best in both high and low situational controls. Relationship motivated leaders perform best in situations in which control is moderate. Fiedler's conclusion is that leaders perform best in situations that match their leadership style. All leaders can be understood as having an enduring style that can be matched to a static environment that can be identified at some point in time. Experience, training, and organizational turbulence are also conditions that can be "fixed" and examined in relation to leader effectiveness.

From *power theory*, leadership is understood as the leader's use of power and influence with a group of people. The power approach, postulated by French and Raven, views leadership as the exertion of power to influence followers behaviors.[105] Accordingly, leaders derive power from five identified sources, or bases, of power. Again, the essentialist notion of the "ideal" shines through as essential power sources and standardized use of those power sources regardless of context.

Social exchange theory proposes that leaders and followers exchange one thing for another. According to the theory, transactional leaders and their followers exchange transactions between task execution and rewards.[106] Transformational leaders cultivate followers' higher needs.[107] In this view, the transformational leadership process is mutual and elevates the follower and leader. The "essence" of leadership according to this theory is social change measured by intent and by the fulfillment of human needs and expectations toward ideal goals. Transformational and transactional leadership are idealized types, characterized by essential, timeless, unchanging features that purportedly can be identified across culture, situation, and context. Finally, this theory posits that it is possible for leaders to identify the "true" and essential needs of followers—exact universal psychological, economic, spiritual, esthetic, and safety needs.[108]

The Contextualist Perspective

In the 1980s, some researchers began to challenge assumptions of universality by examining human phenomena through cultural, cognitive, contextual, and processual lenses.[109] To contextualists, essentialism seemed to be a way of controlling nature and oppressing people. Contextualists believe that a complex system of cultural, social, psychological, and historical differences constitute human experience.[110] They do not deny that phenomena such as leadership exist; however, they posit that such phenomena are more complex, multi-faceted, and varying than previously envisioned.

In the leadership arena, researchers examined cultural differences in an effort to understand whether different countries value different traits or influence strategies. They also examined social differences to understand whether race and gender effected leadership.[111] Researchers in the field of psychology investigated different psychological orientations, for example, different types of cognitive orientations among leaders.[112] Organizational theorists began studying whether different organizational contexts require different leadership—including processual change that occurs in response to distinctive organizational histories and cultures.[113] Historians have begun to examine whether different (historical) periods require different approaches to leadership.[114]

One concept underlying much of contextualist theory is that reality is socially constructed. Social constructivism is the belief that reality is developed through people's interpretation of the world and a denial of essences.[115] Accordingly, reality is a social and cultural construction, not an idealized form beyond our immediate perception. By examining multiple interpretations, a shared sense of reality can be detected; nevertheless, our understanding of reality is always partial and imperfect. Each of us generates our own "rules" and "mental models," which we use to make sense of our experiences.

More recently, contextualist scholars have challenged previously held universal truths and essences because, in this view, there is no objective vantage point (or reality) and our perceptions are the only thing we can come to know.[116] Contextualists also question whether universal essences or truths even exist beyond our perceptions. Instead, knowledge is seen as contingent to local conditions and contexts.

How do contextualists view leadership?

Contextualists believe that leadership is shaped by individual (local) conditions, circumstances, time, and variations of human experience. To contextualists, there are no universal, essential, and transcendent aspects of leadership. Within the contextualist leadership area, the foremost theoretical schools include cognitive, cultural, and processual.

Cognitive theories of leadership describe how leaders have different perspectives or lenses.[117] For example, Bolman and Deal's research[118] demonstrated that leaders tend to examine situations through one or more lens or cognitive orientations (e.g., political, symbolic, structural, or human resource). Building a contingency theory, the researchers demonstrated that different situations might require different cognitive approaches to leadership; a political orientation might serve a leader in one situation while a bureaucratic orientation is important within another. They break from the related, yet essentialist-oriented "situationalist" efforts of matching situation and leader type. Instead, they describe how leaders often try to lead organizations by finding the one best way and then are stunned by the turmoil and resistance that they invariably generate. Bolman and Deal argue that leaders must be passionately committed to their principles, but flexible in understanding and responding to the events, situation, and contexts around them that are constantly shifting and changing. Accordingly, leaders must assume a posture of learning, knowing that leadership is organic and emergent, not static and precise. Research demonstrating that leaders have vastly different cognitive orientations led to more social/cultural studies about other types of differences among leaders' approaches and beliefs.[119]

The social/cultural leadership literature examines gender and race[120] as well as cross-cultural issues.[121] Studies of women leaders have demonstrated that they tend to understand, define, and enact leadership in distinctive ways from men.[122] Women's leadership styles emphasize reciprocity, mutuality, and responsibility toward others. Such relationships are collective and participatory; focus on relationships and empowerment; and highlight outcomes as a central goal of leadership.[123] In contrast to men's leadership styles, women de-emphasize hierarchical relationships, individualism, and one-way power relationships.[124]

Although fewer American cultural diversity studies exist, research on racial or ethnic differences in the United States have found that leadership styles varies from the earlier research conducted on all white, male samples. For example, Native Americans emphasize community, wisdom, and spirituality as important for leadership and African Americans describe a non-hierarchical, community-based definition of leadership.[125]

Cross-cultural studies in the last decade provide superb examples of the contextualist perspectives.[126] One study provides a historical perspective that chronicles a decline in the quest for universal leadership principles and a rise in awareness of differences over the past decade.[127] The research examines issues from differences related to individual countries—to an examination country groupings based on similar contexts or histories.

In general, cross-cultural studies reveal unique ways that leadership is defined among eastern (collective, holistic, spirituality-based) and western cultures (hierarchical, authority-based, and individualistic).[128] Some cross-cultural studies examined difference based on general societal differences such as the tendency to be either individualistic (focus on individual achievement and rights) versus collective societies (focus on collective achievement and rights) and found remarkable differences.[129]

Along with the differing mental models, cross-cultural studies have also examined how the context affects leadership.[130] Some researchers argue that the leadership literature has overemphasized micro perspectives.[131] Conversely, they argue, macro perspectives that take context and complexity into account have received limited attention. Many contextual and processual theories of leadership emerge from anthropological approaches applied to the study of organizational phenomena.[132]

Ethnographic and folkloristic studies illustrate that organizations and societies have particular histories and cultures that affect organizational phenomena, including leadership.[133] It turns out that contexts are so distinctive that comparison across them is often not meaningful. For example, Tierney's analysis of leadership showed that it is like a spider's web – each web being unique to the spot in which it is created.[134] Comparably, leadership is unique within each context and is dynamic, emergent, and evolving over time. Since leadership is a process, it is volatile and sensitive to changes. The conclusion of these cultural studies, to contextualists, is that universal essences have little value in this emergent understanding and context of leadership.[135]

The most recent postmodern leadership theories have moved 180° from the perspective that "leadership" *per se* indwells positional leaders, to the notion that "leadership" occurs as an event interactively within social milieus.[136] The latest of the postmodern theories, *complexity leadership theory*, provides an integrative theoretical framework for explaining interactive dynamics acknowledged by several emerging leadership theories. Viewed this way, leadership is an interactive event in which knowledge, action preferences, and behaviors evolve, thereby provoking an organization to adapt. Leadership is understood as a product of interactive dynamics and leaders as people who influence the interaction between social actors and their environments. Accordingly, adaptive leadership means that leadership occurs (anywhere in a social context) when interacting agents generate adaptive outcomes. Individuals act as leaders in this dynamic when they mobilize people to seize new opportunities and tackle tough problems.

As the situation changes, different people may act as leaders by leveraging their differing skills and experience.

How can understanding both essentialist and contextualist perspectives enrich one's view of leadership?

The appeal of essentialist theory is that it provides a convenient platform on which we can construct ideal leadership models. Being able to create a leadership style that is constructed from such a platform can afford a leader with confidence and provides a handle for meaning-making. Arguably, deriving meaning is an endeavor closely linked with vision, and vision is perhaps the only universal characteristic of effective leadership that appears across all cultures.

The attraction of contextualism is that it has illuminated our understanding of leadership, by showing the diverse contexts in which leaders operate. It has given voice to multiple points of view and shined a light on the obvious—that our globe is full of diverse peoples. Moreover, it provides the answer to why one-size-fits-all does not.

Accepting the coexistence of the notions that constructing an ideal leadership model is practical and, that leadership models must allow for emergent variance, provides leaders with an expansive toolkit. Explicitly stated this means accepting the premise that, underlying fluidity there is regularity, underlying similarity there is diversity.

The Culture–Leadership Link and Intercultural Leadership Competency

The central issue in the study of leadership across different nations is the question of the universality versus cultural contingency of leadership competence. Leadership scholars diverged on this issue, with most assuming absolute positions in the opposite ends of the culture contingency versus universality spectrum solutions.[137] A culture-specific perspective reflects the notion that the occurrence and the effectiveness of certain leadership behaviors are unique to a given culture. The culture-universal position, in contrast, argues that certain leadership behaviors were comparable across cultures and that many universal leadership behaviors existed.

Only recently, has the leadership research community begun to realize universal and culture-specific leadership behaviors were not mutually exclusive categories, but could rather coexist in a single culture simultaneously.[138] The GLOBE research team identified nine cultural dimensions distinguishing one society from another and having implications for managers.[139] Four of the GLOBE dimensions identified (uncertainty avoidance, power distance, institutional collectivism versus individualism, in-group collectivism) overlap with Hofstede's dimensions (see Exhibit 2.1).

Exhibit 2.1

The following five GLOBE dimensions differ from Hofstede's dimensions:

1. Assertiveness, which referred to the extent a society, encouraged individuals to be tough, confrontational, assertive, and competitive versus modest and tender.
2. Future orientation, which referred to the level of importance a society attached to future-oriented behaviors such as planning, investing, and delaying gratification.
3. Performance orientation, which measured the degree to which a society encouraged and rewarded group members for performance improvement and excellence.
4. Humane orientation, which was the extent to which a society encouraged and rewarded people for being fair, caring, generous, altruistic, and kind.
5. Gender differentiation, which referred to the extent to which a society maximized gender role differences.

Can research pinpoint which cultural dimensions are most important for leadership behavior?

Some researchers suggest that individualism versus collectivism could be one of the most important dimensions of cultural variation.[140] Collectivist cultures expect successful leaders to be supportive and paternalistic, whereas individualist cultures more likely value an achievement orientation and participative leadership. Other researchers suggest that power distance is particularly important for leaders.[141] In low-power distance cultures, subordinates expect consultation, whereas in high-power distance cultures subordinates expect leaders to act more direct and autocratic.

Understanding the results of cross-cultural leadership research results could be very helpful to leaders in intercultural interactions. For example, researchers interpreting their results indicate that it would be inappropriate to train leaders in very high-power distance cultures to use participative decision-making since the leaders in these countries are supposed to have all the answers. By inviting subordinates to become involved, followers would see the leader as weak and incompetent. In addition, subordinates in long-term orientation cultures would be more likely than those in short-term cultures to accept development plans that had a longer period.

Prior Research on Intercultural Leadership Competency

At the cognitive level, a leader arrives in a new cultural situation as ignorant, but then moves into the novice level of awareness.[142] The importance of cultural exchange reveals itself to the leader in this novice round.[143] In the next round, the leader transitions to having an understanding and appreciation of the cultural situation. This round also exists as the attitudinal and values level. Moving toward acceptance and internalization, the leader reaches the behavioral level, or mastery round, and arrives at transformation. This was where intercultural competency becomes a leadership practice.[144]

In another view, intercultural leadership competence is the ability to manage uncertainty, create learning systems, and manage cross-cultural ethical issues.[145] A culturally competent individual possesses personal, social, business, and cultural literacy.[146] Such literacy provides the leader with the tools to understand, value, and leverage cultural differences and situations.[147] Moreover, cultural empathy and contextual analysis provide for intercultural competence.[148]

Intercultural competence also occurs when a leader remains aware and deals with complexity.[149] Exemplary intercultural leaders retain the ability to model the way, inspire a shared vision, and enable others to act in any situation.[150] This implies that interculturally competent leaders are able to communicate and motivate others. These leadership competencies occur with the leader retaining an open mind and respect for others.[151]

The first level to build in constructing interculturally skilled leaders is an awareness of the culturally learned starting points in the leader's thinking.[152] This foundation of intercultural awareness is important because it controls the leader's interpretation of all knowledge and utilization of all skills. The need for intercultural awareness seldom appears in the generic training of leaders.[153] The intercultural skilled leader does not take awareness for granted. Sue *et al.* suggested a cross-cultural competency model.

Such proposed cross-cultural competencies and objectives encompass leader awareness of their own cultural values and biases, including attitudes and beliefs.[154] Culturally skilled leaders move from being culturally unaware to being aware and sensitive to their own cultural heritage and to valuing and respecting differences.[155] These leaders are aware of how their own cultural backgrounds and experiences and attitudes, values, and biases influence interactions with others. Such leaders are able to recognize the limits of their competencies and expertise. Culturally skilled leaders are comfortable with differences that exist between themselves and others in terms of race, ethnicity, culture, and beliefs.[156]

Interculturally competent leaders possess specific knowledge about their own racial and cultural heritage and see how such backgrounds affect their definitions of normalcy.[157] Culturally skilled leaders possess knowledge about their social impact on others. They are knowledgeable about communication style differences. This includes how the leader's style may clash with minority groups, with effective leaders knowing how to anticipate the impact it may have on others.[158]

In some nations, leadership means establishing direction and influencing others to follow that direction.[159] Moreover, we know that one of the few universal attributes ascribed to leadership competence is the ability to develop and communicate a vision. An effective intercultural business leader needs to possess clarity of vision to find compatibility with every new intercultural situation.[160] Many competencies are related to being able to understand national cultural differences. Without developing these competencies, an intercultural leader will not be successful in working abroad.

There is a need for leadership theories that both transcend and accommodate culture. The study from which the Geoleadership™, Intercultural Leadership Model was derived sought to determine how business leaders could develop the knowledge, skills, behaviors, and models necessary to interact with dissimilar others in a way that led to mutual appreciation.

In the following chapters, we present the principles of Geoleadership™. We define each principle and describe its attributes as seen through the lens provided by the global interculturalists who participated in the study. Each chapter will also include a brief section related to attitudes and behaviors that support the principle and through presentation of a case study apply the principle to the case.

The Bottom Line

Humans are quite similar as beings in some ways; however, as cultures we vary widely in our worldview. Everything we do is influenced by cultural norms and this includes how we conduct and lead business organizations.

There are important similarities and differences in how cultures perceive leadership. Intercultural leaders must have a solid understanding of how leadership is perceived and practiced in their own cultures and should undertake learning about how leadership is perceived and practiced in other cultures.

While Western leadership theorists largely agree that there is no one-size-fits-all leadership model that can fully prepare a leader for the journey, some do argue that there can be more standardization of leadership practice. Other leadership theorists argue that leadership is bound by the context and no universal principles exist that can properly prepare a leader for all situations. Some argue, and we agree, that there can be a degree of standardization of essential leader practice, but that it is also important for leaders to be adaptive to their dynamic contexts.

3

The Principle of "Care"

Three-fourths of the miseries and misunderstandings in the world will disappear if we step into the shoes of our adversaries and understand their standpoint.

—Mahatma Gandhi

One of the striking repeated themes that emerged from intercultural dialogs in one recent study relates to an apparently widely held perception that too many U.S. business leaders demonstrate little concern or interest in other cultures.[161] Less successful and altogether unsuccessful leaders facing intercultural situations tend to operate from their own cultural background without regards to the cultural context. Successful leaders, on the other hand, operate quite differently.

One theme for discussion in this chapter concerns successful intercultural leaders and the commonalities found among their experiences. Successful intercultural leaders seem to take the time to learn about the cultures with which they come in contact prior to beginning their foreign assignments. In each case we reviewed, the leader read about the culture, took time to visit the foreign country, began learning the language of the host culture, and made a point of getting to know people in the host culture. The majority of the successful intercultural leaders reviewed, purposely demonstrated concern for the host culture by asking questions focused on seeking to understand the interests, values, and goals of the people from the host culture with whom they made contact. We will discuss more about cultural awareness and appreciation in the chapter on consciousness.

Another issue is the tendency to focus only on short-term profit, which can mean long-term disaster. Relatedly, in too many situations, U.S. business leaders appear to be hyper-focused on corporate profit and pleasing share-holders irrespective of any other stakeholder group.[162] In the observation of many intercultural experts, people of many other cultures perceive the tendency for U.S. business leaders to emphasize profit as disrespectful and uncaring. Whether this is true is almost irrelevant because perception often precludes further evaluation.

"Care" Defined

A Geoleader understands the responsibility to consistently balance interest and value for profit and stakeholders. By taking a 360 degree view of the global effects of decisions, the leader can demonstrate not only care for internal benefits but also forethought for any and all external consequences and constituents.

From the GLOBE[163] studies, we know that profit is tied to one of the dimensions measured across culture, namely, performance orientation. While there are several cultures that ranked higher than the United States in performance orientation related to leadership, the majority (of cultures) were less performance oriented than the American culture.[164]

In the American business culture, the tendency toward performance orientation and an emphasis on profit has not gone unchallenged. As early as 1984, when Freeman first introduced the idea of the stakeholder, awareness of multiple interests in business emerged.[165] The term stakeholder is defined as "any group or individual who can affect or is affected by the achievement of the organization's objectives."[166] Other theorists have defined stakeholder more broadly "as individuals and constituencies that contribute, either voluntarily or involuntarily, to wealth-creating capacity and activities, and who are therefore its potential beneficiaries and/or risk bearers."[167] Accordingly, groups like consumers and employees are stakeholders; moreover, society as a whole is also included since whole communities can be affected by the actions of an organization.

Stakeholder theorists claim that all stakeholders have their own intrinsic value, and believe that leaders/managers must account for the interests of all stakeholders. In this view, the ultimate goal of the firm is to balance profit maximization with the long-term ability of the corporation to remain viable as a socially responsible entity.[168] One of the criticisms of stakeholder theory has been the obvious ethical dilemma faced by leaders when trying to balance the various interests of stakeholder groups.

In one study, which enabled multiple stakeholder discourses, the theorists developed a stakeholder-agency perspective to aid leaders in dealing with the stakeholder-balancing act. In this view, the firm is a nexus of contracts between resource holders (stakeholders).[169] A similar approach proposes four structural configurations on the stakeholder/organization relation to explain why different stakeholders influence organizations in different ways. The structural nature of the organization/stakeholder relation, the contractual forms, and the available institutional support influence the extent of stakeholder impact on an organization.[170] The first step is the process of diagramming the intricate, complex web of relations by the compatibility of ideas and material interests. The second step is to identify necessary relations that are internal to a social structure and contingent ones that are external or not integrally connected. In a third step, leaders build decision rules and in the fourth step build outcome scenarios based on the findings from the first three steps.

Implicit in stakeholder theory is that leaders must engage and consult with their various stakeholder groups in all major decisions. This principle is consistent with interculturists' recommendations related to how U.S. business leaders can better operate in other cultures. The prevailing opinion is that U.S. business leaders must demonstrate authentically that they "care" beyond economic indicators, meeting objectives, and *spreading the American way*. A recent study illustrates the point that highly self-oriented bosses are not necessarily good for business to begin with. Exhibit 3.1 provides solid data that suggests that narcissistic leaders probably are not a good fit for intercultural contexts.

Exhibit 3.1

The Brand of Me

Is it bad for business when the boss is in love with himself?

"What's the difference between God and Larry Ellison?" asks an old software industry joke. Answer: God doesn't think he's Larry Ellison. The boss of Oracle is hardly alone among corporate chiefs in having a reputation for being rather keen on himself. Indeed, until the bubble burst and the public turned nasty at the start of the decade (2000's), the cult of the celebrity chief executive seemed to demand bossly narcissism, as evidence that a firm was being led by an all-conquering hero.

Narcissus met a nasty end, of course. And in recent years, boss-worship has come to be seen as bad for business. In his management bestseller, "Good to Great," Jim Collins argued that the truly successful bosses were not the self-proclaimed stars who adorn the covers of *Forbes* and *Fortune*, but instead self-effacing, thoughtful, monkish sorts who lead by inspiring example.

Recently, authors, Arijit Chatterjee and Donald Hambrick, of Pennsylvania State University, examined narcissism in the upper echelons of 105 firms in the computer and software industries.

(Continued)

Exhibit 3.1   (Continued)

To do this, they had to solve a practical problem: studies of narcissism have hitherto relied on surveying individuals personally, something for which few chief executives are likely to have time or inclination. So the authors devised an index of narcissism using six publicly available indicators obtainable without the co-operation of the boss. These are: the prominence of the boss's photo in the annual report; his prominence in company press releases; the length of his "Who's Who" entry; the frequency of his use of the first person singular in interviews; and the ratios of his cash and non-cash compensation to those of the firm's second-highest paid executive.

Narcissism naturally drives people to seek positions of power and influence, and because great self-esteem helps your professional advance, say the authors, chief executives will tend on average to be more narcissistic than the general population. How does that affect a firm? Messrs Chatterjee and Hambrick found that highly narcissistic bosses tended to make bigger changes in the use of important resources, such as research and development, or in spending and leverage; they carried out more and bigger mergers and acquisitions; and their results were both more extreme (more big wins or big losses) and more volatile than those of firms run by their humbler peers. For shareholders, that could be good or bad.

Although (oddly) the authors are keeping their narcissism ranking secret, they have revealed that Mr. Ellison did not come top. Alas for him, that may be because the study limited itself to people who became the boss after 1991—well after he took the helm. In every respect Mr. Ellison seems to be the classic narcissistic boss, claims Mr. Chatterjee. There is life in the old joke yet.

Excerpted from and permission granted: The Brand of Me, August 10, 2006, The Economist print edition.

Related to the practice of considering stakeholder perspectives and profitability is another point repeatedly emphasized by interculturalists, namely, the idea of taking the long view or sustainability view of business. We want to be clear, that we are not suggesting that businesses should not concern themselves with profitability. However, what interculturalists advocate for, and we concur is that global business leaders would benefit from thinking of *both* short- and long-term perspectives. The long view and the sustainability view of business means that businesses should meet today's global economic, environmental, and social needs without compromising the same opportunity for future generations. The movement toward sustainable business is growing and now includes the perspectives of several streams of societal interests including financial investment, responsible business ethics, and of course environmental preservation. We see the boundaries between for-profit and non-profit blurring. We see entrepreneurial spirit moving business organizations closer to taking on corporate social responsibilities evident in the example shown by Bill Drayton in Exhibit 3.2.

Exhibit 3.2

Ashoka's CEO Harvard's 100 "Most Influential"

Recently, HBR editors selected the 100 most influential people. They singled out people who made them think differently about subjects that already interested them, or who made them think about new subjects.

As they assembled the list, they recognized a theme. Everyone on the list has at least a touch of what the HBR editors call "that Robert Kennedy thing"—the impulse to, "dream things that never were and say why not." According to the HBR folks, influence "is more than power, distinct from intelligence, related but not always proportional to fame and fortune, proportional but not always dependent on innovation and originality. Influence is value neutral. It includes an element of public recognition and an element of quiet genius."

On that list is Ashoka's CEO, Bill Drayton, who sparked no less than a social revolution by applying a venture-capital approach to investing in non-profits. Drayton has moved the model for social change from a top-down, government-based approach to a bottom-up, grassroots strategy. "Bill is at the forefront in understanding the way that global society is going to be reorganized in the future."

As a leading thinker on social change, Drayton has pioneered the field of social entrepreneurship. He is founder of Ashoka, a global organization that selects individuals tackling society's most pressing problems with innovative, entrepreneurial solutions and provides initial capital to grow their social ventures. Bill has introduced the world to a fundamentally new model of how ideas can change social systems across the globe with impressive scale.

Excerpted from and permission granted: Ahoka.org, 2007

Taking the long view requires that business leaders envision scenarios that serve both immediate and long-term goals. It requires that leaders not bury their heads in the sand in denial of the uncertainties that the future always holds; but, rather, choosing to imagine the possibilities and planning for how those could be met. The ultimate goal of taking a long view of business is to enable leaders to tolerate ambiguity, accept, and act with the knowledge that the future holds risk and to be prepared even for failure. The degree to which leaders should focus on longer view businesses strategies abroad, should depend on the comparability between the home and host culture. From our experience and from solid research that has shown that all cultures place importance on time,[171] including what is referred to as future orientation;[172] we recommend that leaders investigate how a potential host culture perceives time and the future beforehand.

Also related to the concept of sustainability is the practice of holding a local–global mindset. Although we discuss the principle of context in a later chapter, operating with a local–global mindset does involve attention to context. Operating with a local–global mindset simply means thinking and acting in a local context with an awareness of the consequences to places and people beyond. It follows the simple concept of systems thinking that what is done to one part of the system affects all other parts of the system.

Context awareness, local–global mindset, stakeholder awareness, and sustainability all require a leadership practice that facilitates comprehensive decision-making processes. Without advocating any particular decision process, based on our research, we do recommend that leaders base any business process, including making decisions on the styles of both the host culture and the home culture.

A final element of the Care Principle concerns leaders acting from purposeful rather than habitual approach. Often in our pursuits, we have observed leaders and managers who appear to operate on, what could be described as, autopilot. The mistaken assumption underlying autopilot leadership is that learning stops at graduation or after the first successful job assignment. Our conviction is that leadership, like most professions and life itself, requires continuing education. We recommend that leaders who aspire to or find themselves faced with global, intercultural business assignments devote 20–30% of their time engaged in some type of meaningful learning experience. We discuss more about how leaders can prepare themselves for global assignments shortly.

While our principal audience is leaders and managers of commercial organizations, we recognize, too, that there is a growing number of hybrid organizations, non-profit organizations, and even government and municipal organizations for whom intercultural leadership competency is important. To be quite clear, everything that a leader says and does has far-reaching effects, some more than others. A recent example in the news that played out on the world stage provides an important lesson related to the principle of Care.

Although relations between the faithful of the Muslim and Catholic religious communities had warmed to slightly above tepid during Pope John Paul's reign, icebergs appeared after new Pope Benedict's (XVI) infamous quoting of a 14th century Catholic scholar, incited Muslim anger. Immediately following the September 2006 incident, Pope Benedict's efforts to reach out to the Muslim community were met with further disdain. Many Muslims and other observers as well perceived the Pope's initial apologies concerning his September speech as seeming removed and unremorseful. We would point out that Pope Benedict, in fact, was quite removed from the effect of his comments, and even with his obvious pastoral competence, he initially missed the point. As the news exhibit demonstrates, contact with Muslims in a fence-mending visit to Turkey apparently did wonders to move Pope Benedict to a different place. Pope Benedict, as the leader of one of the world's largest and oldest bureaucratic, global organizations, demonstrated the power of Care (see Exhibit 3.3).

Exhibit 3.3

A Kinder, Gentler Benedict XVI Emerges in Turkey

And then, something historic happened.

Pope Benedict XVI's motorcade arrived in front of us at the entrance of the famed Blue Mosque where the pontiff was greeted by Mustafa Cagrici, Istanbul's Grand Mufti. The two men—resplendent in robes—chatted warmly and posed for pictures. They lingered, like nervous freshmen on the first day of school, before climbing the stairs. At the door, Pope Benedict took off his shoes and became only the second Pope in the history of the papacy to enter a mosque.

A short tour followed and then, in a move that was unexpected but done with such ease, the two men stood quietly in what appeared to be prayer. Both facing Mecca. Two men of different faiths sharing the sanctity of one poignant moment.

It would become the lasting and powerful symbol of the Pope's journey to Turkey.

People had been looking for something to heal the sting inflicted only 3 months earlier when Pope Benedict made comments that were construed as insulting.

In a speech in Germany, he had quoted a Byzantine scholar who characterized Islam as "irrational" and "violent." Understandably, Muslims around the world were outraged.

In the weeks that followed the Pope's comments the Vatican tried gesture after gesture to smooth things over. Even Turkey's Prime Minister, Recep Tayyip Erdogan, insisted he was too busy to meet the Pope so as to distance himself from the inevitable criticism of his party's Islamic roots.

Reconciliation with Muslims it seemed was underway, punctuated by the Pope's visit to the tomb of modern Turkey's founder, his courteous walk through the Hagia Sophia where it is forbidden to pray and that defining moment facing Mecca as his lips quietly uttered words only he will know. Afterwards, the Mufti said it was, "even more meaningful than an apology."

Excerpted from: http://www.ctv.ca/servlet/ArticleNews/story/CTVNews/2007 1229/antarctic_cruise_071229/20071229?hub = World.

Business leaders can help themselves, their organizations, and the other cultures with which they interact by demonstrating concern about the individuals in other cultures and by seeking to understand the other culture's values and interests. American business leaders, in particular, but all leaders must be aware that they are a member of a culture that is just one culture among many without assuming dominance.

Unfortunately, the history of globalization is littered with disastrous examples of how companies, if not whole industries, have blundered into countries without having solidified clear agreements and without having mutual needs in mind. Exhibit 3.4 is a disquieting indictment of the oil industry and the horrific effects on Nigeria.

Arguably, in one of the saddest examples of an intercultural relationship gone terribly wrong, are events that have occurred over the past 50 years in the oil rich region of the Niger Delta. In Exhibit 3.4, we present excerpts from a 2007 issue of the *National Geographic* magazine, which painstakingly journals the effects of misunderstandings, and misguided actions on the parts of oil companies and governments.

Exhibit 3.4

Curse of the Black Gold: Hope and Betrayal in the Niger Delta

The Niger Delta holds some of the world's richest oil deposits, yet Nigerians living there are poorer than ever, violence is rampant, and the land and water are fouled. What went wrong?

Oil fouls everything in southern Nigeria. It spills from the pipelines, poisoning soil and water. It stains the hands of politicians and generals, who siphon off its profits. It taints the ambitions of the young, who will try anything to scoop up a share of the liquid riches—fire a gun, sabotage a pipeline, kidnap a foreigner.

Nigeria had all the makings of an uplifting tale: poor African nation blessed with enormous sudden wealth. Visions of prosperity rose with the same force as the oil that first gushed from the Niger Delta's marshy ground in 1956. The world market craved delta crude, a "sweet," low-sulfur liquid called Bonny Light, easily refined into gasoline and diesel. By the mid-1970s, Nigeria had joined OPEC (Organization of Petroleum Exporting Countries), and the government's budget bulged with petrodollars.

Everything looked possible—but everything went wrong. From a potential model nation, Nigeria has become a dangerous country, addicted to oil money, with people increasingly willing to turn to corruption, sabotage, and murder to get a fix of the wealth. The cruelest twist is that half a century of oil extraction in the delta has failed to make the lives of the people better. Instead, they are poorer still, and hopeless. "I can say this," Asume Osuoka director of Social Action said firmly. "Nigeria was a much better place without oil."

"After 50 years, the oil companies are still searching for a way to operate successfully with communities," says Antony Goldman, a London-based risk consultant. The delta is littered with failed projects started by oil companies and government agencies—water tanks without operating pumps, clinics with no medicine, schools with no teachers or books, fishponds with no fish.

"The companies didn't consult with villagers," says Michael Watts, director of the African Studies Program at the University of California, Berkeley. "They basically handed out cash to chiefs. It wasn't effective at all." No solution seems in sight for the Niger Delta. The oil companies are keeping their heads down, desperate to safeguard their employees and the flow of oil. The military, ordered to meet force with force, have stepped up patrols in cities and on waterways. The militants are intensifying a deadly guerrilla offensive, hoping

(Continued)

Exhibit 3.4   (Continued)

that rising casualties and oil prices will force the government to negotiate. National elections in April could exacerbate the violence, especially if politicians resort to the practice of hiring youth gangs to deliver votes at gunpoint.

Source: National Geographic, February 2007, from the print edition.

The story of the effects of corporate actions in the Niger Delta brings us to a discussion about ethics and leadership of global organizations. The point to make, though, before embarking on a discussion about ethics in organizations is that if we are discussing intercultural contexts and global business we must acknowledge that ethics traditions, as with many other life dimensions, vary from culture to culture. In the following sections, we provide an overview of Western, Eastern, and Middle Eastern traditions.

Taking the High Ground

One tendency in discussions of ethics is that people have ethical perspectives that they generally—unless they have taken courses in ethics or religion—do not understand. Moreover, many people cannot identify the ethical perspectives of other people, and may misinterpret another person's perspective as being unethical when in fact, the other person is arguing from a different ethics tradition. Before discussing the various ethics traditions, we will first define the term *ethics*.

Ethics has two meanings. The first definition is the moral principles that guide and influence behavior (and decisions). The second definition of ethics is the branch of knowledge concerned with moral principles. It is the first definition with which we concern ourselves. Many people think these two terms, *ethic* and *moral* are interchangeable. The simple answer is, not exactly. Ethic (a set of moral principles) is a *noun*. We use moral, an *adjective* to describe the set of principles we use to judge *right* and *wrong* behavior and, *good* versus *bad* human character, or *just* and *unjust* behavior. Therefore, the question remains, where do our ethical perspectives come from, and what are those perspectives?

Ostensibly, we begin early in our lives learning from our caretakers. In the following sections, we provide the answers to these questions without spending much time on the history of these perspectives since this is not a book about ethics. We will first discuss Western ethics traditions, and then examine some other ethics traditions of other world cultures.

In Western cultures, the three traditions of ethics are the ethics of *purpose* (teleology, with its roots in the work of Aristotle) the ethics of *principle* (deontology, with its roots in the work of German philosopher, Immanual Kant) and ethics of *consequence*, sometimes known as utilitarianism (its roots in the work of Jeremy Bentham and John Stuart Mill).

Ethics of Purpose (Teleology)

A teleological perspective is concerned with the "end"—or purpose—of the person. In this view, the person decides what "should be done," and this *end state* is the "good" to which s/he strives. Conduct, which supports that "good" is judged *right*, and conduct hindering that "good" is judged *wrong*. There is a two-step approach in the ethics of purpose. The first is to decide what should be done, and the second is to find the appropriate means to achieve that end.

In the Western vernacular, there is a common expression, "the ends justify the means" which describes this process. Some people have criticized this philosophy, perhaps rightfully so. For believers of this perspective, goodness is judged from having a properly "good" purpose, or *intention,* in mind. For critics of this perspective, intention is not the only criterion with which behavior should be judged.

Let us take the example of Jerrod, a doctor, who responding to an emergency call, gets in his car and drives faster than the speed limit in an effort to arrive at a hospital in time to save the life of a patient. On one hand, the doctor's intentions would be judged as good from an ethics of purpose perspective, regardless of his breaking the prevailing speed law. On the other hand, ethics of purpose cannot justify the law breaking and, in the judgment of teleology's critics, especially if on the way to the hospital, the doctor caused an accident.

Now, purists of the teleological perspective would challenge this last judgment by saying that in the true spirit of Aristotlian analysis, there is a close relationship between the means and the end. In other words, a purely "good" intention, in this case the doctor wanting to save a patient, cannot be separated from the means. Therefore, if the doctor's intention is to save a life, there must be integrity in how he conducts himself in achieving that end. This means that the doctor must act in such a way as to keep the integrity of his conduct in relation to his intention. In this case, breaking speed laws and crashing his car compromise the integrity between his purpose and his actions.

Ethics of Principle (Deontology)

Now while the idea that an ethical perspective based on the notion of principles sounds straightforward, this perspective is a bit complex. Immanual Kant was an academician whose writings posed considerable challenges. His perspective was that all actions must be judged by the premise used to decide the action. If, whatever premise is used, can be judged as universally applicable, then the action, necessarily, must be judged as ethically "right." Consider the following example of how this universal law works.

- All persons have dignity
- Connie is a person
- Therefore, Connie has dignity.

This rationale implies a universal law, what Kant called the "categorical imperative," that can be applied to all persons. These categorical imperatives command us to obey, because we "will" the law, we create the categories to which the rules apply.

Now, let us return to the earlier example of Jerrod the doctor. We have already a categorical imperative which states that it is the duty of all doctors to preserve human life. We know that Jerrod is a doctor. Therefore, it is Jerrod's duty to save life. If in the course of his actions, Jerrod speeding in his car hits a pedestrian in a crosswalk, how would we judge him according to our categorical imperative? We would say that his conduct violated a universal law, and therefore was an unethical act. In other words, we must always act in such a way that we treat humanity, never simply as a means, but always as an end as well. Implicit in this statement is consistency, the groundwork for universal law which is created through "free will."

Ethics of Consequence (Utilitarianism)

In an ethics of consequence, the focus is on the positive and negative effects of a decision or action on the affected people. To judge an act or decision, we need to know what are "the probable consequences" and what those consequences mean for the affected people (or stakeholders). We also need to know how the *positive consequences* compare with the *negative consequences*. With this information, we can choose right action that does the most good for the most people and does the least harm. It is from the utilitarian perspective that we get the expression "the greater good," meaning the greatest utility. Utilitarianism began as a social movement. Ethics of consequences, then, is a public or social ethic. Utilitarians developed an ethic with which they could simply judge whether an action or policy caused pleasure and happiness or caused pain and unhappiness.

One of the classic debates that arose out of the utilitarian movement pits the interests of the individual against the interests of the public. However, John Stuart Mill, who greatly expanded on Bentham's work, believed that neither side, a majority of thousands, nor an individual, could reasonably expect that their perspective be any more or less justified.

Now, for one final review of Jerrod's conduct. According to an ethic of consequences, Jerrod's choice to ignore prevailing traffic laws created a potential to harm any number of people. In addition, by choosing to speed, he took a risk that his conduct could delay his safe arrival at the hospital. In reality, Jerrod hit a pedestrian, and although the pedestrian escaped major injury, he did sustain injury. Moreover, Jerrod was delayed from his objective because he was compelled to treat the injured pedestrian. However, suppose that there were two pedestrians, a little boy, who was hit and his mother, and the mother who was quite disturbed by the driving behavior of Jerrod, hesitated to allow Jerrod to treat her son. Now, we have two pedestrians harmed, a patient waiting at the hospital, a surgical unit frantic because their doctor is late and has not called, and a doctor who has lost sight of his oath. From an ethic of consequence, we must view Jerrod's decision as a wrong one because it caused harm to several people and resulted in no perceivable positive consequences.

Beyond Western Ethics Traditions

For a period of just under 3000 years ago a series of religious, philosophical, and ethical changes took place, which have greatly influenced human morality. Several highly influential "teachers" appeared, each of whom advocated for a moral, ethical, and spiritual wisdom grander in scope and beyond any one society. In China there were Confucius and Lao Tzu; in India Siddhartha Gautama (Buddha); in ancient Persia the Prophet Zoroaster, and in ancient Israel the great Hebrew prophets Jeremiah, the Second Isaiah and Ezekiel. Thereafter, the first philosophical ethics of the Western tradition in the work of people like Socrates, Plato, and Aristotle appeared. These teachers were followed, some centuries later, by the two most influential figures on ethical perspectives, Jesus of Nazareth and the Prophet Muhammad. Quite rapidly, the messages of these highly influential figures led to the growth of major new movements, which are for the most part both ethical and religious with the exception of the ancient Greek moral philosophers.

In the sections following, we overview the major of the non-Western ethical traditions. It is important that the reader keeps in mind that in many societies and cultures around the world, ethical frameworks and practices are based not on secular philosophy, but rather on spiritual and religious doctrine and sacred writings. Therefore, to understand how people of cultures such as Arab, many Asian and Middle Eastern cultures make decisions, one must first understand their religions.

Islamic Ethics

To appreciate Islamic ethics it is vital first to understand Islam, a religion that has its origins in 7th century Arabia. The word Islam itself means "peace" or surrender to God (Allah). The central tenet of Islam involves the acceptance of Oneness, or unity with God and the recognition of Muhammad as the one true prophet. Accordingly, Muhammad, the messenger sent from Allah, is the recipient of the sacred scripture of Islam, which is called the Quran. Islamic Law derives from the Quran.

From the Quran, comes the Islamic ethical tradition. Because Islam does not separate religion from other human pursuits including government and business, ethics, in principle and practice originate from Islamic religious doctrine. Because, as stated already, the doctrine of Oneness is central in Islamic belief, ethics tradition tends to be God-centered. Also in other words, it is God's Will which forms the basis for evaluating human conduct and ethical behavior. Human actions in such a Divine-centered worldview become purposeful, and are driven by the goal to serve, submit, and surrender to God's Will.

The Quran, then, is the primary source in the Islamic ethics, giving guidelines and is the central source for deducing Islamic ethical and moral behavior. These moral guidelines emanate mostly from passages that describe the attributes of the Muslim God. For instance, the Quran presents God as a possessor of Divinely beautiful attributes. Therefore, the faithful are those people who are perceived to have internalized these attributes in their interaction with others. As the embodiment of human perfection, Muhammad's conduct and behavior becomes the norm and standard through which the ethical ideals of the Muslim community are determined. This means, that it is incumbent on people following Islamic Law to try to behave by the standards "known" by the faithful to be Divine attributes. For example, if kindness is one Divine attribute, then the expectation is that people should behave kindly toward one another.

Islamic ethical attitudes toward the environment derive mostly from Muhammad's teachings and personal conduct. If among other definitions, ethics is the codification of the rules for behavior, the way we make decisions about right and wrong, and the values that underlie such decision making then, represents a vital resource of reference for a systematic regulation of Muslim life and activity. In other words, all rules concerning prohibitions and what is permissible, stretching from rules governing ritual observances, social transactions (like commercial and family laws), are supposed to be sanctioned by Islamic Law. Islamic Law has classified human actions into five basic categories.

1. Obligatory acts (the five daily prayers, fasting during Ramadhan, or a pilgrimage to Mecca)
2. Recommended acts (caring for the sick, kindness to animals, and respect for the environment)
3. Reprehensible but not forbidden acts (silence against injustice)

4. Forbidden acts (stealing, bribery, cheating, or dishonesty)
5. Morally neutral (liking baseball but not football).

The implications of the Islamic codification of human actions are that there is some ambiguity and that there is a close relationship between ethics and law. Ambiguity is evident in the actions that are categorized as recommended, reprehensible, or indifferent/morally neutral. In the case of the ambiguous categories of human actions, the law becomes neutral. In other words, Muslim conduct that may be classified under these categories, although in some instances it may be judged undesirable or harmful, it is nevertheless exempted from civil penalties.

Islam is often described as an "action based" religion meaning that beliefs must be accompanied by necessary actions. The ethical implications of this, is that human intention alone to "do good" is insufficient. From the Islamic perspective, good intentions must translate into good actions. For example, and continuing with our story of Jerrod, it is not enough for Jerrod to say that he intended to remove broken bottles on the road; he should actually remove them. Otherwise, if any individual were endangered, Jerrod would be morally responsible. The point is that good intention must be acted out and not confined to an individual's thoughts.

Like most traditions, Islam is not free from diverse points of view. One to consider is the imperative to apply and enforce God's will through application of Islamic Law. Is that simply influencing the practice of God's laws, or is it enforcing morality? For example, Muslim countries such as Saudi Arabia and Sudan have made Islamic Law, civil law. Similarly, even in countries where Muslims live within secular democracies, Muslims have not shied away from demanding that Islamic Law should govern them. In other words, as the symbol of human excellence, Prophet Muhammad represents the ethical ideal. Based on this centrality of Muhammad within the Islam, parallel to legal or Islamic Law-based ethics, a less legalistic ethics has emerged that stresses the compassionate side of God rather than the punitive dimension of God.

In summary, morality in Islam is based on the following basic beliefs and principles. Allah is the source and creator of all goodness, truth, and beauty. Human beings are representatives or agents of God on earth. All things in creation are created for the service of humans. Allah as a just God does not place unnecessary burdens on humans. All that humans do must be done in moderation. Except for the explicitly forbidden, all things are permissible. The ultimate goal is to attain the pleasure of Allah. Accordingly, Islam has lain down in the form of religious and social duties regulations that have moral and ethical implications for organizing human life. These are meant to assist Muslims in their quest toward moral progress and improvement of inter-human relations. A critical reflection on

Islamic ethics indicates that Islamic morals are goal driven. The ultimate goal and concern is the desire to attain the pleasure of Allah. Such a view has led some Muslims to assert that morality cannot be imposed by human authority but must emerge from the World of the individual.

Hindu Ethics

The ethical tradition of Hinduism is a cultural and historical tradition so rich and complex that some see it as a federation or plurality of religions rather than a single religious stream. An amazing variety of religious beliefs, practices, customs, and trends can be found within the wider Hindu community.

There are a number of ways or paths in Hinduism that will enable the seeker to achieve final spiritual liberation from the problems of suffering, bondage, and ignorance. A Hindu may choose whichever path fits his/her circumstances. The three main paths are:

1. The path of works done in the right spirit, a spirit of unselfishness.
2. The path of inner spiritual realization.
3. The path of loving devotion to a personal God (e.g. Shiva, Vishnu) or the great Goddess.

Following one or more of these three paths will eventually bring the seeker to a genuine realization of, and encounter with, the one Divine Reality, which has numerous manifestations: Shiva, Vishnu, Krishna, Durga, Ganesh.

There are many Hindu Scriptures, and a Hindu may choose to focus on any number of these Scriptures as his or her preferred holy book; this might be the popular Bhagavad Gita, the time-honored collection known as the Four Vedas, or the Ramayana.

Hinduism is a constellation of traditions, and the diversity continues into modern times. Hinduism has been described as a tolerant and flexible spiritual tradition. Religious and social practice in Hinduism is crucially important; Hinduism is a tradition in which "doing and acting" are more fundamental than "believing." This doing can take many forms: popular worship, various ritual performances, yoga, prayer, chanting, good deeds, participation in festivals, pilgrimages, and many other things. One important context in which Hindu religion has been learned and lived out over the centuries is within families.

Many current Hindu philosophers today perceive an act as truly amoral only if it is taken out of *informed* choices that are *freely* made. Hinduism, some argue, is perhaps the most spiritual of the world's religions. Yet the tradition contains a full range of worldly and otherworldly values. For example, Bhagavad Gita describes the four goals of life: Moral and ritual action; Economic and political activity; Desire and pleasure; Ultimate spiritual liberation. One significant teaching of the Gita is that you do not need to leave the world and society behind in order to find God; you can continue to act fully in the world in all manner of ways, but you should do so in a spirit of action without attachment. This means action without desire, without ambition, without selfishness, without vested interest.

Hindus live by two important principles.

1. Karma *actions* (i.e. any actions, whether right or wrong) coupled with the consequences of actions.
2. Dharma *right/appropriate actions* (including moral actions, and appropriate ritual actions).

Karma effectively means, as you sow, so shall you reap. Act morally, and this will affect your future lives for the good; act selfishly and negatively, and in your future lives you will experience negative and miserable circumstances. Consequently, moral considerations are based on whether or not the person's desire to do something either provides insurance for a good next life, or provides a strong enough motivation to outweigh the thought of future life repercussions.

By contrast, Buddhists believe that karma is generated only by intentional human actions. Karma in Hinduism does not involve some fatalistic belief that there is no human freedom, that everything is always pre-determined. Although what a Hindu is now is a result of past (and unchangeable) forces and influences, from this moment on the Hindu is relatively free to shape his or her own future destiny.

Dharma is a very important principle in Hindu traditions and has two contextual meanings. Applied to the universe, dharma implies orderliness and coherence of the universe and of nature. Applied to the human and social realms, dharma implies proper action, right action, and moral action.

The link between these two meanings is simply that dharmic action is right action that conforms to the order that lives in all things.

Some dharmic virtues are universal and obligatory for everyone (e.g. honesty, temperance, patience, hospitality, and kindness), while other applications of dharma are contextual, depending on the caste to which you belong (Brahmins, Rulers/warriors, Farmers/traders, Servant workers), or the stage-of-life you are passing through (Spiritual student, Married householder, Contemplative forest-dweller, Holy wanderer).

There are a number of traditional social practices in Hinduism that are based simply on a principle of, do not do things because you feel that you must do them; do them when you understand and sincerely accept the call of genuine moral obligation.

African Ethics

It is important to understand that it is not possible to generalize across African cultures, given the large number and variety. Nonetheless, for our purposes here, we provide as much universality as possible without compromising accuracy. There is agreement among scholars that there are a number of patterns in most African cultures. For example, all African cultures share the concept of ancestor veneration.

The importance given to ancestors is demonstrated by the fact that ancestors are the perceived guardians of ethics and *morality*. Arguably, such a view stems from the understanding that since ancestors are those who have lived exemplary lives in the world of the living, they continue to be pre-occupied with regulating the affairs of their communities even in their temporary absence. In a sense, they are still concerned about the moral integrity of their communities. For disregard of what constitutes moral virtues renders the community vulnerable to harmful spirits, misfortune, and subsequent destruction. Relatedly, a universal concept across African societies is that the notion of what is wrong and right, desirable and undesirable, acceptable and disliked is evaluated based on whether it has the approval or non-approval of the ancestors. In other words, in deciding on a course of action, the question becomes how conduct will invite the pleasure or earn the wrath of the ancestors.

Given that African ethics and morality are based on the veneration of ancestors, the general character of African ethics, the central concern, is the management of life and maintenance of well-being within society. Individual ethical choices are made within the context of the community, that is, community in the inclusive sense. In such a context, individual actions are evaluated and judged based on the effect that they have on the life of the community. In particular, within the South African context, this view finds expression in the concept of *Ubuntu* and a similar notion is expressed in the Shona concept of *Ukama*, implying the relatedness between humans, environment, god, and ancestors. Simplified, the concept underpins the very communal nature of African society and by extension its ethics. The well-being of the individual and his or her interests are possible through the community where the community becomes a web of relationships. This is well expressed in the Zulu saying, *Umuntu ngumuntu ngabantu* (You are a person through others). In other words, the well-being of the individual and its interest is possible through the community. As an ethical principle, *Ubuntu* then places a high value in sound human relations. Therefore, in traditional societies no one was a stranger, hospitality to strangers and the spirit of sharing were respected values of a community. Likewise, cruelty, murder, cheating, or stealing was sufficient to warrant ostracizing the individual through public censure (i.e. for the shameful or immoral act). Therefore, in a sense the act of ostracizing the individual served as some kind of a form of deterrent punishment.

In ethical terms, it is the collective wisdom of the ancestors and elders that becomes the basis or point of reference for moral decisions or choices that the individual or community makes. Morality is the creation of the community and emerges from its social institutions. It is lived within the community so what an individual does directly or indirectly affects the whole society. Therefore, tradition demands that those who have done shameful or immoral acts must be cleansed before they can be accepted back into the community. In summary, the community's history and life experience are the sources of African ethics. This source may vary and evolves from social customs, religious beliefs, regulations, social taboos, proverbs, and certain symbols.

Confucianism

Confucianism is a philosophy concerned with humans, their achievements and interests, rather than with the abstract beings and problems of theology. In Confucianism, man is the center of the universe: man cannot live alone, but with other human beings. For human beings, the ultimate goal is individual happiness. The necessary condition to achieve happiness is through peace. To obtain peace, Confucius discovered human relations consisting of the five relationships that are based on love and duties. Great Unity of the world should be developed. All humans are good and always striving to be better, be loyal, and live morally. The focus is on comprehensive truths rather than logic. They feel the more comprehensive the closer it is to the truth. Confucianism emphasizes sympathizing for others when they are suffering. They are always searching for a higher sense of sympathy for people. This belief system also entails the belief that the ultimate personal harmony in life is the relationship one has during human existence.

Taoism

Taoism is a constellation of related Chinese philosophical and religious traditions and concepts. These traditions influenced East Asia for over two thousand years and some have spread internationally. Taoist propriety and ethics emphasize the Three Jewels of the Tao; namely, compassion, moderation, and humility. Taoist thought focuses on wu wei ("non-action"), spontaneity, humanism, and emptiness. An emphasis is placed on the link between people and nature. Taoism teaches that this link lessened the need for rules and order, and leads one to a better understanding of the world.

The word *Tao* means the "path" or "way," but in Chinese religion and philosophy it has taken on more abstract meanings. Tao is rarely an object of worship, being treated more like the Central Asian concepts of dharma. Most traditional Chinese Taoists are polytheistic. Nature and ancestor spirits are also common in popular Taoism. Organized Taoism distinguishes its ritual activity from that of the folk religion, which some professional Taoists (*Daoshi*) view as debased. This sort of shamanism is eschewed for an emphasis on internal alchemy among the "elite" Taoists.

The Moral You

Supporting all ethical traditions, there is a system of morality. Morals are the principles we use to judge right and wrong, just and unjust behavior, and good versus bad human character. It is our moral principles that guide our behavior and with which we form our opinions about our behavior and that of other people. No matter what culture you are from, you possess a set of morals.

Previously, we discussed ethical frameworks and the bases for the various ethical perspectives to which people subscribe. Further, we also noted that our ethical perspectives develop in us from an early age through our interactions with caretakers, religious institutions, schools, and general societal influences (television, media, role models, etc.). If our moral principles guide us and we learn them through interaction with our caretakers and early influences, the question remains of how we develop moral principles.

In this section, we discuss the prevalent Western theory of moral development to date as refined and researched by Lawrence Kohlberg, a professor of Education at Harvard University. Kohlberg based his theory on the earlier work of Piaget done in the 1930s. Kohlberg posited his refinement of Piaget's theory in the early 1960s and actively continues his research today.

The Formation of Moral Principles

An important aspect of any developmental process is that it occurs over time. In other words, development means something transforms. Moral development is no exception to this rule. People progress forward—never backward—through stages of moral development. What transforms is the person's cognitive structure. Simply put, the way that people intellectually construct their thoughts, evolves over time due to the influences of their environment and their own personality formation.

The research on moral development demonstrates three important characteristics. First, people exhibit consistent moral judgment through each stage. This means that during any stage, a person will behave similarly in character with that stage. They do not move backwards, and they do not suddenly behave as though they were in an advanced stage and then retreat to a far earlier stage. Second, people pass through the stages sequentially; they do not go forward, then slip back, then move forward again, unless they experience extreme trauma. Third, as people progress through the stages, they incorporate the essential aspects of earlier stages. However, they tend to use the highest stage understood.

The result of this developmental process is that people progress from a simplistic moral perspective of right and wrong to an increasingly complex and differentiated model of moral reasoning. What causes some individuals to progress and others to remain in earlier stages has to do with many factors such as the ability to empathize with other people, and their capacity for remorse. Generally, when an individual is stuck at a psychological level they will be stuck at a moral development level as well. Next, we describe each of Kohlberg's three stages of moral development. The three stages in human development are Preconventional, Conventional, and Postconventional. Within each of these stages are subsets, which we describe as well.

Level One: Preconventional

In this stage, children respond to cultural rules of right and wrong by perceiving the connection between behavior and physical pain or pleasure.

Stage One: Punishment and Obedience Orientation. People (children) in this stage of moral reasoning equate right and wrong with the dictates of authority and the punishment associated with a given action. In other words, the consequences of the child's action determine how s/he interprets the goodness or badness of those actions. The child seeks to avoid punishment and respects authority based on the avoidance of punishment, not based on a value for elders.

Stage Two: Instrumental Relativist Orientation. Children in this stage of reasoning begin to factor their own wants and needs in their choices. If something satisfies the child's own needs, then it is worth the risk of punishment. Simply put, the child in this stage begins to understand that s/he can satisfy his/her needs through behaving in an approved manner. S/he will behave in such a way because s/he is convinced that there is reward—a *quid pro quo relationship*. Occasionally in this stage, the child even considers the needs of other people.

Level Two: Conventional

Once children reach the conventional stage, they begin to associate their own behavior with maintaining the expectations of their social groups. In this stage, they learn conformity and loyalty to the rules of their families and other important social groups.

Stage Three: *Interpersonal Concordance Orientation*. Children in this stage of reasoning are often entering adolescence, and become concerned with what is good for others. There is a pre-occupation with being a "good" girl or boy. They have a larger perspective, and see themselves as part of a society with its rules and regulations.

Stage Four: *Law and Order Orientation*. Individuals in this stage of reasoning have an increased sense of social order. They tend more to rely on "the rules" as laid out by the society to make their moral choices. Maintaining social order and doing one's duty are important.

Level Three: Postconventional

Once individuals enter this stage, they begin to evaluate moral values and principles in terms of the merit of the rule or value apart from the particular authority or group.

Stage Five: *Social Contract-Legalistic Orientation*. Individuals in this stage maintain their emphasis on social order, but they see it less as a black-and-white set of rules and more as mutually agreed upon standards. They also factor in the individual's rights when making moral choices. They do not see the social system as perfect, but believe that it is still necessary to avoid chaos.

Stage Six: *Universal Ethical-Principle Orientation*. Kohlberg's final (and most controversial) stage represents the epitome of human moral reasoning. Individuals in this stage realize that sometimes what they choose democratically is not necessarily in the best interest of the society. They make their moral choices based on their internal ethical standards, which take into account the universal good.

Kohlberg's Classic Dilemma

In the next section, we provide an example of how to understand and use Kohlberg's model of moral development. Kohlberg used this particular example in his research. Kohlberg's description starts with children who receive their orientation to values and ethics. However, as a person matures, the individual should expand upon this original psychological construct. As one grows, so should this moral sense of responsibility.

Heinz Steals the Drug.   In Europe, a woman was near death from cancer. One drug might save her, a form of radium that a druggist in the same town had recently discovered. The druggist was charging $2,000, ten times the cost of making the drug. The sick woman's husband, Heinz, went to everyone he know to borrow the money, but he could get together only about half of what the drug cost. He told the druggist that his wife was dying and asked him to sell the drug cheaper or let him pay later. The druggist said "No." The husband got desperate and broke into the man's store to steal the drug for his wife. Should the husband have done that? Why or why not?

Level One: Preconventional—In this stage, personal needs determine right or wrong. Favors are returned along the lines of "You scratch my back; I'll scratch yours." In the Heinz case, the person wants to avoid apprehension—either for stealing the drug or for not doing enough to save his wife. Wanting to avoid punishment will be his main motivator.

Level Two: Conventional—Someone operating from this level will value both following the law and doing what is best for a person. They would see the situation as either "it is against the law to steal" or "it is okay to steal the drug because he is trying to help his wife."

Level Three: Postconventional—Someone operating from Level 3 has altruistic ideals in mind. They value human life over a potentially arbitrary law and they would believe that you have to consider the situation.

Kohlberg's theory is value-free. Heinz could have stolen or not stolen the drug with moral reasoning from *each* level.

Moral Responsibility

Does understanding the stages moral development help us understand better the behavior of organizations? Does it help us understand our own behavior? Can we better grapple with the issues facing our business world today?

From our perspective the answer to all these questions is, yes. As members of organizations, we carry the expectations that we, as adults, are fully prepared to make appropriate decisions. By understanding our own moral reasoning and understanding that we have in our grasp the cognitive tools to make appropriate decisions, we necessarily assume responsibility for our actions. Along with other cultural biases, intercultural leaders must be aware of their own ethical and moral principles. As we have indicated with other organizational considerations, intercultural leaders must be aware that ethics and moral standards differ across cultures and this area of knowledge and understanding must be learned at a local level along with language and other cultural norms, laws, and customs.

Integrative Ethics Model

In any situation, there are nine elements to consider, the person or "agent" (who), the act (what, including all potential consequences), alternative acts (all options considered—which does the greatest good for the most people, causing the least harm to the fewest number of people) the "agency" (how it will be carried out), the scene (where), occasion (when), the purpose (why), the actors (all stakeholders to whom something is or may be done), and consent and/or notification.

When all nine of these elements are considered, and all the ethics traditions are linked together, the strengths of those traditions enable us to build an integrated ethical framework. Such a framework gives us a comprehensive basis with which to make decisions. For organizations, it can provide a methodology and practice that can allow members to avoid disagreements and help decision-makers prevent harmful conduct. Making ethical decisions must start at the top of the organization and be practiced throughout the organization. Michael Hackworth stated in his *The Buck Stops Here* presentation for the Markkula Center for Applied Ethics related how he models ethical leadership in his role as CEP of chip manufacturer Cirrus Logic, "employees take their cue from the CEO," he said. "In every situation, they ask, 'What does the boss want?' They give him what he wants when they talk about the business, when they talk about the law, and when they talk- or don't talk-about ethics. In general, people line up behind what the CEO wants."

In Exhibit 3.5, the Pegasus International case study is presented. Using the integrative ethics framework above, imagine how leaders might confront the challenge of their company planning to expand into a country where bribe-taking is considered a normal part of doing business.

Exhibit 3.5

The Case of the Million-Dollar Decision

Pegasus International Inc. is a leading manufacturer of integrated circuits (chips) and related software for such specialty markets as communications and mass storage, as well as PC-based audio, video, and multimedia. With a focus on innovation, Pegasus is committed to "technology leadership in the new millennium." Its long-standing strategy has been to anticipate changes in existing and emerging growth markets and to have hardware and software solutions ready before the market needs them. The company has also made significant strides in wireless communications.

The systems and products of Pegasus' wireless business have been selling well in its already existing markets in the United States, Japan, and Europe. But, like any company, Pegasus is eager to grow the business. At a strategy session with the Wireless Division, Pegasus CEO, Tom Oswald, and division managers decide to explore the potential of expanding their business to China.

Initial research indicates that China is likely to develop into a huge market for wireless because its people do not currently have this capability and the government has made spending on wireless a priority. Wireless is really the only choice for China because of the high cost of burying the communications cables necessary in wired systems; further, in underdeveloped countries, copper wires are often stolen and sold on the black market.

Subsequent research does raise one concern for Pegasus wireless managers. They tell Oswald, "We have this problem. China allocates frequencies

(Continued)

Exhibit 3.5   (Continued)

and makes franchise decisions city by city, district by district. A 'payoff' is usually required to get licenses."

The CEO says, "A lot of companies are doing business with China right now. How do they get around the problem?"

His managers have done their homework: "We believe most other companies contract with agents to represent them in the country and to get the licenses. What these contractors do is their own business, but apparently it works pretty well because the CEOs of all those companies are able to sign the disclosure statement required by law saying that they know of no instance where they bribed for their business."

"I wonder if paying someone else to do the crime is the same as our doing the crime," Oswald says. "I'm just not very comfortable with the whole question of payoffs. So, let me ask you, if we don't expand into China, how much business will we lose, potentially?"

His Wireless Division manager responds, "It will be huge not to do business in all the countries expecting payoffs. China alone represents easily $100 million of business per year. It's not life and death, but it is a sizable incremental opportunity for us, not to mention potential Japanese partners who will make significant capital investments. All we have to do is add our already-existing technology. When you consider all that, we have a lot to gain. What will we really lose if our local contractors are forced to make payoffs every now and then?"

Oswald wants his company to succeed, he wants to maximize shareholder value, he wants to keep his job, and he wants to model ethical leadership. He has made an effort to build a corporate culture characterized not only by aggressive R&D and growth but also by integrity, honesty, teamwork, and respect for the individual. As a result, the company enjoys an excellent reputation among its customers and suppliers, employee morale is high, and ethics is a priority at the company.

The Pegasus International mission and values statement is:

Pegasus International has always placed a high premium on its relationship with its employees. Although the nature of our business and markets may change as the company evolves to meet different market conditions, a strong emphasis on ethical behavior and respect for each other will remain constant. Our behavior is guided by these simple but important values:

- Be honest with yourself and others
- Tell it all and tell it like it is
- Protect our intellectual property
- Face the facts
- Keep your commitments make it happen
- Take personal responsibility and be accountable
- Think beyond boundaries and leverage your activity
- Value each other's contributions/ opinions/perspectives
- Attack the problem, not the person

(Continued)

Exhibit 3.5   (Continued)

- Be prepared for meetings
- Do not waste others' time
- Listen actively
- Seek others' participation
- Create value for customers
- Promise what you can do and do what you promise
- Build quality in and improve continuously
- Meet/exceed customers' requirements
- Create long-term successful customers.

Source: Adapted from: Hackworth and Shanks (2007). Santa Clara University Markkula Center for Applied Ethics website.

The Principle of "Care" in Practice

A Geoleader can demonstrate the principle of Care through the following practices and behaviors:

- Clarify and understand the membership of each stakeholder group
- Meet with representatives of each stakeholder group to understand their interests, values, and goals
- Communicate commitment and concern for stakeholder perspectives and interests
- Analyze all business decisions from the perspective of each stakeholder group
- Develop decision rules to be used in making business decisions that consider stakeholder interests
- Develop outcome scenarios as a step in strategic planning.

Case Presentation: eBay Enters Japan

How do you design a business venture and build a relationship with another culture that reflects respect and mutuality? The answer to that question is evident in Exhibit 3.6 (eBay Japan), and illustrates an important point about how American business leaders can engage other cultures with the principles of Care.

Exhibit 3.6

eBay Company Profile

eBay, Inc., through its subsidiaries, provides online marketplaces for the sale of goods and services, online payments services, and online communication

(Continued)

Exhibit 3.6   (Continued)

channels to a diverse community of individuals and businesses in the United States and internationally. It operates in three segments: Marketplaces, Payments, and Communications. Marketplaces segment provides the infrastructure to enable online commerce in various platforms, including the traditional eBay.com platform, as well as other online platforms, such as Shopping.com, Kijiji, Gumtree.com, LoQUo.com, Intoko, Marktplaats.nl, mobile.de., and Rent.com. This segment's eBay.com platform includes traditional auction format; fixed price format; and eBay Stores that provide various tools for sellers to build, manage, promote, and track their business.

Its services comprise trust and safety programs; feedback forum; safeHarbor program; verified rights owner program; PowerSeller program; customer support; and tools and services. Payments segment offers PayPal, a payments platform that enables individuals or businesses with an email address to send and receive payments online. Its services include joining the network, verification of its PayPal's account holders, withdrawing money, and trust and safety programs.

Communications segment consists of Skype, an Internet communication product that enables voice over Internet protocol calls between Skype users, as well as provides Skype users connectivity to traditional fixed-line and mobile telephones. This segment offers its software in 28 languages. The company was founded in 1995 and is headquartered in San Jose, California.

Source: Yahoo! Finance, eBay, http://finance.yahoo!.com/q/pr?s = EBAY

---

eBay is not just an online auction site; it is an industry within itself. It has changed the way we shop, the way we spend our leisure time and the way that we do business online. Millions of users and billions of dollars in revenue over its brief history clearly prove that the founders' vision is solid and its leadership talented. The company has had astounding growth in an extremely competitive industry and it thrived even through the dotcom disaster years. It is reasonably safe to say that eBay is a "household word" in the United States and even in other parts of the world.

The company vision, as set forth by the eBay founders has been to continue growth, and to develop new territories. Company leadership looked toward the Japanese market that up until recently had been untested in online auctions. Pundits considered the Japanese market a risky venture because no one was sure how the Japanese people would react to buying "used" goods. Japan is considered by some to be an extremely image conscious society and buying someone else's old computer did not seem to fit into that culture. All the major players in online auctions were sitting on the fence, waiting to see if they should take action.

The eBay leadership decided that it was time to jump in and Yahoo! caught word of it. Yahoo!'s management had the philosophy that if the Japanese market failed, it failed; but if it succeeded, the riches would go to the first company in. The story goes that Yahoo! leadership took the chance. The company leaders and staff spared no effort in mobilization and

(Continued)

Exhibit 3.6   (Continued)

had their site together and operational in a mere 4 months. By all accounts, Yahoo!'s site was an overnight success.

There were still high hopes for eBay's launch however, and it was the intense faith in eBay's CEO Meg Whitman that fueled those hopes. A graduate from Princeton and Harvard, Meg Whitman used her considerable presence and assuring confidence to lead her through a distinguished career at some of the top organizations in the United States. She had taken eBay from a somewhat popular online destination with 30 employees to an Internet behemoth. Ms. Whitman had proven herself fully in the past; there was no reason to think that she would not hit another home run. She hand-picked Merle Okawara to head up eBay Japan. Ms. Okawara was a prominent Japanese business leader, being one of the only female executives in the male-dominated (Japanese) business arena. She was famous for having rejuvenated a failing frozen food manufacturing business and had experienced a thriving entrepreneurial career. Together, these women were determined to maneuver eBay Japan into the next cultural phenomenon.

By the time the eBay site was ready for launch, it was more than apparent that there was a thriving market for online auctions in Japan. It was an instant attraction for all of the memorabilia collectors at a time when the Japanese people were beginning to realize that the economy was faltering. They did not have the same cash flow they had enjoyed in previous years and the deals found on the Internet were appealing. Yahoo!, being the only major player for the previous 5 months, was soaring in popularity. eBay went live and almost immediately fizzled out. It turned out that the golden child of dot com had somehow managed to get everything wrong. They had allowed Yahoo! the opportunity to develop a strong, loyal consumer base, who was now accustomed to no user fees. eBay had decided to stay with their customary format and charge all the fees as in the North American market.

Paying a fee was not a great incentive for Japanese consumers who were already feeling cash strapped and were happy where they were. It made no sense to switch to eBay. However, fees were not the only Japanese complaint with the new eBay Japan site.

The physical layout of the site was apparently wrong as well. Designers poorly planned the search function and did not include extra features that attract a Japanese user; things like horoscopes and cartoons. No one at eBay, not even Ms. Okawara, seemed to understand that the Japanese *youth* did not have access to the credit cards like their Western counterparts did. They liked to pay cash, so the pressure to pay with PayPal or credit cards was a complete turn-off.

Initially, Meg Whitman tried to put it off to growing pains and vowed to persevere in the market; they were in it for "the long haul." Nonetheless, it became very apparent that their moment of opportunity was gone. Nothing was going to salvage eBay Japan and both Meg Whitman and Okawara had to admit to a very public defeat. They could have stayed and fought it out, they could have poured millions of dollars into it, but being great leaders, they knew that they had to care about all of the stakeholders and get out. They did not admit permanent defeat however;

(Continued)

Exhibit 3.6   (Continued)

they used this as a learning experience and changed their growth strategy. They have since started purchasing their way into the markets, as they did in a $9.5 million deal with Neocom in Taiwan and a $50 million dollar deal with Baaazee in India. They now save the time it takes to build a site from scratch and they delete the cultural learning curve. Interestingly enough, neither new site charges user fees.

How could eBay have succeeded in Japan?

Case Perspective: Care Applied

In an interview with Newsweek magazine in October 2002, CEO Whitman was asked what went wrong in Japan. She replied that eBay "didn't have the first-mover advantage in Japan." However, she went on to say that she believed that "With 20–20 hindsight, I don't think we executed as well as we might have…we were a much less experienced company in early 2000 than we are today."

While it is true that Yahoo!'s first-mover position gave the company a huge advantage over eBay and it is also true that by the time eBay arrived the Japanese economy had turned downward; other cultural factors probably played a significant role in eBay's missteps in Japan as well. Arguably then, eBay's first misstep was its late arrival in the Japanese market. Its second misstep was in *how it entered* Japan in that second position.

Unless a company is entering the Japanese marketplace with no competition and there is a pent up demand for particular goods or services, it is wiser to enter unobtrusively at first and then move more aggressively once established. Companies that have entered Japan in competitive markets successfully have done so by taking the culturally proper approach and built strong networks and relationships prior to starting operations. While eBay leadership wisely chose to hire a bicultural businessperson to lead eBay Japan operations, doing so was not enough, especially since Yahoo! had already established itself. Additionally, the newly appointed President of eBay Japan, Merle Okawara was born and resided in Hawaii, and while she had attempted to start a business in Japan, and was known as a businessperson who turned around a failing food business, to the Japanese, she was still a relative outsider. As a Japanese-American, Ms. Okawara would have had to approach the Japanese in a similar way than any other foreigner.

The company's third misstep was not properly preparing for the Japanese consumer. For eBay, sinking significant funds in development would have been fruitful had they also taken the time to network with the Japanese and build solid relationships with consumers and local businesses. Further, taking time to engage with Japanese people in a meaningful way should have provided eBay leadership with an understanding of the interests, needs, preferences, and goals of potential Japanese consumers. While there has been some convergence of Western and Japanese cultures over the past 40 years due to globalization, the Japanese culture holds to a number of distinctions from Western cultures. By considering and involving Japanese consumers in the design and building of the eBay interface, eBay most likely could have constructed a pleasing product.

During the initial start-up period of eBay Japan, the company's marketing and public relations department and Ms. Okawara invested time and energy in publishing articles and press releases about how the Japanese needed to master the Internet and suggested that the Japanese were ready to embrace the concept of purchasing used goods. It is clear that Ms. Okawara had the ability to promote herself and represent eBay's interests. However, was it the most interculturally perceptive networking? Was a cultural mindset altered? Probably not.

Case Presentation: Cost Versus Care

The subject of this chapter is the principle we refer to as "Care." It is simply the idea that leaders and managers, in fact, all business people, would serve humanity and themselves better by having honorable intentions behind decisions and actions taken.

The organizational practice of outsourcing has been commonly used for over a decade. Originally, the practice was created as a cost-saving measure to avoid hiring and employ people in functions that an organization was not particularly expert. In the following *Economist* article, we see some interesting new trends. When we read the article that we present in Exhibit 3.7, we immediately thought of Fredrick Winslow Taylor, who is often credited with being the father of "scientific management" and his particularly timely speech made before the U.S. Congress in 1912, in which among other brilliant things, said, "Scientific Management is not any efficiency device, or a time saving device, or a pay system, it is not a scheme, or a time and motion study. Now, in essence, scientific management involves a complete *mental revolution* on the part of all parties engaged in any particular establishment or industry—a complete mental revolution as to their duties toward their work, toward their fellow men, and toward their employees [or bosses]."

Exhibit 3.7

Old Assumptions Are Being Challenged as the Outsourcing Industry Matures

At the start of the decade anecdotes began to circulate about the perils of sending white-collar work abroad. One apocryphal tale centered on Indian

(Continued)

Exhibit 3.7 (Continued)

workers who had been given the job of keying the results of the latest British census into a database. The work was done quickly. Everyone was satisfied until the entries were reviewed and it emerged that the most common surname in Britain was "Ditto." But the initial amusement about offshoring soon gave way to fear. The threat that cheap labor in India and other low-wage countries posed to costlier workers in the developed world was a central theme of America's 2004 presidential campaign.

Several years on, the politics of offshoring are still childish: Recently, a leaked memo from Barack Obama's research staff referred to the Illinois senator's main rival for the Democratic nomination as "Hillary Clinton (D-Punjab)." Yet the outsourcing industry, the conduit for much offshored work, is maturing. (Outsourcing refers to work contracted to an outside firm; offshoring is the shift of work abroad.) And as it grows up, it is changing in many ways.

For a start, the industry is growing less rapidly than before. Offshore work is a component of most outsourcing contracts, but jobs no longer flow only from richer countries to poorer ones. Cost savings are still the principal motivation to outsource, but performance is becoming the main battleground between providers. Even the language is changing. Vendors refer to themselves as partners. Labor arbitrage is out; "intellectual arbitrage" is in. Some even recoil from the word "outsourcing" itself. "It gives the impression of just throwing something over the wall," says Ross Perot Jr., chairman of Perot Systems, a computer services firm based in Plano, Texas.

Start with the numbers. The latest quarterly report on the state of global outsourcing from TPI, a consultancy, was published recently. It showed that both the number and value of contracts awarded during the first half of this year had declined in comparison with the same period in 2006. In 2007 the total value of contracts awarded in the first 6 months was the lowest since 2001 (see chart).

Critics argue that the TPI numbers understate levels of activity. They do not include public-sector deals, deals worth less than $50 million or contracts renewed without the use of an adviser, of which there are an increasing number as relationships between customers and suppliers deepen. Some parts of the industry are also much bubblier than others: demand in Europe is robust, for example. "We're not in the land of scarcity," says Kevin Campbell, who runs Accenture's outsourcing business. According to Ian Marriott of Gartner, a market-research firm, the industry has settled into a pattern of single-digit growth.

As growth slows, it is clear that making money is becoming more difficult for outsourcing firms. Competing on price is getting ever harder. Established vendors are hiring workers in the same low-cost locations as their offshore rivals—the likes of Accenture and IBM have been furiously ramping up their operations in India, for example. One response is to keep searching for ever-cheaper locations, both within India and outside it, but a race to the bottom on price threatens both the quality of service and profit margins. For the top-tier providers, the way to stand apart from the crowd is to deliver more valuable services.

(Continued)

Exhibit 3.7   (Continued)

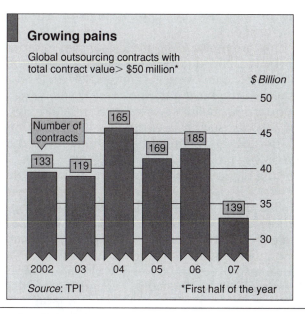

Growing pains

Global outsourcing contracts with
total contract value > $50 million*

$ Billion

Number of contracts

133   119   165   169   185   139

2002   03   04   05   06   07

Source: TPI   *First half of the year

Figure 3.1 Growing Pains

In part that means moving into more sophisticated areas of activity. As well as managing clinical-trial data for pharmaceutical clients, for example, Accenture is starting to monitor people's reactions to drugs. Xansa, a British service provider, not only processes expenses for its clients but also analyses the numbers to help them spot anomalies. And it is working on a way to manage absenteeism among clients' employees by having a nurse call people at home after they have been off sick for a couple of days.

All this has the effect of making consulting and industry expertise a more important part of providers' armory. It also leads to changes in the way that outsourcing firms are measured. Jean-Hervé Jenn of Convergys, a provider of back-office services, points to a shift in call-centre outsourcing contracts away from quantitative metrics, such as the duration of calls, toward more qualitative measures based on customer satisfaction. (Despite popular perceptions, that does not mean an end to offshore call centers. According to Mr. Jenn, when technical knowledge counts for more than familiar accents, it may still be better to sent calls to overseas agents.)

The industry's reward systems are also under scrutiny. Traditional pricing models have been based on a mark-up over the cost of labor (which is a risk to the client) or on a fixed cost for delivering the service (which is a risk to the vendor, particularly given rising wages and stronger currencies in many emerging markets). But attention is gradually shifting to "gains-sharing" arrangements, whereby outsourcing firms and customers both benefit from performance improvements. Neeraj Bhargava, boss of WNS, an Indian provider that started life as a unit of British Airways, points to the example of vendors being able to recover debts that are too small for big companies to

(Continued)

Exhibit 3.7   (Continued)

collect efficiently on their own. A share of the extra revenue recovered can go straight to the vendor.

Outsourcing firms are moving into more countries in order to deliver the right mix of cost, risk, and quality. As Western providers concentrate on beefing up their presence in low-wage centers, Indian vendors are focusing on the markets where the buying decisions are made. Physical and cultural proximity is important for building closer client relationships, for delivering certain types of services (such as unscripted selling) and for soothing concerns about data security and confidentiality. Hiring locals also has the effect of cutting down on visa hassles.

Wipro, one of the big three Indian providers (along with Infosys and Tata Consultancy Services), is close to reaching an agreement with the authorities in Atlanta, Georgia, to set up its first software-development centre in America. The three other cities shortlisted during the selection process—Austin, Texas; Raleigh, North Carolina; and Richmond, Virginia—stand a good chance of hosting other centers. Azim Premji, Wipro's Chairman, says that the proportion of local employees (as opposed to visiting Indians) in the company's overseas locations will rise from 10% to one-third over the next 3 years.

Few providers expect the topic of offshoring to lose its political sting—despite plenty of evidence, including a recent OECD report on the subject, showing that it is not a big cause of job losses and has an overall positive effect. But the maturing of the outsourcing industry ought to mean that scaremongering about jobs flowing from rich countries to poor ones will sound less and less convincing.

Adapted from and permission granted: *Outsourcing: External Affairs*, July 27, 2006, The Economist print edition.

Case Perspective: Care Applied

Outsourcing has become the new business trend globally. Companies continue to venture to countries wherein costs are lower and profit margins are high. Currently, China and India are leading the way, with many firms adopting a "ChIndia" strategy to capture the labor advantages in country. The interesting side note to this now is that some large Chinese and Indian firms plan to actually to "offshore" their own work back to the countries which began the offshoring in the first place. Not only will U.S. business leaders have to be culturally competent within the cultural context of their offshoring counterparts, but also learn how to deal with these same counterparts when they return to the U.S. market. Care from all sides must be shown, to employees and customers alike, in order to understand the respective stakeholder viewpoint. Will the offshore management staff in India, for example, have the same concerns as those in China? How will these concerns change if these same managers are relocated to the United States?

US business leaders will need to be in constant and clear contact with all stakeholders to show a firm commitment as well as understanding from the perspective of each stakeholder group. Whether business decisions are made online or offline, a set of rules needs to be developed to analyze how each decision will affect each stakeholder interest. In doing so, leaders can attempt to plan more strategically in order to achieve desired outcomes. Profit seems to remain the guiding principle in most business dealings, but it is changing the way leaders view the conduit for profit (i.e. global employees) that is vital. There needs to be a thought shift from currency to care in order to sustain long-term relationships in markets that have not yet been fully developed and promise untapped opportunities.

The mental revolution to which Taylor referred was that the antagonism and conflict between management and worker had to stop. Management, and ownership, had to stop focusing on increasing their profit at the expense of worker and consumer. Workers had to stop focusing on increasing their wages at the expense of the company ownership and management and the consumer. Taylor said it best, " The great revolution that takes place in the mental attitude of the two parties under scientific management is that both sides take their eyes off of the division of the "surplus" (profit) as the all-important matter, and together turn their attention toward increasing the surplus"...through mutual effort, cooperation and honorable intention. Recently, Warren Buffett stated, "the reason for making profit was to use it to benefit all." The intention should never be on purely increasing profit, or decreasing cost. The intention must be to maximize profit through mutual collaboration for the benefit of all and the exclusion of none.

The Bottom Line

Sensitivity, concern, and appreciation for other cultures are primary requirements for the new intercultural leader—we call this the principle of Care. Leaders can improve both profit and intercultural relations by adopting a "long view" or sustainability view of business strategy. Adopting a local–global dialectic ability can help leaders to demonstrate their commitment to both corporate and regional needs. By dialectic ability, we mean that leaders should engage in the perspective talking dialog necessary to consider all stakeholders.

Making decisions is an essential task of leaders and adopting a context-based decision and problem-solving process is vital. Our recommendation is that intercultural leaders involve local people from the beginning of any foreign business venture and that stakeholder involvement is part of all future decisions.

Leaders must adopt a purposeful rather than habitual behavior pattern. The lesson learned from most global business failures is that what works on home turf will not necessarily work in another culture. Moreover, what works in one foreign culture will not necessarily work in yet another culture. Leaders must consider the differences as well as the similarities across cultures in order to be successful in all cultures.

4

The Principle of "Communication"

If you talk to a man in a language he understands, that goes to his head. If you talk to him in his language, that goes to his heart."

—Nelson Mandela

The prevailing theme of this chapter is that business leaders need to engage with individuals from other cultures in order to understand their own cultural background and biases. Past research indicates that culturally skilled leaders move from being culturally unaware to being aware and sensitive to their own cultural heritage and to valuing and respecting differences.[173] These leaders were aware of how their own cultural backgrounds, experiences, attitudes, values, and biases influenced interactions with others. Theorists suggest that leadership is central to the human condition, and further that the follower is a social animal.[174] Intercultural experts concur that through engaging with diverse cultures, a leader becomes more aware of a personal cultural framework.[175]

"Communication" Defined

In order for business leaders to lead effectively in intercultural situations, they must engage and interact with those cultures in whose countries they work with a desire to understand and appreciate that culture and its people

Intercultural competency experts agree that building intercultural understanding is the top priority for American business leaders.[176] The more leaders know about cultural influences, the better they are able to direct the organization by understanding the behaviors of both their own employees and others outside the organization.[177] Theorists suggest that effective intercultural leaders are able to communicate and motivate others. These competencies occur when the leader retains an open mind and respects others.[178] Leadership also results when an individual can influence, motivate, and enable others to contribute toward the effectiveness of an organization.[179]

Interculturalists agree that on the social level, effective communications remain the top competency for global business leaders.[180] Research informs us that the ability to communicate clearly is paramount for a globally competent leader.[181] Additionally, exemplary intercultural leaders are able to communicate and motivate others[182] and are knowledgeable about communication style differences.[183] Effective communication remains crucial as the forces of globalization are pulling all cultures into a virtual and time-independent business zone.[184]

The problem for American business is that too many organizations have operated with an ethnocentric approach to their ventures abroad. Operating with an ethnocentric mindset means that U.S. business leaders tend to consider language, values, and behaviors as standardized and homogenized throughout the world.[185] Dealing with language involves an interaction between the text on the one hand, and the culturally based world knowledge and experientially based learning of the receiver on the other. Exhibit 4.1 provides a good example of the mindset and practice of an intercultural leader who epitomizes the concept of communication.

Intercultural Communication

All communication is cultural. People communicate by drawing on learned patterns, rules, and norms. When people interact, two factors influence the nature and quality of the relations, namely, *situation* and *disposition*. We discuss situational factors in chapters devoted to context, contrast, and immersion. In this section, we discuss the dispositional (psychological and sociological) factors that influence interpersonal contact, specifically related to *intercultural communication*. Intercultural communication is the management and transmission of messages for creating meaning across cultures.

Intercultural communication difficulties are the cause of many problems in global business contexts. The way people communicate varies widely between, and even within, cultures, let alone between and among regions, professions, socio-economic classes, genders, and organizational cultures. At a basic level, communication between humans involves desire (intention plus motivation) and prediction (calculation plus expectation). In other words, people make communication decisions based on their desire and the expected response from the receiver, whether or not they are conscious of this intricate process.

At a psychological level, people base communication strategies on their assessment of the receiver, whether s/he is different, or similar to others with whom the sender has previous experience. On a sociological level, people base communication strategies on assessment of the receiver's similarity to the sender (i.e. within group) or aspirational group affiliation. In addition to these psycho-cognitive and socio-cultural processes, culture affects several aspects of communication interactions. Language, even between same-language speaking groups (e.g. France and Quebec, United Kingdom, United States, and Australia), is the most obvious difference; however, there are a number of other equally important cultural distinctions.

The areas of cultural variability, related to intercultural communication, include non-verbal communication (facial expression, gestures, and posture) tone and volume, pace, social distance (how far apart are the speaker and receiver), time orientation, uncertainty-avoidance, locus of control, conflict orientation and worldview.

Intercultural communication involves situations where there is communication between persons with different cultural beliefs, values, or ways of living. Cultural differences may be minimal, for example between a German and an Austrian, or may be great, as between a Scot and a Malaysian. At best, intercultural communication can be difficult if the communicator and the receiver share few mutual language and practices.

The culture of a receiver of communication acts as a filter through which he/she interprets the message. This filter may color the message to the point that the message received may not match the message sent. The source of the communication will most often be within the context of the sender. Ostensibly, culture influences every facet of the communication experience. The message that is received is actually more important than the message that the communicator sent. In other words, effective communication depends on the accuracy of the message received.

Non-verbal communication, particularly in relation to verbal channels, is highly culture dependent and relies on cultural heritage. Every person is influenced on how to move and communicate from a very early age. Hence, it plays a significant role with regard to intercultural communication and in fully understanding what is being communicated.

Hall differentiated between low- and high-context communication. Low-context communication focuses on verbal elements and is characteristic of cultural groups from North America, United Kingdom, and Germany. High-context communication blends verbal messages with a lot of bodily behavior, motions, and signs; this typifies Central/Eastern Europe, the Mediterranean region, South America, among others.

> ### Non-verbal behavioral elements include
>
> - Eye contact
> - Facial expression, posture, and gestures
> - Distance between interlocutors
> - Influence of odors
> - Tempo and time factors
> - Touch
> - Artifacts and environmental objects.

Much like verbal communication, non-verbal communication, including posture and bodily expression, carries a meaningful message that other people receive and process. Similarly, words have multiple meanings to people and so too do behavioral messages sent through other non-verbal channels. Messages sent through non-verbal channels tend to mean different things by various cultural groups, often crossing the borders imposed by verbal language restrictions, but also generating new challenges in societies with multiple cultures.

Daniel Goleman identified five domains of emotional intelligence (EQ), namely: self-awareness; self-regulation; motivation; empathy; and social skills. The estimate is that 90% of emotional communication is a non-verbal component. This includes body posture, movements and gestures, facial expressions, eye contact, touching, interpersonal distance and greetings.[186]

General knowledge about cultures and EQ facilitate the following important aspects of intercultural communications, all of which are necessary for intercultural leaders.

- Developing an understanding of basis of cultural differences (categorization, differentiation, in-group/out-group distinction, learning styles and attribution)
- Understanding the influences that culture has on communication and associated behaviors
- Acquiring a level of intellectual curiosity, openness, tolerance, and empathy towards foreign cultures and their inhabitants.

EQ, through its emphasis on intercultural awareness, empathy, self-awareness, and social skills, can strongly aid intercultural communication competences. This begs the question of what constitutes intercultural communication competence and how all this relates to the concept of communication within the Geoleadership framework.

Competent intercultural communication requires behaviors that are effective and appropriate. Effective intercultural communication means that people are able to achieve desired personal outcomes. To do so, competent intercultural leaders should be able to interact within a social environment to obtain mutually accepted goals. This presumes that competent leaders, as communicators, are able to identify their goals, assess the resources necessary to obtain those goals, accurately predict the other communicator's responses, choose mutually workable communication strategies, enact those communication strategies, and, finally, accurately, and mutually assess the results of the interaction. Before continuing this discussion, we present an example of an intercultural leader who has impressed others with his leadership (Exhibit 4.1).

Exhibit 4.1

David Radcliffe's Neck: ABC Europe Excel Award Winner Talks About Engaging Employees and Reaching Out to Other Cultures

To understand the secret behind Excel Award winner David Radcliffe's passion for employee communication, we have to go back to his childhood and a busy street in London. On their way home from school, David and his brother regularly met Mr. Joseph, the elderly Jewish owner of a bookstore. Not only would he help them to get into their building, but he would also check what they had learned in school. One day, a big black car came speeding down the road, nearly hitting Radcliffe. Mr. Joseph, who caught the boy in time, remarked: "You know, young David, one day you'll have a big black car like that. Always stop for people!"

Radcliffe has not forgotten his old friend's precious advice. He is now the chief executive of the UK-based Hogg Robinson. With 7,500 employees and 3,000 offices in 200 countries, Hogg Robinson is a leading provider of corporate and employee services, as well as Europe's third-largest international travel management company. Its businesses offer outsourced pension payments, employee benefits consulting, corporate event management and e-commerce. And it was Radcliffe's interest in his employees' needs and his dedication to internal communication that landed him the first IABC Europe Excel (Excellence in Communication Leadership) Award, presented in Brussels, Belgium. His ease with people was clearly evident at the awards dinner, joking at being in a room full of communicators: "It is like meeting a hangman. He looks at you and says that you've got a really nice neck."

Asked what the award means to him, Radcliffe does not hesitate to put it in perspective. "What really pleases me is that the award should go to the company," he says. "I have stolen all the ideas from the people who work for me. I may have added one or two myself. But all I have done is make it happen." Radcliffe believes that a company gets free ideas from every employee. And when an organization succeeds in harnessing those ideas, it not only gets a lot of free advice, but also creates a culture of exchange.

(Continued)

Exhibit 4.1   (Continued)

Radcliffe digs for innovative ideas in both formal and informal discussion platforms. He spends two days every six weeks meeting with employees in their offices around the world. "Rather than going around one of our buildings with 200 people, I am better to get 20 of them for an hour and say, 'Ask me questions,'" he says, explaining that those 20 will then relate their conversations to the 200.

He also meets regularly with 12 people from throughout the company. They fly in for a few hours to discuss different matters with him and other senior directors. The participants are guaranteed confidentiality. When Radcliffe became chief executive in 1997 and launched this initiative, most of the questions were about local issues and tended to focus on the individual, such as "Why is my manager never talking to me?" "Why am I never given a chance to talk about my career?" or "Why are you being unfair to that person?" Today, the comfort level has improved so that people's concerns are now more about the company and its acquisition plans and growth prospects. "This happened because the local issues have already been dealt with," says Radcliffe, citing yearly staff appraisals, Internet-based feedback programs and internal publications that cover these areas.

Radcliffe attended the IABC award dinner in Brussels on a stopover to Australia. "Next week, I will see three locations in Australia, Singapore and Hong Kong. I will be having lunches, breakfasts, and dinners with everyone to make sure that they have time to talk to me. It is a week of my life—wasted or well spent?" he muses, but he already knows the answer. When he leaves, he says, those employees will say, "The chief executive actually listens to what I have to say."

Cross-cultural communication

Another program Radcliffe is proud of is interchange. "No matter where I went, I used to hear, 'Why aren't there more chances to work abroad?'" he says. That was when Hogg Robinson came up with the idea of inviting employees to apply for a "job" in another country. They usually stay for a month, experiencing a different culture and learning to work in it.

Radcliffe also leads Business Travel International (BTI), a corporate travel management company that is partially owned and managed by Hogg Robinson. BTI recently set up majority-controlled joint ventures in China, Hong Kong, Macau and Taiwan. BTI Jin Jiang is the only corporate travel management company to have obtained licenses to do business in China's major cities—a vast advantage in a country whose corporate travel market has experienced double-digit growth in recent years as a result of both direct foreign investment and the expanding domestic economy.

As CEO, Radcliffe made sure he learned about China's culture as well as its business prospects. "China's culture is much older than any other, so they've got to have something right," he says. "Go and find out what that is, and then blend it with what you want…. When you go into a different country, with all the best technology in the world, you still encounter a huge history, and that means that different people have different needs." Radcliffe's mantra, he adds, is "never assume you have the right answer."

Source: *Communication World,* March–April, 2005 by Silvia Cambie.

As the David Radcliffe example demonstrates, appropriate communication necessitates the use of messages that are expected in a given intercultural context, and actions that meet the expectations and demands of the situation. This criterion for communication competence requires the leader to demonstrate an understanding of the expectations for acceptable behavior in a given situation. A competent intercultural leader must recognize appropriate communication means recognizing the constraints imposed on their behavior by different, culturally defined, sets of rules, avoiding violation of those rules with inappropriate (perceived as impolite or offensive) responses, and enact communication behaviors in an appropriate (e.g. clear, truthful, considerate, responsive) manner.

The two criteria of effectiveness and appropriateness combine to influence the quality of the interaction. Recently, Spitzberg suggested four communication styles based on these criteria:

1. Minimizing communication is both inappropriate and ineffective, and would obviously be of a low communicative quality.
2. Sufficing communication is appropriate but ineffective, that is, it is highly accommodating and does nothing objectionable, but also accomplishes no personal objectives. The suggestion is that the sufficing style is sufficient to meet the basic demands of the context, but accomplishes nothing more.
3. Maximizing communication occurs when an individual is effective in achieving personal goals, but at the cost of being highly inappropriate contextually. This style may include verbal aggression, deception, the infringement of others' rights, or the degradation of others.
4. Optimizing communication occurs when the participants simultaneously achieve their personal goals and fulfill the normative expectations of the context.[187]

While seemingly simplistic, this framework provides understanding of the dialectics of the competence criteria in intercultural social contexts. When communicators interact effectively and appropriately, they are co-orienting and coordinating their behaviors (verbal and non-verbal) to accomplish social functions, obtain personal goals, and conform to the normative expectations of the situation.

Interestingly, though some researchers examining "interculturality" suggest that intercultural communication is an interactive process whereby cultural differences are established not through external forces, but rather from the interactants themselves.[188] In other words, cultural identity is constituted by, through, and during intercultural exchanges. The implication is that in our intercultural conversations, cultural identity is situationally emergent rather than normatively fixed. Despite there being sometimes obvious physical differences between two conversants (i.e. a person of Asian race and a person of Caucasian race), we do not enter intercultural communication interactions with dossiers printed on our foreheads that provide each other with cultural identification. In short, intercultural relationships require effortful, meaningful, and (dialectical) exchanges. In an excerpt of a *Business Week* article about innovative companies (Exhibit 4.2), we find examples of companies that in theory and practice endeavor to connect with other cultures.

Exhibit 4.2

Learning Journeys Lead Global Innovators

Learning journeys can be interesting. Starbucks Corporation uses them, and while the coffee company began performing ethnographic analysis in 2002, it focuses on its army of baristas to share customer feedback. The firm has started venturing out with product development and other cross-functional company teams on inspirational field trips to gain customer viewpoints and patterns. One Starbucks's senior manager took a team to Paris, Düsseldorf, and London to visit in-country Starbucks and other restaurants and cafes to learn more about local cultures, behaviors, and fashions. Such trips provide different ideas and different ways to think about things that may not be readily apparent when sitting in a cubicle back home.

Here is an example of trying to see the value of customer research. A Finnish engineer is trying to design a mobile phone for an illiterate customer in India. That was the problem Nokia personnel dealt with when the firm started producing low-cost phones for developing markets. A combination of clear ethnographic and lengthy user research in several Asian countries assisted Nokia in understanding how illiterate people exist in a world full of numbers and letters. Nokia found the answer. The firm created a new "iconic" menu that lets illiterate customers find contact lists consisting of images.

More innovation followed. By paying attention to customer feedback in less-developed nations, Nokia personnel found that phones need to be very durable, since phones often the most expensive item these customers will purchase. For use in tropical climates, Nokia made the phones more moisture-resistant. Such Nokia phones also used special screens that are more legible in bright sunlight.

Do You Really Believe You're Multicultural?

The early 21st century is conspicuous with contradiction, a time of both tremendous globalization and retrenchment of old cultural biases. Consider two recent studies concerning the state of multiculturalism and race relations in the United Kingdom and United States.

A 2003 report on the status of multiculturalism in United Kingdom, commissioned by VSO (Voluntary Service Overseas), an international charity organization, showed that that 80% of those asked believe that a new British society cannot be built without interacting with different cultures.

Yet, that same report showed that 77% of respondents agree that different cultures in United Kingdom merely coexist and do not connect. Only 13% said they wanted increased contact with other cultures. Over half, 52%, feel that it is easier to live in a cultural ghetto isolated from people who seem different. Interestingly, the same study revealed that of their own international charity workers 92% consider their overseas experience has made them more confident in engaging with different cultures. More than two-thirds, 69%, have had more contact with people from different cultures in their home country because of their experience of being put into intercultural situations in which they had to engage with other cultures.

A survey of 1,207 U.S. residents (328 blacks and 703 non-Hispanic whites) conducted in December 2006 by Opinion Research Corporation for CNN indicates that whites and blacks disagree on how serious a problem racial bias is in the United States. Almost half of black respondents—49 percent—said racism is a "very serious" problem, while 18 percent of whites shared that view. Forty-eight percent of whites and 35 percent of blacks chose the description "somewhat serious." Asked if they know someone, they consider racist, 43 percent of whites and 48 percent of blacks said yes. However, just 13 percent of whites and 12 percent of blacks consider themselves racially biased. This survey represents the legacy of black–white tension in the U.S., and the bad news is that new racial divides have opened between mid-eastern, especially those of Muslim faith, and other cultures within the U.S.

By now, it may seem to the reader that we have characterized global business vis-à-vis globalization as a destructive force, in other words, the problem. On the contrary, we view global business as the potential unifier of societies. A good resource on this topic is our conviction is that people of diverse cultures can peacefully and creatively cohabitate, indeed thrive, without altogether losing each their unique character. To accomplish such a splendid transformation though, businesses and country governments must approach the process mindfully.

The Principle of "Communication" in Practice

A GeoLeader™ can demonstrate the principle of connection through the following practices and behaviors:

- Break out of your cultural comfort zone—put yourself in a minority position within an unfamiliar culture—engage with that culture on their terms.
- Volunteer your time with an organization that serves a culture with which you are unfamiliar.
- If you can afford it, travel to an unfamiliar country—don't be satisfied with touristic experience—meet people and summon all of your curiosity to find out about the worldview of this unfamiliar culture.

Case Presentation: Wal-Mart in Canada

What happens when conventional business wisdom—that proposes the best approach is to create a distinctive competitive advantage and stick to it—fails in a new market? Exhibits 4.3 and 4.4 highlight such a case as Wall-Mart.

Exhibit 4.3

Wal-Mart Company Profile

Wal-Mart Stores, Inc. operates retail stores in various formats worldwide. It operates in two segments, Wal-Mart Stores and SAM'S CLUB. The Wal-Mart Stores segment comprises supercenters, discount stores, and neighborhood markets, as well as an online retail format, offering apparel; domestics, fabrics, stationery and books; shoes; housewares; electronics; furnishings; appliances; auto accessories; horticulture; sporting goods; toys; pet food and items; cameras and supplies; health and beauty aids; drugs; jewelry; optical, and photo processing. The neighborhood markets include dry grocery, meat, produce, deli, bakery, dairy, frozen foods, pharmaceuticals, photo processing, health and beauty aids, household chemicals, paper goods, general merchandise, and pet supplies departments. The SAM'S CLUB segment comprises the warehouse membership clubs in the United States and samsclub.com, offering hardgoods, software, electronics, jewelry, sporting goods, toys, tires, books, groceries, and private labels. As of January 31, 2006, the company operated 1209 discount stores, 1,980 supercenters, 567 SAM'S clubs, and 100 neighborhood markets in the United States and internationally. It operated 11 units in Argentina, 295 in Brazil, 278 in Canada, 88 in Germany, 398 in Japan, 774 in Mexico, 54 in Puerto Rico, 16 in South Korea, and 315 in the United Kingdom, as well as 56 stores through joint ventures in China, as of the above date. Wal-Mart Stores was founded in 1945 and is based in Bentonville, Arkansas.

Exhibit 4.4

What would Linda buy? Wal-Mart needs to know

At the new Wal-Mart Supercenter, it's all about Linda. She's the prototypical Canadian customer for whom the massive stores are being designed, right down to where the bras are displayed. "Linda" is 30 to 45 years old, has two or three children, a husband and a career. She's a soccer mom who multitasks, and she's time-starved. So when she heads to Wal-Mart for the family shopping, she'd like to pick up some cosmetics for herself, a prescription for her son, diapers for the baby and dog food for the pet. All in that order. Then she'd like to get some grocery shopping done at the same time. She might even have noticed a parka or a pair of pants at the nearby fashion section. Or spotted a cellphone across the way that looked appealing.

(Continued)

Exhibit 4.4 (Continued)

But at her regular Wal-Mart, she's not completely comfortable in the lingerie section. It's next to a busy aisle, and across from electronics. Men often frequent that department, and that may mean that she spends less time there than she otherwise would.

Wal-Mart Canada Corp.'s research on "Linda," who represents its core customer, has played a big role in the planning of its new Supercenters. The object is to get customers in and out of the stores as quickly as possible, while ensuring that they buy as much as possible. "When we put together a new service or product, we say, 'Let's check with Linda,'" Wal-Mart Canada chief executive officer Mario Pilozzi said in an interview as he toured the new Supercenter in Stouffville, Ont., which opens Wednesday. "She's very real…. Our whole organization has to understand that customer. So we give the customer an identity." The identity is a quintessentially Canadian one. "Linda" is a home-grown creation, initiated a couple of years ago at Wal-Mart Canada in Mississauga, said Jim Thompson, senior vice-president of merchandising. She is the personification of the company's target customer, and she's the focus of what most of its Supercenter work has been built around. Her picture is a familiar one at head office. She generally wears jeans and a smart sweater, and there are even cardboard cutouts of her that executives take to meetings when they talk strategy.

Wal-Mart is launching the new Supercenter concept in Canada starting with three in Ontario, with plans for about 14 more next year and what analysts expect to be dozens across the country. In the Supercenter in Stouffville, north of Toronto, the retailer has placed cosmetics at the front, and to the right, on the supermarket side of the store (rather than by the general merchandise entrance). Shoppers tend to automatically turn to the right when they enter a store, research has found. Cosmetics sales also provide Wal-Mart with higher profit margins than many of its other products.

The cosmetics is part of a big pharmacy section which has been moved from the right side of a standard Wal-Mart, to the front near the grocery entrance. That makes it convenient for to get prescriptions and then move on to the infant and toddler section, and then to the pet department, Mr. Thompson said. At traditional Wal-Marts, the pet department is at the other end of the store.

As for the bras, they've been moved away from the electronics, to a quieter aisle next to the shoes. The placement is strategic and could prompt women to buy more shoes, he said. That's because while lingerie is often a have-to purchase, shoes tend to be bought on impulse. When they're looking at the bras and underpants, they may just notice a pair of high heels that catches their fancy.

There have been other subtle adjustments in a bid to cater to the core customer. She is looking for healthier foods, so a nutritional honey almond crisp cereal has been placed next to the bananas—with the thinking that cereal and bananas are a natural fit.

Jams and juices have been added to the cereal aisles so that shoppers' breakfast needs are all in one place. And for a quick, simple Sunday morning

(Continued)

Exhibit 4.4   (Continued)

family breakfast, the frozen sausages—which are typically carried in the meat department—are displayed by the frozen pancakes and other breakfast items. It's also an attempt to make it easier to find everything in the same aisle.

In the home section, bed, bath, and kitchenware have been organized in sections of contemporary, traditional, and ultra-traditional styles, so that the customer can differentiate them quickly. And taking a page from IKEA and other home furnishing retailers, the Supercenters have set up small "vignettes," such a fully made-up bed and fully set dining table, to show how products look together. Toys have been moved next to electronics, because so many toys now have a technological twist and are becoming electronic gadgets.

"Linda" has a hectic life, and anything that Wal-Mart can do to make it easier is a feather in its cap. "Linda is like the CEO and the CFO [chief financial officer] of the family," Mr. Thompson said. "We've got a lot of respect for this lady. She is balancing her kids, her husband, her career.... We look after her and we become her one-stop shop, her destination for all her needs. Linda wins, we win and our shareholders win."

Source: Adapted from *Globe* and *Mail* (Canada) Marina Strauss, November 8, 2006.

Case Perspective: "Communication" Applied

Our perspective on Wal-Mart's cultural adaptation strategy related to Wal-Mart Canada is a mixed one. Although their deference to "Linda" demonstrates that Wal-Mart has acquired some hard-learned business shrewdness, enough to pay attention to its local customers, the question is whether it will be enough to convince wary Canadians.

In several countries where the corporate colossus ventured, the native cultures have not always responded enthusiastically. Take Wal-Mart's experience in Japan for example. Despite buying a state in Seiyu Limited in order to ease into the Japanese market, Wal-Mart's retail pricing policy was not well received by Japanese consumers who traditionally perceive low-cost pricing with low quality. The retail giant faced similar consumer difficulties and failures in South Korea. In Germany, where Wal-Mart's failure has reached folkloric stature, the retailer simply underestimated another obvious cultural characteristic, the strength of German labor unions. How could the world's largest retailer miss such obvious consumer attitudes? The answer is simple; they failed to connect.

Wal-Mart's historic success within its domestic culture is based on a simple formula: rock-bottom prices, zealous control of inventory, and a vast array of products. The problem in countries such as Japan and South Korea is that while there is an avid interest in all-things-American, there are stronger cultural attitudes that supersede the Asian fascination with a capitalistic United States.

The early reviews from Canadians appear to be less than promising for Wal-Mart. Moreover, Canadians seem determined not to copy their American cousins south of their border. The early financial results from the autumn 2006 reported in several Canadian newspapers appeared bleak. The Canadian public has a plethora of media sources that seem eager to expose Wal-Mart's failings in important areas such as employee benefits and human rights violations in some manufacturing shops that supply Wal-Mart with cheap goods. In sum, it is too early to tell whether Wal-Mart's new strategy in broad consumer profiling will pay-off or cause the company to abandon another foreign market.

Case Presentation: EMEA—America, a Culture Clash

Europe, the Middle East, and Africa, usually abbreviated to EMEA is a regional designation used for government, marketing, and business purposes. It is particularly common among North American-based companies, who often divide their international operations into regions. Increasingly, companies are separating their Eastern European business from the rest of Europe, and refer to the EEMEA (Emerging Europe, Middle East, and Africa) region as separate from the European region because of increasing expansion into these areas. Exhibit 4.5 focuses on the collision of cultures within this area.

Exhibit 4.5

EMEA—US culture clash

"We were like young teenagers kicking and screaming!" That was the cathartic realization, expressed by European team members of a U.S.-based service industry multinational. They were looking back at the poor communication and cultural misunderstanding between the EMEA (Europe, Middle East and Africa) group and the U.S. headquarters, following a series of rapid mergers and acquisitions. Despite an action oriented and results focused shared culture, there was an EMEA perception that "business was suffering

(Continued)

Exhibit 4.5   (Continued)

from unproductive time and ineffective working relationships," claimed the EMEA management team. Yet there was a critical need to build an effective global team. EMEA managers were constantly involved in long conference calls and e-mails that made no allowance for time zone differences. Not only was this a pressing issue for the individuals involved on a daily basis, it was equally vital to their customer's experience of seamlessly global delivery. It became critical to move beyond local silos and deal with rapid transition, work overload, and cultural clashes with the parent company.

Six months later, team members reported, "we managed to make a major psychological switch... and learned to release and channel negative energy into a positive passion for change." They also reported that their "cultural norms of formal politeness and sardonic humor misfired in the USA and that a new mindset and behaviors would be needed to shift the team dynamics." So, what caused the shift? As an independent consultant at the time, I remember beginning to work with the team. Time pressure would not allow for whole training days, and we could see what was needed was more than just a one-off awareness workshop. I decided to introduce a new, updated approach to action learning, what I now call "REAL," or "reflective, evaluated, action learning," to the team. Action learning was originally developed by Reg Revans in the 1940s and enjoyed a revival as a cornerstone of Peter Senge's learning organization in the 1990s. While the traditional approach to action learning is to take a day a month—yes, a working day out of the work routine—in 2005 this kind of time is a scarce commodity. REAL introduced shorter, more regular meetings and allowed for sustained incremental learning, and the practice of behavioral changes between sessions. This was an approach suited to geographically co-located teams and addressing organizational issues. Hence Boshyk (2000) calls this "business-driven" action learning in his book of the same name where the organizational issue is the priority.

In another example to the one I am writing about in this article, REAL was used in a small consultancy to look at the development of its rapidly changing culture, and its determination to retain and nurture its values and sense of community, as it grew larger. So, while action learning has long been used for personal development and for team building to great effect, it has rarely been used to tackle diversity issues and examine cultural behaviors and breakdowns. It is only now beginning to be recognized as an ideal tool for developing the diversity skills needed to work with global customers, manage an increasingly diverse workforce, and as a more effective alternative to the now clichéd "one-day diversity workshop."

One or two day diversity training programs can develop awareness but cannot change behavior patterns established over a lifetime. Despite increased training efforts—and significant advances in embedding diversity policies and procedures—it has proved much harder to develop inclusive behavior and a deep understanding of how differences impact how work gets done and also can actually benefit organizations. Even the best diversity policies do not automatically reach hearts and minds. Mentoring and coaching can address individual issues—but profound and organization-wide change must be sustained, supported and incremental. For this to happen,

(Continued)

Exhibit 4.5   (Continued)

the ongoing support and challenge of a group of diverse colleagues can be more powerful than any training. It is vital to address the real issues which are happening regularly in the work place, and are often just below the surface. Short-term cultural orientation programs or diversity awareness programs may raise awareness of issues, but only a sustained incremental approach can demonstrate results in actions into the workplace.

With the support, confidentiality and challenge of their action-learning group, the EMEA team began surfacing entrenched assumptions, prejudices and behaviors over several months. In the initial meetings, they believed they could solve problems at a rational level, but they were derailed with frustration with U.S. HQ. The REAL process enabled the EMEA team to take time to reflect on assumptions and experiment with style and behavior.

They learned to accept that "it is a U.S. cultural norm to be assertive/talk loud and use an upbeat tone" on conference calls, whereas EMEA staff prefer to use irony and humor which did not "play" in the U.S. HQ. They learned that a long ironic e-mail to California was a waste of effort. So their awareness was raised, but what were they going to do about it?

"This is where traditional, classroom training falls down," claims Cari Caldwell, director of—and a fellow diversity consultant at—Future Considerations. "Although heroic efforts are made to include experiential exercises and approaches to training, nothing can replace the depth of learning that occurs in that moment of trying a new behavior with real people in a real situation. This is what working with 'difference' is all about."

"Putting yourself, your career and reputation on the line by daring to try things differently is different from what you would culturally, normally do. You need the support of peers, input, and guidance on what to try—and the confidence to be able to make mistakes." Relevant incidents in the work place were logged every week and raised in the group meetings, where participants were able to reflect on their own analysis of them. Group members brought their own challenges to the assumptions and offered alternative options for action. Thus did the meetings provide an opportunity for a second attempt at modified action or behavior in the workplace.

The REAL process opened up completely new insights into the situation. As the team examined their assumptions and cultural blocks, they challenged and re-framed their own behavior. For example, the British communication style was far more reticent, so that they felt undermined and undervalued compared to the more direct and assertive style of their U.S. counterparts. They began to question whether they could style-switch enough to shape the agenda, change the dynamic and contribute to the discussions without losing their identity. They tried it. They tested different approaches on conference calls and e-mails and began to change the dynamic. They learned to switch styles of communicating without feeling they had "become American." From the REAL process they became empowered and proactive.

They claimed, "It has enabled us to define our responsibility as a non-HQ location." The responsibility was to create constructive relationships within the global team, instead of complaining about the U.S. HQ's approach. Not only did the team members report a shift in learning, but because the

(Continued)

Exhibit 4.5   (Continued)

program was being rigorously evaluated, they had the numbers to demonstrate their learning to management.

Few applications of action learning include the evaluation aspect that REAL brings. Critical incidents that participants faced were regularly logged via charts and a "narrative" of the meeting distributed electronically, to remind participants of the learning they had undergone and of their commitment to new actions. Participants evaluated the development of their learning and changed behavior in the workplace at the end of each session; this meant they could see the pattern of change—both through graphs and analysis of their comments.

Action learning is known for being an empowering methodology, but it was also motivating for the team to demonstrate its learning to senior management. The results below show the transfer of learning to the workplace and illustrate a similar pattern in two quite separate REAL programs in different companies.

A questionnaire was completed by each set of participants at the end of each REAL meeting over eight to ten sessions spanning several months. Each question could be answered with a score from 0 (never) to 8 (very often). As a means of analyzing the results, the scores for each question were averaged after each meeting and plotted over the period, thus giving longitudinal results.

The average responses were interesting to the most significant question, "How often are you applying action learning points in the workplace?" Results showed a clear increase in the frequency of REAL applications, thus demonstrating transfer of learning into the workplace.

In another example of the REAL process with a completely different company—again a questionnaire was completed at the end of each meeting—results showed average responses obtained to the question, "How often have you caught yourself doing something different in the workplace as a result of the REAL set?" The responses to this question again demonstrate a significant increase of application of learning in the workplace.

This kind of evaluation offers significant support to "capturing the slippery experience" of intercultural learning. In the end, specific business outcomes included new communication protocols between the team and HQ, and team members gained the ability to shift their communication styles to be effective when working with other cultures. The program also motivated the groups to feel that retention had become a key issue. A questionnaire conducted nine months later reported that participants were still using the skills—every day—that they had learned.

The REAL approached offered a time-efficient solution in a corporate environment where there was typically little time for reflection and where action learning might not be an obvious choice. It offered more tangible evidence of results that could be demonstrated quantitatively as well as in business plans. It also offered a way to address global diversity issues which promises to be more rigorous in changing counter-productive behaviors and turning difference into a strategic competitive advantage.

Source: Adapted from and permission granted. *EMEA—US Culture Clash, Industrial and Commercial Training*, 2005, vol. 37 by Corinne Rosenberg.

Case Perspective: Communication Applied

Even though business leaders speak different languages around the world, the need to be understood is universal. Humor, for example, does not always translate well. Many U.S. firms have flat leadership structures wherein informal communications prevail and colloquial discussions take place daily. When you add in a global layer of staff who do not share the same verbal and non-verbal language cues, misunderstandings increase. Training can take place in order to teach the meanings of different words and phrases in another language, but if a common tongue is chosen (i.e. English), there will be varying degrees of language meaning. For example, native U.S. English speakers may not understand the conveyed message of someone who learned English in England, India, or New Zealand.

As this case demonstrated, diversity training is a start to build communication awareness, but it is a sustained commitment to understand that what is said is not always, what is meant. For example, there is the classic example U.S. business leaders have learned that in Japan, "yes" can actually mean "no." The topic of body language can also add in another layer of complexity. It is common that the issue of communication such as this does not cross the leader's radar until problems arise. Miscommunications can be minimized by initially having all those involved in the situation to actually meet each other face to face. In this era of virtual communications, misunderstandings increase because messages are mostly judged on their context and tone and not on the sender or his/her proficiency in all possible cultural connotations.

Given the spread of communication technology, it becomes imperative that situations such as those shown in the EMEA case study above be taken into consideration. Simple things such as recognizing time differences can be the first step in realizing that any one firm contains a plethora of individuals with differing communication styles and tones. It is best not to readily judge a note from a foreign counterpart on the base level only if there is an initial negative reaction. By meeting those with whom you will communicate regularly will be integral to build a necessary foundation for future dialogs.

The Bottom Line

The essential message in this chapter is that you must connect with people from other cultures to understand them. To understand people who are different from us, we must engage in meaningful communication. For the intercultural leader this means developing a keen general understanding of how communication works. Beyond this however, the intercultural leader must learn the communication styles of other cultures so that s/he can know how other cultures operate and can learn how to discuss communication with other cultures. In other words, intercultural communication skill means being effective and appropriate within intercultural situations. Working toward mutual understanding and agreement is a necessity. Being an effective communicator means having the ability to achieve desired outcomes. To do so, competent communicators should be able to influence their social environment to obtain those goals. This presumes that competent communicators are able to identify their goals, assess the resources necessary to obtain those goals, accurately predict the other communicator's responses, choose workable communication strategies, enact those communication strategies, and, finally, accurately assess the results of the interaction.

Appropriate communication entails the use of messages that are expected in a given context, and actions that meet the expectations and demands of the cultural situation. This criterion for communication competence requires leaders to demonstrate an understanding of the expectations for acceptable behavior in a given situation. Appropriate communication means the leader must recognize the constraints imposed on their behavior by different sets of rules, avoid violating those rules with inappropriate (e.g. impolite, abrasive, or bizarre) responses, and enact communication behaviors in a culturally appropriate (e.g. clear, truthful, considerate, responsive) manner. When communicators interact, they are co-orienting and coordinating their behaviors (verbal and non-verbal) to accomplish social functions, obtain personal goals, and conform to the normative expectations of the situation. To the extent that the communicators do these activities effectively and appropriately, they are considered competent communicators.

At a greater level, business leaders must adjust their mindset from simply trying to move into a new market to engaging with the culture for mutual benefit. Such benefits can derive from looking at what similarities exist between mindsets rather than the differences. Starting from a positive and appreciative viewpoint when dealing outside one's own cultural comfort zone aids greatly in communicating more effectively.

5

The Principle of "Consciousness"

Everyone thinks of changing the world, but no one thinks of changing himself.

—Leo Tolstoy

The Tolstoy quote above sums up conveniently what many astute people have advised for centuries, and was beautifully said by Socrates, "…the unexamined life is not worth living…know thyself." The fact is we could fill up pages with clear and unequivocal messages from true sages all admonishing us that real knowledge comes from being aware of one's own ignorance. This sage advice is true for all people, and what is important for ordinary people is critical for extraordinary people and those who are in positions of great leadership.

In a recent study of intercultural specialists, researchers asked the experts to define the competencies needed by intercultural leaders and their top response was "self-awareness." Above all other competencies in the inter-personal competency category, participants reported that a business leader's ability to be self-aware of his or her culture, as well as that of others, should be of primary importance.[189] This finding reinforces the assertion that a leader arrives in a new cultural situation as ignorant, but then should move into the novice stage of awareness and should continue to evolve in knowledge through building awareness.[190] Building competence about a target culture means that leaders acquire a hands-on knowledge and skill base in combination with self-awareness.[191] In sum, the quality and level of a leader's awareness largely determines his or her performance.

It turns out that a good number of studies have determined that competency occurs when an individual recognizes cultural differences and ultimately reconciles them by transforming conflicting values into complementary values.[192] Some researchers have concluded that the first level of interculturally skilled leadership is an awareness of the culturally learned starting points in the leader's thinking.[193] This intercultural awareness becomes the foundation of the leader's decision-making ability, through which the leader interprets knowledge and utilizes skills. However, the problem is that until very recently, intercultural awareness has not been a subject for study in the generic leadership training.[194]

To Daniel Goleman, whose groundbreaking research led him to propose the concept of Emotional Intelligence,[195] self-awareness is perhaps the most important of all EI competencies. As Goleman notes, and we agree, the higher a leader climbs in the organizational hierarchy the more important EI, and therefore self-awareness, becomes. Self-awareness means being tuned into one's own cognitive and emotional states, core values and beliefs, personal preferences, and biases. Self-awareness also means being able to assess how one's behavior affects other people, which is particularly important in building trusting work relationships with subordinates, both managers and individual contributors. In one recent study, the researcher found that emotional competence was a better predictor of leadership effectiveness than was Intelligence Quotient (IQ).[196]

"Consciousness" Defined

The point of consciousness, or self-awareness, is its use as a tool of exploration, receptivity, and compassion rather than as a device for self-judgment and self-loathing—it is not another channel for your internal critic. Self-awareness is a reflective practice meant to be a means to enhance your intentionality, higher order thinking, and interpersonal skills. Despite what you may think, interpersonal skill begins with learning how to interact effectively with *yourself*. Largely, self-awareness is an internal process; however, its effect is to both, relationship with self, and relationship with others. The objective is actually to become more, *you* Paradoxically, the more you understand yourself, the more open and receptive you can be with other people. Only with a high level of self-awareness can intercultural leaders engage the trust and commitment of others that is necessary to sustain organizational excellence.

Interculturalists have identified several interpersonal skills associated with self-awareness, determined necessary for intercultural leaders.[197] The list of skills and attributes include curiosity, observation, reflection, adaptability, empathy, and perspective taking. To these, we add mindfulness and taken all together, we categorize this skill area as consciousness. Consciousness is the quality of *being* in a state of total awareness.

Mindfulness

Before we discuss mindfulness, it is first important to differentiate it from the related term, "concentration." Concentration is the willful extended focus of one's attention to something. It is the particularization of one's attention. Concentration is an important skill, but is not our focus here. On the other hand, mindfulness is the fully opened and freely receptive quality of observation, and it is a vital skill.

Mindfulness is the state of complete awareness achieved through receptivity and observation. There are four areas of mindfulness: awareness of one's body and all of its functions; awareness of sensations and feelings; awareness of thoughts, beliefs, and attitudes; and lastly, awareness of mental and emotional hindrances.

In many world religions and spiritual orientations, mindfulness is taught as a practice through such methods as meditation. While we are not making recommendations for religion or spirituality, we do note that neuroscientists have studied the brain functioning of meditators (people practicing various meditation techniques including mindful meditation)...and found that they are healthier than non-meditators because they are able to shift their mental focus from the stress-prone right frontal cortex to the calmer left frontal cortex. Additional and important information of such studies for leaders is that meditators (people practicing various meditation techniques including mindfulness meditation) were able to shift their mental foci more readily than those who do not meditate.

Curiosity

Curiosity is a natural function of human consciousness and it can be developed to enhance intelligence and leadership ability. Quite simply curiosity leads people to consider both life within themselves and life outside themselves. Effectively, it is a process of inquisition, of questioning what, how, when, where, and why phenomena exist. Leaders require a certain level of skill in being curious about the world in which they live in order to be able to observe, assess, derive meaning, and envision a future. Psychologically speaking, curiosity is a primary driver of human motivation.

The success of a leader's influence in compelling others to follow is in their ability to question, which then leads them to the best answers for each situation. Good leaders take time to listen, engage, imagine, and investigate alternatives. They inspire others through their own curiosity.

Successful intercultural leaders set their curiosity loose in new cultural settings to satisfy a thirst to discover the possibilities. In the classic Bennis text on becoming a leader,[198] on becoming a leader, The Art of Leadership, the management guru discusses the virtue of curiosity in several facets of leadership from desiring to understand their own thinking process, to an insatiable desire to discover all that can be known.

Curiosity leads us to discovery and coupled with human compassion will compel leaders to engage people from different cultures from a place of genuine interest. Curiosity coupled with intelligence forms the cornerstones of vision. Curiosity coupled with discernment prepares a leader to evaluate and make ethical decisions. Curiosity coupled with imagination creates the fertile ground of innovation. Interculturally competent leaders develop a sense of wonderment. The capability and capacity for wonderment often dissipates in people after childhood; brilliant leaders, and interculturally competent leaders, enhance their sense of wonderment rather than lose it. Curiosity is an important element in adaptation skills. It prompts us to explore new frontiers.

Observation

Closely connected to curiosity is the ability to observe. Leaders, in fact, have a lot to observe. They must build perceptual abilities that enable them to perceive behavior in their staff, consumers, and beyond; they must be able to perceive and scan what is going on in the marketplace; they must be able to perceive trends; they must perceive a complex array of data; and they must be able to accurately describe, analyze, and make meaning out of what they observe. Organizational members look to their leaders to help make sense of what is going on in the world around them.

Because meaning-making is an important aspect of leadership, leaders in intercultural contexts face greater complexity in deriving meaning from multiple layers of context (e.g. local, global, intercultural). The complexity lies in the layers of pan-cultural languages, norms, symbols, attitudes, beliefs, and laws. Facing such complexity, the leader must perceive issues, problems, opportunities and threats from his/her own culture, the host culture, as well as the regional, national, and global perspective. In such situations, leaders must be able to discern whether, for example, a threat is only perceived as a threat in certain stakeholder groups and not others due to naïveté, culture, or something else.

Observation skills require first that the leader has awareness of his/her biases and filters (generation, gender, ethnicity, orientation, profession, religion, etc.). Secondly, perfecting observation skills means learning how to observe descriptively and evaluatively. Descriptive observation means creating a picture of a situation in as neutral a manner as possible. Evaluative observation means being able to discern risk, danger, opportunities, and possibilities. It is a quality of astuteness.

Reflection

Reflection is the ability to learn through careful consideration. Often, reflection means considering previous actions, events, or decisions. Two foci of reflective activity are important for leaders: external and self. In reflecting on external life, leaders should consider all aspects of their responsibilities, including financial, strategic purpose, structure, corporate culture, and stakeholder groups. Self-reflection is an introspective activity in which one poses and answers provocative questions toward examining one's values, attitudes, beliefs, and biases. Self-reflection must include the leader's sense of his/her job, so that positional power does not infect interactions. In Table 5.1 is a self-reflection survey to assess your leadership effect.

Adaptability

Adaptability has always been important for leaders and managers. However, in an increasingly complex global society and marketplace, adaptability is the crucible. Without adaptability a leader and his/her organization faces extinction. In an environment that is constantly in flux, leaders must be able to respond to, if not predict, change. Change brings novel situations, which in turn require leaders to understand that what worked before may not work again. In other words, novelty places people in learner mode where prior experience is tested. This means that a significant ingredient in adaptability is learning agility—being able to learn something newly adeptly and swiftly.

Several elements comprise adaptability: learning agility (cognitive flexibility, curiosity, memory, recall, synthesis); attitudinal adjustment; and behavior modification. In order for an adaptation to quicken, the person must align values, attitudes, beliefs, thoughts, and behaviors. Unless the leader aligns an adaptation in all of these areas, the resulting misalignment creates incongruent behavior. Often, organizational personnel will interpret the leader's incongruent behavior as lack of integrity. Such interpretations by personnel can create an atmosphere of mistrust.

In a global context, where leaders are responsible for intercultural enterprise, layers of culture create even more complexity to the leader's adaptive competence. In intercultural situations, the leader is adapting to or within a cultural context. In such cases, the leader's alignment of cognitive, attitudinal structure, and behavior must take into consideration the cultural expectations.

Perspective Taking

In a recent study, the Center for Creative Leadership[199] set out to ascertain what the current perspective was concerning differences in managerial effectiveness between domestic and global managers. One quality that had paradoxical consequences for leaders working in intercultural contexts, was perspective taking, the ability to empathetically understand someone else's perspective and worldview. It was paradoxical in that, while this

Table 5.1 Leader Self-awareness Assessment

Behaviors	Seldom 1	Sometimes 2	Often 3	Frequently 4	Always 5
1 I recognize the effect of my emotions on work performance.					
2 I recognize the effect of my emotions on relationships with others.					
3 I recognize my personal impact on group and team functioning.					
4 I can describe my strengths realistically.					
5 I can describe my weaknesses realistically.					
6 I work to understand others' perspectives.					
7 I take time to discern the dynamics of all stakeholder groups.					
8 I listen to others actively, checking to ensure my understanding.					
9 I discern non-verbal communication accurately.					
10 I use a variety of techniques to inform my self-reflections.					
11 I seek feedback from all relevant constituencies about my behavioral impact.					
12 I show an interest in others who are different from me.					

Your score: Add together all of your circled values for a grand total and compare to the chart below:

51–60 = Excellence   41–50 = Constructive awareness

31–40 = Opportunity   21–30 = Behavioral and attitudinal change required

characteristic portends a successful performance of a leader working within an intercultural context, it also portends a negative rating of that leader by his/her domestic peers.

Perspective taking requires more from the leader than mere concern about other people. It requires that the leader tangibly recognize and understand the experience of other people. Exhibit 5.1 contains a brief perspective-taking survey.

Exhibit 5.1

Leader Perspective-taking Assessment

The following statements inquire about your thoughts and feelings in a variety of situations. In the space before each item, indicate how well it describes you by choosing the appropriate number on the scale at the top of the page. Read each item, reflect on it before responding, and answer honestly.

Scale:
Describes   **Does not describe Me**
Me well   **at all**

| 1 | 2 | 3 | 4 | 5 |

_____ 1. Before criticizing somebody, I try to imagine how I would feel if I were in his/her place.

_____ 2. If I'm sure I'm right about something, I don't waste much time listening to other people's arguments.

_____ 3. I sometimes try to understand my friends better by imagining how things look from their perspective.

_____ 4. I believe that there are two sides to every question and try to look at them both.

_____ 5. I sometimes find it difficult to see things from the "other guy's" point of view.

_____ 6. I try to look at everybody's side of a disagreement before I make a decision.

_____ 7. When I'm upset at someone, I usually try to "put myself in his shoes" for a while.

There is no score for the leader perspective-taking assessment because it is meant to provoke reflection only. There is no right or wrong and no profile associated with it.

The Principle of "Consciousness" in Practice

A Geoleader can demonstrate the principle of consciousness through the following practices and behaviors:

- Practice mindfulness techniques: Meditate
- Expand your awareness quotient: Periodically assess and review your awareness of your environment and yourself
- Build and enhance your natural curiosity: Take critical thinking or creative thinking courses.

The Case of Flextronics Expansion: The Principle of Consciousness Applied

How do truly intercultural leaders become effective in working in intercultural contexts? Consider the case of Flextronics and its successful expansion into foreign countries. In his own words, CEO Michael Marks describes how his company has grown from a small technology company to a global player in Exhibit 5.2. We use the Marks piece as an example of a leader who demonstrates "Consciousness."

Exhibit 5.2

Flextronics Company Profile

Flextronics International Ltd. (Flextronics), incorporated in May 1990, is a provider of electronics manufacturing services (EMS) to original equipment manufacturers (OEMs) in industries, including computing; mobile; consumer digital; industrial, semiconductor and white goods; automotive, marine and aerospace; infrastructure; and medical. The Company provides a range of vertically integrated global supply chain services, through which it designs, builds, and ships a packaged product for its OEM customers. The Company's services include printed circuit board and flexible circuit fabrication; systems assembly and manufacturing; logistics; after-sales services; design and engineering services; original design manufacturing (ODM) services; and components design and manufacturing. As of March 31, 2006, its total manufacturing capacity was approximately 15.8 million square feet in over 30 countries across four continents. Flextronics has retained a 15% stake in the software business. During the fiscal year ended March 31, 2006 (fiscal 2006), the Company sold its Semiconductor division to AMIS Holdings, Inc. The Company has established a network of manufacturing facilities in the electronics markets, including Asia, Europe and the Americas. During fiscal 2006, Flextronics' net sales in the Americas, Europe and Asia represented 22%, 22% and 56% of its total net sales, respectively. Its customers include Casio, Dell, Ericsson, Hewlett-Packard, Kyocera, Microsoft, Motorola, Nortel, Sony-Ericsson and Xerox.

Michael Marks is the CEO of Flextronics. About ten years ago, right after NAFTA took effect, I had the idea of locating a Flextronics manufacturing plant in Mexico. I clearly remember people saying to me, "Don't do it. That's a siesta culture," implying that any labor or other cost savings to be gained there would be offset by the workers' laziness. I made a trip anyway and checked out three factories, one making cables for the auto industry, one making toasters, and one doing electronic assembly. I came away thinking, "It's not humanly possible to work harder than these people or to produce products faster than this." We built a plant near Guadalajara in 1997, and within five years, its revenues grew to more than $1 billion.

(Continued)

Exhibit 5.2   (Continued)

I tell the story because it underscores the corrosive effect of stereotypes and how they undermine good decision making in a business that needs to globalize. To me, the most important criterion for a business leader is that he or she be free of such strong biases. If I heard evidence of that kind of stereotyping in conversations with a job candidate, that would be a big red flag. Usually, of course, the stereotyping is more subtle. Managers often pick up the impression that the Chinese are good at this, the Germans are good at that, and so on. But I have learned that in every place we operate, in every country, the people want to do a good job. They simply need training. If you show people, for instance, what great manufacturing is, they will work toward it—and I have found that there is no place where people can't do a world-class job.

This isn't to say that we approach every region with a cookie-cutter uniformity. We may need to train workers differently in different parts of the world. We discovered this early on in Guadalajara because the demographics of Mexico are very young—a large percentage of the workforce is under the age of thirty-five. The contrast with Japan, a country with a relatively old workforce, is striking. Training becomes a different proposition when you cannot rely on tacit knowledge transfer from seasoned fifty-year-olds to greener thirty-year olds. Mexico might require a more intense training regimen or a longer time commitment.

Running a global company also means learning how different countries are governed, and being able to work with their leaders. This is particularly true for a manufacturer like Flextronics, because most countries, whether developing or developed, tend to want the manufacturing jobs we have to offer. As a consequence, we must be in frequent contact with senior government officials, addressing issues like tax holidays and dollars for training. Consider an issue that the head of our European operation is currently dealing with. A few years back, the Hungarian government agreed to give us a ten-year tax holiday as the result of a $50 million capital investment there. The problem is, Hungary is now trying to gain admittance to the European Union, which won't allow such tax holidays. What will we do about this? It will get worked out, but it's complicated. The head of European operations has to have the skills to deal with such high-level political issues—skills that don't develop in people automatically.

How do we choose leaders with the cultural breadth to conduct such negotiations—and to get past the kind of stereotypes I discussed earlier? The most capable executives I've known have traveled extensively, learned other languages, and have often been educated abroad. But most of them gained their broad perspectives in the course of their work. Flextronics' top management team orchestrates manufacturing activity in twenty-eight different countries and leads sales operations worldwide. The peer group includes a CFO from New Zealand, a CTO from Grenada, a sales executive from Ireland, and business unit heads from Sweden, Great Britain, India, Singapore, and Hong Kong. It's hard to work in such an environment and remain provincial in your outlook.

(Continued)

Exhibit 5.2   (Continued)

Increasingly, though, we are seeing that our more junior executives have this kind of multicultural exposure as part of their upbringing. Today's thirty-year-olds grew up in a different world from their parents, with much greater ease of travel, more education abroad, and technologies like the Internet and cell phones affording more lines of global communication. Dream résumés that show, say, an upbringing in Paris, a Harvard MBA, and summer internships in Japan are becoming more and more common among young job applicants.

As a result, there is much more uniformity among young managers around the world. Imagine pulling together thirty people from thirty different countries, all in their thirties. Chances are, they would all interact quite easily—and that isn't because young people tend to be fairly open-minded. It's because there's been a major shift in thinking from the last generation. And that shift will make the task of developing global leaders easier with each passing year. In another two decades, an American is not going to stop to consider that he is dealing with someone from Japan. A strong leader will be just that—a strong leader—whether Brazilian or Malaysian. The global part of leadership will be given.

Source: Adapted from *Should You Be A Global Manager*, September 1, 2003, Working Knowledge for Business Leaders by Marks and Meiland.

Case Perspective: "Consciousness" Applied

From the perspective of intercultural competence, the Michael Marks discussion on his company, Flextronics, exemplifies "the right stuff." What we perceive is a clear alignment between values, attitudes, beliefs, and behavior. Further, Marks' portrays an enlightened respect for all cultures. In our experience, it is difficult, if not impossible, to portray such respect and cultural competence unless it is genuine. Marks' statement, that what is most important to him in evaluating leadership is that a leader is "free" of cultural bias, is resounding evidence of the essential elements of leadership consciousness. The reader will note clear evidence of perspective taking, self-awareness, curiosity, observation, reflection, and adaptability in the Marks' discussion.

Marks' comments demonstrate an understanding that culture provides both an avenue for understanding and a path to misunderstanding. When he investigated Mexico as a potential site for a manufacturing site, Marks' inclination was to go to the country to experience first-hand the culture and its people. He suspended making any pre-conceived judgment about Mexican people, and further, he overlooked those dire warnings he had received from people. In his investigation, not only did he discover that the warnings were inaccurate in describing the Mexican people he observed, he also discovered that the behavior that was described in the warnings was opposite. Far from being the "siesta culture" attributed to them, the Mexican workers Marks observed performed at an extremely high level of productivity.

Another important message Marks conveys in his discussion concerning the tendency of leaders and managers to become caught in stereotyping cultures, is that generalizations amount to grand assumptions. Imagine the competitive advantage a company has that bothers to investigate a potential manufacturing site in Mexico compared to a similar company that dismisses out-of-hand the option of Mexico because of misconceptions—misconceptions based on stereotypes and assumptions. Minimally, competent leaders and managers objectively investigate assumptions to confirm or disconfirm their accuracy.

The next point that Marks makes that warrants a few words is his observation that no matter where on this planet he has observed people at work, people across those cultures, when given the proper resources, training and tools, aspire to do good work. We want to emphasize two points. First, that Marks is drawing on direct experience. Second, is that in observing similarities across cultures with which he has had experience, Marks is building a knowledge base which can allow him the ability to draw people together over common ground.

We also support Marks' viewpoint that there is a "global culture" emerging with a new generation of workers, a global culture that operates through the explored commonalities across cultures and that honors the rich gifts that each culture contributes to the global societal tapestry.

The final point to make on the Marks piece is that he argues the case for attainment of intercultural leadership skills through immersion and direct experience. Michael Marks exemplifies the characteristics we attribute to "consciousness" and in his discussion; we perceive the skills of a true interculturally competent intercultural leader.

Case Presentation: Proflowers

In the following case, we present an organization that demonstrates a practice of going global with mindfulness (Exhibit 5.3).

Exhibit 5.3

Company Profile: Proflowers

Following is an interview with Bill Strauss, CEO of Provide Commerce, Inc. which operates ProFlowers, Cherry Moon Farms, Secret Spoon, and Red Envelope in more than 50 countries. Mr. Strauss founded the company in 1998 and they took it global in 1999. The company's annual revenue is about $250 million.

(Continued)

Exhibit 5.3   (Continued)

Provide Commerce operates an e-commerce marketplace of supplier to the customer at competitive prices. The company combines an online store-front, proprietary supply chain, management technology, and established supplier relationships to create a market platform that bypasses traditional supply chains of wholesalers, distributors, and retailers. They have operations and procurement in other countries.

What is your biggest international issue with other countries (i.e. South America)?
The two main issues are political stability and the exchange rate.

How do you manage employees/vendors/customers overseas?
We have vendors and employees that we have carefully selected and worked with over the years and these relationships are built on mutual trust and respect. We manage them through a team in our Miami facility, which is our main importing center.

How stable is your international product supply?
We consider it very stable due to the variety of vendors in a variety of countries that we have been doing business with for years.

Has Proflowers always bought flowers from other countries (i.e. South America)?
We began sourcing flowers outside of the United States shortly after we began our business. Our direct business model allows us to go anywhere in the world to find the best products for our customers.

How do you deal with foreign governments and how is that different with dealing with the U.S. government?
We do not deal directly with the foreign governments and have not had any issues different from our government. We follow policies and procedures for importing and have worked well within the established system.

Where have been your biggest international successes and why?
We believe procuring flowers from South America has been a huge home run due to the high quality of the product. We have conducted surveys amongst American flowers consumers for the traits they most value in a rose and South American roses exhibit those qualities above any other roses we have found: large heads that open up fully and last a long time.

Where have been your biggest international problems and why?
We have not had many problems working internationally on procurement. On another note and (another) aspect of our business, we are waiting to expand our marketing efforts internationally due to the differences in consumer behaviors and taste on flower buying.

(Continued)

Exhibit 5.3   (Continued)

How do you think U.S. business leaders must change their style of leadership when going into foreign markets?
Our operating principle is always to conduct business fairly and to seek "win-win" partnerships. I don't believe that that changes based on geography.

In the Geoleadership Model below, which of the seven capabilities do you think is most important for u.s. business leaders when operating abroad? Why?
Given our future aspirations for international consumer marketing, I would say "Care" and "Communication" based upon the high cost of marketing and the importance of customer focus.

Case Perspective: "Consciousness" Applied

ProFlowers has been successful in leveraging foreign counterparts for domestic gains. The company operates a large facility in Miami, Florida, wherein English and Spanish are the common communication vehicle. Retaining positive relationships with such counterparts, despite the different languages, is vital to the firm's success. By consistently keeping the customer in mind, the company seeks to expand more globally, while still being aware of the cultural differences in product preference. By doing so, the firm can continue to build alliances and reach out to develop mutual expectations and cooperation with customers, employees, and suppliers.

As also shown in the case of ProFlowers, there will be a certain amount of change when new markets are entered. Managing such change promotes innovation and enlists others in generating, initiating, and sustaining change. By remaining conscious of the differing cultural contexts, the leaders can empower others to delegate responsibilities along with the authority necessary for success and encourage employee participation in decisions that will affect such change. Instilling accountability across the board globally establishes the necessary measures and creates process ownership by continuously holding oneself and others accountable for the process and results. Leaders who realize that change is difficult, but necessary for future gain, can coach followers in such things as the transfer of knowledge, the support of skill development, and the recognition of performance. Individuals, despite rank, wish to be viewed positively for their contributions. Leaders who keep this in mind when dealing with different global constituencies will be well served.

The Bottom Line

Living in a global culture means trying to balance two powerful yet ostensibly opposing factors: the rapid development of globalization itself and the counter-globalization fueled by political and religious factions. No one is sure what globalization will lead to; however, most authorities and theorists believe that globalization will continue. Some observers have speculated that globalization is an innate drive in humans based on the basic motivation that propels people to connect with each other, to profit by trading, to spread their beliefs, to exploit resources, and to dominate others.

In the past, leadership theory and practice have tended to be from a universal, essentialist, one-size-fits-all strategy. However, it seems clear that working in global and intercultural contexts requires leaders of a different kind. While it may be impossible for individuals to be expertly prepared to lead across all cultures, some characteristics and skills do seem to fit in all cultural contexts.

The critical message of this chapter on leader consciousness is that leaders working in intercultural contexts must develop the skills of a sage individual. To build such a high level of sophistication in leadership requires that the leader becomes adroit in mindfulness, awareness, observation from a 360° perspective and from an objective perspective of self. Keen curiosity, observation, awareness, and mindfulness skills are mandatory for leaders to be able to deal with the "contrasts" and ambiguity of intercultural leadership. In the next chapter, we explore the topic of contrasts.

6

The Principle of "Contrasts"

If I take refuge in ambiguity, I assure you that it's quite conscious.
—Kingman Brewster

Contracts Defined

Ambiguity, from the Latin *ambigere*, which means "to wander," does not just mean, "Having two or more meanings." It also means "doubtfulness or uncertainty as regards to interpretation." In other words, ambiguity means that there is doubt, disagreement, tentativeness, or contrasting perspectives.

To say that we live in a world that is complex and seems at times rife with ambiguity would be an understatement. The fact is that our lives are lived amidst contrasts from the most mundane to the exotic. For leaders and managers, the modern business environment presents either routine or novel situations. While this always has been true to some extent, in the modern business world, leaders and managers face a changeable continuum in the ratio of novel to routine. As we have discussed in previous chapters, a leader faces ambiguity as a normal aspect of the role and intercultural leaders face increased ambiguity because of the complexity dealing with multiple layers of culture.

What is ironic is that the more ambiguous the situation the more leadership is needed. Consider your own experience in routine work situations: do you feel confused? Chances are that you do not. Now consider what happens in novel work situations, when you encounter something you have never encountered before and you do not have an explanation for what is occurring: how comfortable are you in these situations, especially if you are required to make a swift decision? Chances are that you desire some type of assistance; most likely, you desire guidance. The more urgent the situation, the greater the desire for relief. That is what leaders do, they provide relief, meaning and the path forward—from the front-line supervisor who answers a novel procedural question, to the enterprise president, who steps up to the podium to address personnel when two competitors merge, seemingly ending life as usual.

The truth is, leadership is all about deriving meaning out of a *living* context and the capability to envision a plausible future. In order to derive meaning, a person must be able to discriminate one event or phenomena from another. Basic physics of Field Theory informs us that humans are in a constant state of discerning "figure" from "ground." This simply means that we perceive reality via a dimensional picturing during which we select, through our various sensory capabilities, that which we deem important against that which we perceive as unimportant. The "rightness" or "wrongness" of our interpretations may very well be reliant upon our ability to convince ourselves and other people of the reality that we perceive. Enter culture, which effectively, presents cultural members with "automatic" interpretations according to some previously estimated principle or truth.

Contrasts and ambiguity commonly occur in the eyes of the beholders, when multiple (cultural) interpretations are represented in the situation. The degree of effect of cultural differences on people depends on the level of cultural sensitivity and openness of the parties involved. The perceivers in any situation act based on choices determined through, albeit brief, interpretive exercises, where the perceivers choose the (figurative) lens with which they make their choices. Again, culture provides convenient solutions to the dilemma of deriving meaning. Choosing convenience too quickly presents the possibility that the chooser closes themselves off from greater potential, or opportunities.

Leaders face contrasts and ambiguity at multiple levels in their roles. While ambiguity typically feels uncomfortable for most people, the discomfort occurs because of uncertainty, of not knowing the outcome. What is helpful for people is realizing that ambiguity occurs because people recognize that there is more than one answer, more than one way forward. Rather than perceiving this as negative, effective leaders perceive ambiguity as an opportunity to create something new in the place of what used to be.

Ambiguity Zones

Values and beliefs form most of our perceptual experiences, and as discussed previously, culture plays a significant role in shaping our values and

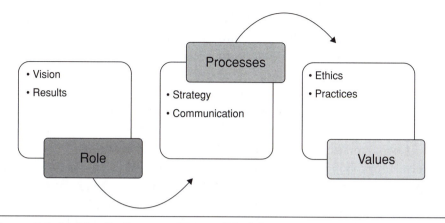

Figure 6.1 Ambiguity Zones as Process Model

beliefs. In organizations, leaders face ambiguity in three areas: role, process, and values. Role elements refer to those aspects of leadership that involve the leader's role, the leader–follower relationship, vision, and results. Role elements are the *content* of leadership. Process elements include strategy, communication, decision, and problem solving. Process elements are the *method* of carrying out leadership responsibilities. Value elements include values and operating principles, ethics, and corporate citizenship. Value elements are the *importance* attributed to life issues. Ambiguity zones are modelized in Figure 6.1.

Role Elements

In chapter two, we briefly discussed the point that leadership is conceived differently across cultures. How leaders, working in an intercultural context, conceive their *role* and how intercultural stakeholders perceive their leaders' role is a matter to be socially constructed rather than assumed. In any context, leaders must be aware of their role within the organization, how they, and their behavior, affect other organizational members. Leaders wear many hats in executing their jobs. They must understand that they do not have all of the answers and give latitude to other organization members to do their jobs. However, even this wisdom, as true as it is for leaders working in U.S. contexts, does not apply across cultures. In intercultural contexts, leaders must be aware that their perception of their role and how they developed their identity as a leader was constructed from a culturally based orientation. Working across cultural boundaries requires what sociologists refer to as "code shifting." Code shifting means that a person shifts his or her attitudes and behaviors when they enter a different culture. An intercultural leader's attention to cultural context also means that how they communicate aspects of their role to organization members requires special attention. While an egalitarian or democratic leadership style may be appropriate in one culture, in another culture, the leader may need to take on a more authoritarian style to be congruent with the expectations of the host culture. Although, even when a directive leadership style is warranted to fit a host culture, a leader in such a context would need to be mindful to consider stakeholder groups and establish practices that would facilitate interaction with those groups, yet use decision styles and other support behaviors that would match the authoritarian style.

Since *vision* is a capability that requires leaders to foresee, scan, and interpret the environment around them, leaders must be aware of their own cultural and background biases that tint their perspectives. We do not mean to suggest that what is perceived, interpreted, and transformed by a leader is necessarily ripe for rejection by intercultural stakeholders simply because of a cultural bias. There is more that binds people together across cultures in the way of similarities than sometimes we bother to acknowledge and leverage. What we do mean to suggest is that leaders, who by the nature of the delicate relationship between leader and follower, already have quite a significant challenge in communicating and inspiring followers to own and actuate a leader's vision for the future. The challenge is that what is interpreted as "good" or "bad," "right" or "wrong," "worthy" or "unworthy," "plausible" or "implausible" is in the eyes of the beholder. Hence, what the leader determines is worthy and plausible may seem off the mark to organizational stakeholders from different cultures. Consider for example the eBay case study from a previous chapter when the company perceived it to be attractive for Japanese to provide a web experience that replicated the American version only to discover that the Japanese consumers largely were interested in more options and did not want to pay fees, given the Yahoo! free option available. In the eBay case, as we saw, even hiring a person of Japanese heritage did not help the company because that leader was not in tune with current Japanese consumer desires nor had any localized experience in Japan (given that she was from Hawaii and not Japan).

The outgrowth of a clearly articulated and executed vision in all organizations is *the result* that which is achieved at a predetermined point in time. There are wide variances across cultures about what constitutes appropriate results for spent labor, although there is less variance than during the Cold War era, when the worldwide economy was dominated by two opposing forces, capitalism and Marxism. Even within capitalist countries, there is variance in how the people of cultures perceive the concept of results. Achieving results involves values, beliefs, and worldview.

Such cultural issues as power distance (see Table 6.1), assertiveness orientation (see Table 6.2), performance orientation (see Table 6.3), future orientation (see Table 6.4), gender egalitarianism (see Table 6.5), individual versus collective orientation (see Table 6.6), and time orientation all

Table 6.1 Power Distance Orientation

Social Inequities	• Multiple classes • *Large Middle Class*
Power bases	• Stable & Scarce • *Transient & Shared*
Role of Power	• Provides Social Order • *Source of Corruption*
Social Mobility	• Limited Upward • *High Upward*
Information Control	• Localized • *Shared*
Governance	• Differentiated • *Democratic*
Independence	• Highly Influenced • *Native Influence*
Civil Freedom	• Weak Liberties • *Strong Liberites*
Resources	• Few & Controlled • *Vast & Mass Use*
Consumption	• High Growth & Coordination • *Mature Growth & High Purchasing Power*
Technology	• Mass Use Supports Power Distance Reduction • Need for Specialized

Source: Adapted from Culture, Leadership, and Organizations: The GLOBE Study of 62 Societies. 2004. Sage.

Table 6.2 Assertiveness Orientation

High	Low
• Aggressive & Tough Behavior of all Members	• Value Modesty & Tenderness
• Recognize Strength	• Sympathize with Weak
• Value Competition	• Value Cooperation
• Driving Work Ethic	• Value Friendship
• Direct Unambiguous Communication Style	• Indirect Communication
• Explicit	• Value Face-saving
• Value Success & Progress	• Value Subtlety
• Value Expression	• Value Detachment
• Value Justice	• Negative View of Aggression
• Control Environment	• Stress Equality & Quality
• Value Capability & Reward	• Value Tradition
• Value Trust based on Capability	• Value Personhood
	• Value Trust based on Predictability

Source: Adapted from Culture, Leadership, and Organizations: The GLOBE Study of 62 Societies. 2004. Sage.

Table 6.3 Performance Orientation

High	Low
• Value Development	• Value Relationships
• Emphasize Results More than People	• Loyalty & Belonging
• Competitive, Assertive & Materialistic	• Respect Quality of Life
• Set Demanding Targets	• Emphasize Experience
• Believe in Individual Control	• Value Harmony Over Control
• "Can Do" Attitude	• Performance Appraisal Values Integrity, Loyalty & Cooperation
• Reward Individual Achievement	• View Appraisal Feedback as Judgmental
• Performance Appraisal Emphasize Achieving Results	• Assertiveness is Socially Unacceptable
• See Feedback as Necessary	• Money Motivation is Inappropriate
• Bonuses & Financial Rewards	• View Merit Pay as Destructive
• Hard Work Pays	• "Attending Right School" is a Success Criterion
• Education is Critical for Success	• Emphasize Tradition
• Value "Doing" More than "Being"	• Value Sympathy
• Age is not Factored	• Associate Competition with Defeat & Punishment
• Direct & Explicit Communication	• Who You Are is Valued Over What You Do
• Approach to Time is Monochrome	• Value Age in Promotion
• Sense of Urgency	• Value Subtlty & Ambiguity
	• Poychronic Time Approach
	• Low Sense of Urgency

Source: Adapted from Culture, Leadership, and Organizations: The GLOBE Study of 62 Societies. 2004. Sage.

Table 6.4 Future Orientation

High	Low
• Higher Rates of Economic Success	• Lower Economic Success
• Save for the Future	• Spend Now, Save Later
• Psychologically & Socially Well-adjusted	• Less Well-adjusted Individuals
• Greater Intrinsic Motivation	• Shorter Strategic Horizons
• Organizations have Longer Strategic Horizons	• Maladaptive Structures and Managers
• Flexible & Adaptable Structures	• Perceive Dualism between Material & Spiritual—Trade-offs are Mode of Operation
• Material & Spiritual Fulfilled are Linked	• Instant Gratification
• Defered Gratification	• Habitual Leadership patterns
• Favor Visionary Leaders	

Source: Adapted from Culture, Leadership, and Organizations: The GLOBE Study of 62 Societies. 2004. Sage.

Table 6.5 Gender Orientation, Egalitarianism High versus Low

High	Low
• More Women in Positions of Authority • Higher Status of Women in Society • Women have Greater Role in Societal Decision-making • Less Gender-based Job Segregation • Higher Female Literacy Rates • Similar Education Levels between Genders	• Fewer Women in Authority • Lower Societal Status • Lesser Role in Societal Decisions • Lower Number of Women in Workforce • Lower Female Literacy Rates • Lower Education Level of Women

Source: Adapted from Culture, Leadership, and Organizations: The GLOBE Study of 62 Societies. 2004. Sage.

Table 6.6 Individual and Collective Orientations

Individual	Collective
• Singular Focus on Self & Family • Autonomous Self • Individual is Priority • Personal Needs Determine Behavior • Emphasis on Rationality • Industrial & Gathering • Fast Pace Lifestyle • Higher Subjective Well-being • Nuclear Family Units • Love is Weighted Heavily in Marriage • Direct Communication • Engage in Solo Activities • Short Social Interactions • Less Distinction between In-groups and Out-groups	• Individuals are Integrated within Cohesive Groups • Self is Seen as Interdependent • Group Goals Preside • Obligation & Duty Determine Behavior • Emphasis on Relatedness • Economies Agricultural & Developing • Lower Subjective Well-being • Extended Family Structures • Love is Less Weighted in Marriage • Indirect Communication • Group Activities • Fewer Social Interactions of More Intimacy • Greater Distinctions between In-group & Out-group

Source: Adapted from Culture, Leadership, and Organizations: The GLOBE Study of 62 Societies. 2004. Sage.

contribute to how people conceive of results. For definitions for each of these cultural domain areas see Table 6.7. The point is that in a world of constant change, a global leader is somewhat tentative in his or her evaluations and decisions. Such leaders avoid being dogmatic, but are open to change and new cultural perspectives.

Table 6.7 Uncertainty Avoidance

High	Low
• Tend to Formalize Interactions	• More informal Interactions
• Document Agreements	• Rely on "word" of Person Rather than contracts
• Keep Meticulous Records	• Rely on Memory versus Recorded Documentation
• Formalize Policies, Rules & Procedures	• Informal Interactions
• Take Moderate Calculated Risks	• Risk Taking is Less Calculated
• Inhibit Innovation	• Foster Innovation thru Less control & More Risk Taking
• Stronger Resistance to Change	• Less Resistance to Change
• Less Tolerant of Rule Breaking	• Less Rule Oriented to Control Behavior
• Seek Predictable Behavior	• More tolerant of Rule Breaking

Source: Adapted from Culture, Leadership, and Organizations: The GLOBE Study of 62 Societies. 2004. Sage.

Process Elements

If people can agree on what is to be done, they next have to consider how it will be done. In the same way that people can experience conflicts about results, they can also experience conflict related to method and approach. Related to vision is the task of developing a clear business *strategy* from the vision. Strategic and tactical aspects of organizations require planning, organizing, and executing. Cultural orientations that may affect processes can include future orientation, uncertainty avoidance (see Table 6.8), and individual versus collective orientation.

While we have covered *communication* as a critical element in intercultural leadership competency previously, here we discuss communication as a process element of leadership. The act of communicating is an event of leadership, which emerges purposefully in support of both tangible (directives, procedures, and policies) and intangible (values, emotions, and concepts) pursuits. Communication is instrumental because it represents energy, which is focused and directed. In fact, communication is similar to currency; it is an energy source through which humans think and create their futures. Yet, the act or event of communicating is a process, and therefore reliant on the social actors' approach.

Support mechanisms such as *decision-making* and *problem-solving* present additional challenges for intercultural leaders working in intercultural settings because these elements also are heavily influenced by cultural norms.

Table 6.8 Culture Dimensions Definitions

Power Distance
- The degree to which members of a collective expect power to be distributed.

Uncertainty Avoidance
- The extent to which a society, organization, or group relies on social norms, rules, and procedures to alleviate unpredictability.

Humane Orientation
- The degree to which a collective encourages and rewards individuals for being fair, altruistic, generous, caring, and kind to others.

Institutional Collectivism
- The degree to which organizational and societal institutional practices encourage and reward collective distribution of resources and collective action.

In-Group Collectivism
- The degree to which individuals express pride, loyalty, and cohesiveness in their organizations or families.

Assertiveness
- The degree to which individuals are assertive, confrontational, and aggressive in their relationships with others.

Gender Egalitarianism
- The degree to which a collective minimizes gender inequality.

Future Orientation
- The extent to which individuals engage in future-oriented behaviors such as delaying gratification, planning, and investing in the future.

Performance Orientation
- The degree to which a collective encourages and rewards group members for performance improvement and excellence.

Source: Adapted from Culture, Leadership, and Organizations: The GLOBE Study of 62 Societies. 2004. Sage.

Values Element

A lot of what informs people's decisions and actions are their beliefs and *values*. Values are the principles by which people live, they indicate the worth and importance we place on aspects of life. They capture our attention and motivate us toward goals. No human being reaches adulthood without having formed values. Culture plays a significant role in the values people adopt. Values are either implicit or explicit, depending on the person, group, and culture. Leaders typically demonstrate their values through their behavior. When values are known and followed between people, they form the basis of trust. When values are unclear, or incongruent, mistrust occurs.

Some organizational researchers have concluded from their comparative studies the possibility that successfully performing organizations tended to have a leadership style based on values.[200] The common element of high-performing organizations is that values are prioritized over purely profit.

According to Ann Gordon, Canadian Nuffield Scholar (2004), values and leadership style are strongly linked. Further, values orientation across countries and cultures differs, and those countries whose values (and therefore leadership styles) are similar find an easier fit. Gordon's article, Exhibit 6.9, provides an excellent background on the importance of values congruence and intercultural leadership competencies. Ms. Gordon's research and report provide further evidence that it is important that the training and preparation of leaders and managers must be localized to the particular intercultural context within which the leader/manager is expected to work.

Exhibit 6.9

Intercultural Leadership

There is a whole variety of opinions out there regarding global leadership qualities. If you look at all this, it can be very overwhelming. For simplicity sake, basically there are two ways in which people look at leadership. There is a group of people who believe that you are born with leadership skills, or rather "natural-born leaders." This type of leadership is one-way: leaders influence others to follow. The other school of thought believes there is much more interplay going on between leaders and followers; their behaviors and situations influence each other towards certain goals. Some feel the traits are inherited and others feel that characteristics are learned.

"Learned characteristics" seem more relevant, particularly transformational leadership, which is a style of two-way influence. Charismatic Leadership is a familiar style to most people because the leader's charisma is the focus. A special appeal, visioning abilities, values and the influence of the leader to get others working together to believe in and attain this vision are important behaviors in this style. Transformational leadership also has a charismatic component emphasizing strong beliefs, values, and vision. The difference is that in the process of transformational leadership, both leader and follower are developing personally or transforming as they work towards a greater goal and together can even transform entire organizations or institutions.

An example of a transformational leader would be Gandhi. His leadership and behaviors changed a lot along his path and transformed others to go beyond self-interest, for the betterment of society. Everyone is born with certain abilities that are different from others. A question of whether a person acts on those abilities and enhances them makes the difference.

(Continued)

Exhibit 6.9   (Continued)

A good leader in Canada or the U.S. automatically means a good leader in China or Brazil? It depends on their orientation to the kind of leadership style they have. For instance, if my style is more of a transformational leadership style, it tends to be more accepted in the Anglo cluster in the world as well as in Latin America. If you look at the Middle East, for example, they would probably be farthest away from that particular leadership style. A number of studies found that values are critical in leadership. The values that the Anglos hold are very different from the Middle East values. China and Canada rate Charismatic Leadership quite similarly.

Common traits can exist among leaders regardless of cultural differences. Studies done so far have looked at things in a few ways. Such studies look at values across cultures, and those cultures with similar value orientations would probably accept and respond to similar leadership styles. The other way to do it is to take some of those leadership theories that are mostly North American, have a western bias, and apply those leadership traits in an intercultural context. The third way is by combining values and specific leadership styles.

There can be differences, for example, in selecting a manager to work in Shanghai and another in Brazil. A theory is that of the eight skill groups listed in the intercultural leadership framework, one or more of those eight areas will be more important depending on the cultures involved. There is a sort of weighting process to be done. For example, in the research in the Canada/China context, relationship-building skills were the most important. After that, knowledge of the host country, intercultural communication, adaptation, and innovation skill areas are most important. Thus, if such research was performed again in Brazil, there might be that relationship-building skills are not as important as intercultural communication. People have suggested that relationship-building skills will appear everywhere, and that might be true, but this is not for certain.

Leadership skills can be learned over time. The other thing to remember is that a leader should always be learning themselves and always adapting. One is never there, because that would be a state of perfection. Sometimes there are good leaders but people put such leaders up on a pedestal. Yes, they are good leaders, but if they are to continue being good leaders, they are changing, growing, and improving. Some of the skills that they possess come naturally, but then they improve them and acquire new skills as well. Most people who have been in leadership positions for a number of years will tell you that there are lots of things that have not worked. When things are not working, when an approach is not working, some self-analysis should be done about the way things are being handled. That is where a leadership framework can be helpful because you can sit down and look at the skill list and perform a self-evaluation.

An organization can become more interculturally competent. Leaders can train their staff. They can have them assess themselves against intercultural leadership skills and how they can improve their skills if necessary. By considering and then addressing these issues, they will maximize the performance of the organization within a specific cultural context. Therefore, the organization is more apt to attain its objectives.

Source: Adapted from *Intercultures Magazine, Center for Intercultural Learning,* July 13, 2007.

What Can Go Wrong

It appears that people who are comfortable with higher levels of ambiguity are also more interested and comfortable with contexts that feature diverse groups of people. People with low tolerance for ambiguity, who find themselves in intercultural situations, can make costly mistakes.

Risk aversion occurs when leaders are inexperienced or ineffectual; however, several potential causes underlie ineffectual issues. One issue, previously discussed, is the difference in how people of different cultures conceptualize a situation as a problem, or not a problem. This can become problematic in situations such as personnel performance evaluations, where culturally bound behaviors are interpreted as "good" and "bad" be the different cultures present at the table. Another issue is that people can perceive something as a problem, or not, based on the amount of uncertainty that is created (potentially) by perceiving something as a problem. For that matter, the same issue comes up in intercultural assessments of opportunities. A last issue that can occur is when people, such as a group of leaders within an organization, unconsciously and subjectively narrow the potential solutions because of fear of uncertainty, which raises the risk factor in the minds of the participants.

Auto-pilot decision-making occurs when leaders seek to govern and direct from a place of operating by precedent. In such cases, a leader may perceive the complexity inherent in a particular situation and seek to avoid their own discomfort and will make a decision based on something they did in the past. These types of decisions typically conform to cultural norms.

Decision paralysis occurs when leaders in intercultural contexts face their own inexperience along with the good intentions of acting with integrity and wanting accommodate local culture, but without the benefit of other intercultural competencies in place to support their efforts.

Overcomplicating occurs when inexperienced leaders have the desire and intention to act in consideration of all stakeholders, but perceive that the situation has no solution that will be appropriate. Usually, this occurs when the leader lacks the skills necessary to bring all parties to the table and negotiate solutions.

Reactionism occurs on both the emotional and/or the behavioral level when novice intercultural leaders have built little or no self-awareness, and little or no awareness and appreciation of and for other cultural perspectives. A high performing career professional has many competencies. Above all, the global leader has to have managerial and technical competencies. In addition, here are three areas of competence to cultivate.

Competencies

Regulating emotions is critical for leaders. We do not mean to suggest that leaders should not ever show their emotions, because at times allowing a window to one's feelings helps normalize situations for followers. The challenge for leaders is to know their own sensitivity areas as well as where they may have emotional blinders. Emotionally intelligent leaders can identify what emotional state they are in at any time and understand the affect this is having on their perceptions of a situation, their behaviors, and their cognitions. Leaders with less emotional intelligence are more likely to be at the mercy of their emotions in that they will color and change their perceptions of reality, their behavior, and the way they think and think about their thinking and emotions without being aware of this.

Monitoring behavior is closely related to regulation of emotions, since behavior is the outgrowth of thoughts and feelings. It is unrealistic to think that leaders will never behave in a way that they regret, or in a manner that causes some type of negative reaction or response from followers. However, and to extend the point made above, when leaders are able to build awareness of their emotions and know their own biases and emotional triggers, they have a better chance of acting from an informed rather than impulsive frame of mind.

Cognitive flexibility means that leaders perceive "reality" as something co-created rather than fixed by precedent. Harken back to our earlier discussion about mindfulness and flexibility. Leaders working in intercultural contexts must be able to switch back and forth between their own perspectives and taking in the perspectives of other stakeholders.

The Leader Ambiguity Aptitude Continuum

Leaders who are able to cope well with situations of high contrast and ambiguity without undue stress also tend to value a diversity of people to challenge and inform their thinking. Conversely, leaders with low tolerance for ambiguity, those who prefer the comfort of more stable environments tend to prefer to work with people who are like them. They tend not to like being challenged by different thinking and ideas that do not accord with their own. For the ability to accept and value diversity is to read the ability to accept and value a diversity of thinking. Essentially, there appears to be a link between cognitive broad banding, tolerance for ambiguity, and an understanding that diversity can help to extend ones thinking and help with problem solving. The following exhibit (Table 6.9) provides a description of levels of ambiguity comfort and approximates the behaviors one

Table 6.9 Leader Ambiguity Aptitude

Basic	Intermediate	Advanced	Proficient
Copes with change and novelty, shifting when necessary and with support	Copes with change and novelty, shifting with relative ease	Perceives effects of change and novelty on self and others, prepares to shift responsively	Anticipates effects of change and novelty, directs self and engages others in effortlessly shifting emotions, behaviors and cognitive patterns
Suggests solutions, plans and acts without having considered stakeholder/other perspectives	Decides and acts to compensate with some consideration of stakeholder perspectives	Uses creativity to adapt useful alternatives in collaboration with stakeholders	Predicts and communicates the opportunities from a stakeholder-aware perspective, engages stakeholders in co-creating new and mutually agreeable realities
Tolerates and reacts to risk and uncertainty after some disruption	Handles risk and uncertainty with minimal disruption	Embraces risk and uncertainty	Prospers self and others by maximizing benefits and lessening effects of risk and uncertainty

could expect from leaders working at each level. However, this schematic is culture-bound to the extent that the underlying assumption is that high ambiguity tolerance is valued.

All leaders and managers who are considered for positions within intercultural contexts should be assessed for their level of ambiguity tolerance. Those who may have the desire, but who do not assess at higher ambiguity tolerance levels should be given the opportunity to expand their ambiguity tolerance through coursework and special mentored assignments. Those who demonstrate the flexibility to develop higher ambiguity tolerance could be considered for further development. Those who are not comfortable with ambiguity and do not demonstrate an interest and flexibility to develop this ability should be considered for stable environments only.

The Principle of "Contrasts" in Practice

A Geoleader can negotiate the principle of Contrasts through the following practices and behaviors:

- *Deflate stress*: Analyze what makes you anxious, and short-circuit the process before it takes hold. Drop the issue for a short while if you get emotional.
- *Embrace change*: Be willing to let go of one way of doing things to try something new. Invite new ideas, and experiment until you are comfortable with change.
- Go on a trip to a foreign country you have not visited before. Rather than a touristic trip, take a cultural trip to immerse in the culture.
- Manage a temporary group of resisting people in an unpopular project.
- Assemble a team of diverse people to accomplish a difficult task.
- Take on a task that you have never done before.
- Teach others something you do not know well. Pick something new, different, and unfamiliar.
- Be a "researcher" of other people. Study their behavior and what they do differently from you. Adapt what you learn to change your behavior.
- Be alert to your behavior and emotions when faced with transitions. Review what is similar and what is different before transitioning between old and new situations.
- Monitor yourself more closely and get off your autopilot. Look at each situation from a fresh perspective. Ask yourself questions consistently, and try new solutions for old problems.

Case Presentation: USAHP Expansion into Mexico

How does a leadership group lead the effective acquisition of a foreign company? How is employee resistance deal with? And how do differences in national cultures, regional cultures, and in culturally based technologies affect employees' and leaders' ability to deal with ambiguity? Consider the case of USAHP's acquisition and its successful expansion into an a-typical Mexican region (Exhibit 6.2).

Exhibit 6.2

Case Study on Culture and the Implementation of Manufacturing Strategy in Mexico

Mexico is the number-two exporter to the United States, and the codependence of the two nations is obvious. United States investments in Mexico have grown considerably over the past years, especially since the North American Free Trade Agreement (NAFTA) began promoting industrial development when it came into effect in 1994. Initially, many U.S. firms moved to Mexico in search of cheap labor, in spite of evidence that cheap labor itself rarely enables companies to compete successfully in the global marketplace. Many of these firms subsequently moved from Mexico to South Asia and Southeast Asia, attracted by even lower wage rates. Other firms have moved to Mexico to establish long-term relationships that secure a profitable place in developing Latin American markets.

Consequently, the acquisition by a U.S. multinational (USAHP) of the Mexican plant (from PAMEX) discussed here was exceptionally challenging. To expand its activities, USAHP purchased a plant in Axcala, Mexico, from a Mexican group called PAMEX. At that time, the plant had more than 500 employees and had a production of a million cases of products per month. The plant had state-of-the-art technology with almost completely automatic lines. The two companies had very different ways of conducting business. PAMEX management believed that its employees should learn by experience and trial and error. PAMEX hired local employees, more because of established relationships than on education and expertise. As a result, many of its employees had only an elementary education. On the other hand, USAHP relies heavily on systematic training and expertise when it makes hiring decisions, and only hires people who have at least some technical education. It prefers to hire outstanding new graduates who have studied in selected universities (mostly private universities), and it requires them to be very proficient in both written and spoken English. Selection decisions are made through a standard U.S. process-applicants are given a test to measure their ability to solve problems and then the few who pass that test go through a series of interviews.

As a result, getting a job in the Axcala plant became much more difficult than before, especially for local people. The region where the plant is located has some technical schools that supply the labor force for local industries, however, the area lacks good universities. Therefore, USAHP largely recruited its new administrative personnel from neighboring, more developed, and culturally distinct (Mexican) states. Workers at the PAMEX plant suddenly were confronted by newcomers who were both outsiders (either U.S. citizens or from neighboring states) and different in terms of their backgrounds, education, and experience. Expatriates from the U.S. were doubly alien—they were U.S. citizens and they chose to live in neighboring states because of its more attractive climate and educational institutions.

For the managers and engineers remaining from the previous company, the culture change accompanying USAHP's acquisition of the Axcala plant was enormous. Most of the employees felt, accurately, that their jobs were in jeopardy because of the remarkable differences in philosophy between

(Continued)

Exhibit 6.2   (Continued)

the two companies. PAMEX promoted, rewarded, and retained employees based on their loyalty to the firm and to their immediate supervisors, and based on interpersonal (usually family) connections. In contrast, USAHP's policy was to hire technical experts to start as supervisors and then grow within the company up to managerial positions. Similar differences were apparent in the reward systems of the two companies. Under PAMEX, managers' salaries were based on their friendships with the owner or the board of directors of the company.

As a result, their salaries were far larger than the USAHP salary structure allowed, given their training, performance, and experience. Meanwhile, most of the technicians had salaries that were far below USAHP's standards. To bring the new plant into line with company standards, USAHP froze the salaries of the overpaid managers and fired those whose jobs were primarily based on their personal relationships with the previous owners. The managers whose salaries were frozen were unhappy with the change, but they were happy to keep their jobs. However, one of USAHP's first steps raised questions about the fairness of the company's reward system. In the new plant, rewards, promotions, and retention were based on objective measures of individual performance. Each of these changes was appropriate given the strategic model within which USAHP operated. But, for PAMEX employees, the changes created uncertainty and ambiguity and directly threatened their job security. To make matters worse, outsiders, who in many ways had thus inadvertently exaggerated their alien status, imposed the changes. As a result, the changes created an exceptional level of uncertainty for employees whose society is especially focused on uncertainty avoidance.

Implementing the Total Productive Maintenance Concept

The new owners also required operators to learn a completely new way of working. Workers were accustomed to being mere button pressers and were not required to write or document anything. With USAHP, the workers had to change their everyday practices and adhere to strict working standards that required constant documentation. Because of these changes, many of the older workers accepted voluntary retirement packages because they just could not adapt to the new working systems. The ones who remained found ways to delay or short-circuit the implementation of the change.

USAHP uses Total Productive Maintenance (TPM) in its plants to remain competitive. TPM is a manufacturing strategy of Japanese origin that includes different working methodologies.

The First Years of AM in USAHP Axcala

To begin the AM implementation, USAHP started training at the top managerial level as a way to convince the rest of the plant that autonomous maintenance was so important that even managers would get their hands dirty working on the machines. For the startup of AM, all the leaders of the plant including the plant manager cleaned their assigned work centers and documented the status of their work. The next step was to involve all of

(Continued)

Exhibit 6.2   (Continued)

the plant to work in autonomous maintenance. An exchange of personnel from different sites where AM was already in place was promoted. The company provided all the necessary equipment, such as computers, for exclusive AM use. Autonomous maintenance was first applied to those operations and equipment identified as most critical for the manufacturing process. On the one hand, one would expect top-down change fostered by recognized experts to be readily accepted by members of a high-power distance (PD) society. However, the key personnel involved in this change were outsiders, not members of the operators' existing "in-groups."

Ruben Salas was the AM leader chosen by the plant leadership team. He was transferred from another Mexican site where autonomous maintenance had been implemented successfully. Forty teams were formed to pilot the AM project. However, from the beginning, Salas had leadership problems with the production department.

Arturo Suarez was the production department's manager. He was local to the region, had worked in the factory for over 10 years, and had gained the respect of the workers in the plant. Suarez started as a supervisor when the plant was owned by PAMEX and worked his way up to his current position. Suarez was under constant management pressure to meet the production requirements set by the sales department. As a result, he opposed having the department's employees go to AM training sessions because their absence could jeopardize meeting production quotas. The production workers also noticed that the managers could not come to an agreement on the importance of autonomous maintenance. The new managers had no direct experience on the shop floor and could not produce persuasive evidence of the positive effects of the system on the workers' lives. As a result, the workers decided to listen to Suarez, the boss with whom they had worked for more than a decade and whom they were loyal to. They did not embrace the autonomous maintenance philosophy and thought that cleaning the equipment was pointless because "it would get dirty again anyway."

During this time, the company struggled to provide AM training to its employees. The employees were negatively influenced by Suarez, never understanding why they had to go to training. It seemed like a waste of time to them, and they chose not to go or showed up late. In fact, the implementation of AM seemed to penalize the operators because it eliminated their piece-rate reward system, and now they could not blame the maintenance group for any production losses due to machine breakdowns. They believed it was unreasonable for the managers to ask them to fix their own equipment when they had no maintenance experience and previously had been served by a specialized maintenance department. Furthermore, they thought there was no reason to change the current methods because "they had worked fine" all this time for PAMEX.

In summary, the workers had no incentives to implement autonomous maintenance and had significant disincentives for doing so. The workers' resistance to AM was also related to the ambiguity of the system itself. There are no predefined, detailed recipes on how to apply AM. Instead, the methodology relies heavily on active worker involvement, a common feature

(Continued)

Exhibit 6.2 (Continued)

of many methodologies of Japanese origin. For instance, the guidelines state that one should achieve zero defects without explicitly saying how to achieve that goal. The methodology states that every member of a work group is responsible for finding and implementing new solutions. In contrast, Mexican workers are culturally predisposed to obey established rules procedures and to follow a leader. Both predispositions provide stability and protection in uncertain situations. Because most of the workers from PAMEX had, at best, elementary school educations, the new managers decided that the work standards and procedures should be created from the supervisor level instead of from the workers themselves, as required by AM. During this initial attempt to implement AM, the combination of cultural preferences and a badly designed reward system probably doomed the system from the outset. After two and a half years, only six groups out of 40 had progressed enough to be moved to step two of the seven-step AM methodology procedure.

Source: Adapted from *Journal of Manufacturing Systems*, 2004.

Case Perspective: Contrasts Applied

Organizational change inevitably generates resistance. In even the best of circumstances, change creates uncertainty and ambiguity, and employees respond to those anxieties in myriad ways, many of which can undermine the organization's objectives. Resistance to change is related to national culture in two ways. First, cultural assumptions influence the way in which multinational corporations approach expansion into a new country or market. There are many possible forms of expansion. In terms of potential cultural integration, the two extremes are (1) "greenfield" starts and (2) acquisitions. In the former situation, a multinational company sends a small group of expatriates into an area to hire locals and gradually build a business. The potential for cultural clash is minimized, and the opportunity for the expatriates to learn the nuances of the new culture is maximized.

At the opposite extreme are foreign acquisitions, in which a multinational firm purchases a local company or plant. Acquisitions are quick but fraught with potential for culture clash. In the worst-case scenario, the acquiring firm blindly imposes its own way of doing things on members of a very different culture with little consideration of those differences or for the values of employees of the acquired firm.

As a result, cross-cultural acquisitions tend to fail significantly more often than other forms of expansion, especially when the cultures of the acquiring and acquired firms/plants are substantially different.[201] For a variety of reasons, most of which are related to the political, legal, and economic situation that characterizes the society in which a multinational is based, national culture and mode of intervention are strongly correlated. U.S. firms tend to acquire foreign firms or plants, and tend to place the burden of adaptation on members of the acquired firm/plant rather than accepting that burden themselves.[202] The potential for resistance is increased by differences in cultural assumptions within organizations. Arguably, the most important dimension that differentiates national cultures is Uncertainty Avoidance (UA)[203]—the intensity with which each culture's members feel Years of delays in the successful implementation of autonomous maintenance could have been avoided if USAHP's management had a better understanding of PAMEX's national and regional cultures. In particular, the case study illustrates differences among U.S. business and Mexican and Axcalan cultures in uncertainty avoidance and power distance as related to rules, leadership, teamwork, work ethics, and workforce educational level. This section will discuss these differences and their impact on TPM implementation.

The new reward system uses rules to manage worker uncertainty, instead of using the relationship culture of Axcala. The rules themselves are clear and known to all and are a welcome improvement over the ambiguities and uncertainties of the past two and a half years; however, just as importantly, the rules are implemented in a manner that relies on in-group links instead of threatening them.

A main flaw in the initial attempt to implement TPM was that USAHP overlooked how differently people in United States and Mexican cultures relate to leaders in a company—that is, power-distance (PD) differences. The initial resistance to implement autonomous maintenance (AM) was very high because of the failure to recognize the importance of getting "in-group" leaders (such as Arturo Suarez) to wholeheartedly accept the TPM philosophy, and the failure to recognize that the workers were not responsive to the expertise, status, or power of outsiders. The workers were culturally predisposed to follow Suarez as a local leader. In the second attempt, USAHP eliminated this resistance by removing Suarez from the leadership.

Another cultural issue disregarded by USAHP in the initial implementation was the different predisposition that Americans and Mexicans have for working in self-managed teams. In the United States, most people leave their parents' home early in their lives, either to go to college or once they get their first jobs after high school graduation. It is very different in Mexico, as in most Latin American cultures, where most people live with their families until they get married, even if this is long after they could be financially self-sufficient. Therefore, early in their lives, U.S. workers learn to trust coworkers with whom they have no personal or family relationship, while Latin American workers are more used to the security of being surrounded and supported by family and tend to distrust strangers. As a result, Americans are more predisposed to become effective working in teams, while it may take longer for Mexicans to trust arbitrarily assigned teammates.[204] Conversely, the extreme individualism of American culture makes it difficult for those from the United States to understand the responses of more community-oriented cultures like those of Latin America.[205] The United States has the highest ranking in individualism when compared to every other country in the study; Mexico scores on the opposite side of the same scale. In the workplaces of an individualist society, others' are seen as "resources," and "tasks" prevailing over "relationships," making teamwork a natural work method. It is conjectured that this difference is more obvious in less-educated layers of the society, thus the significant resistance of the workers to outsider managed teams in the USAHP case. In the second attempt, USAHP gave more power to the team leaders, and the reward system directly penalized team members for not participating in the autonomous maintenance program.

The former type of system, like the one used by USAHP, largely maintains a centralized structure of power and authority. Therefore, the system is one that would be minimally upsetting in a culture with high-PD. USAHP's management modified its implementation of some autonomous maintenance methods to those that were more appropriate to the Axcala plant. Because the company's initial goal was to use the same practices in all of its plants, this willingness to adapt is both surprising and a credit to its management. The results suggest that successful implementation would have occurred sooner if those involved had recognized the impact of regional cultural differences from the beginning.

To understand the Mexican culture fully, one needs to differentiate among the regions of the country. Experts in intercultural communication have recognized for some time that treating a nation as a homogeneous culture is unwise.[206]

USAHP made a rational decision to apply a production system that had been successful in its other plants, including some in Latin America, to its new acquisition in Axcala. Increasing the educational level of its workforce, redesigning its reward system to focus on productivity rather than interpersonal ties, and implementing a proactive system of equipment operation and maintenance all are consistent with modern management and operations theory. Additionally, there is no sense that, even if USAHP had been thoroughly knowledgeable and exquisitely sensitive to the overall differences between AngloUS and Mexican cultures, it would have understood and adapted at first to the nuances of the local culture of the Axcalan plant.

Fortunately, USAHP was willing to recognize that its change effort was failing and to make appropriate adjustments, something that is unfortunately rare among U.S. organizations.[207] As a result, USAHP was able to succeed when it had been on the brink of failure. Finally, just to highlight the importance of the cultural aspects when trying to implement a new manufacturing system, since the new implementation the company has been able to reduce machine stoppages by more than 50%, which can represent significant savings for the company running a high-volume, continuous process.

Through analysis of this case, we can see that even with the best intentions and with having, some knowledge of a national culture does not necessarily portend a successful acquisition venture. Leaders of the USAHP organization needed to spend the requisite time in the region, as part of the "due diligence" of the acquisition. The layers of complexity in this case were greater because of the insularity of the local culture, because of the manner in which the U.S.-based company leaders approached the situation initially, and because of the additional complexity of using a Japanese manufacturing style. We might suggest in such a situation that the acquiring organization could have called in cultural consultants, if appropriately skilled leaders were not available to conduct the initial due diligence. What we are suggesting here, is that the due diligence process of mergers, acquisitions, and expansions, always include a significant phase devoted to assessing the various cultural characteristics of each organization, its region, and nation.

The cultural quality that will be most needed by firms in the future is awareness of contrasts. As firms expand their businesses internationally, the senior management must be aware of the cultural and social climate to make the correct business decisions. Often time, management is not aware of all of the nuances of a country and tries to integrate only to find that their business philosophy was not in line with the cultural or social structure. If a business plans to succeed, they must be aware of the climate and adapt their philosophy to accommodate. Furthermore, once a firm has established its business internationally, they must continue to be aware of the cultural changes and keep their employees aware so that they can make proper day-to-day managerial decisions. Awareness by both senior management before expanding into a foreign country and by the management to know how to deal with specific situation in that culture is essential to a business' success.

Case Presentation: Islamic Finance

In this chapter devoted to contrast, we have identified areas of difference between cultures and their varying values and norms related to difference and ambiguity. Exhibit 6.3 presents a case that highlights uncertainty avoidance, risk, and future orientation.

Exhibit 6.3

When Hedge Funds Meet Islamic Finance

One recent afternoon, New York money manager James Rickards presented Sheik Yusuf Talal DeLorenzo with a dilemma: Could his hedge fund be Islamic-friendly?

Islam prohibits all kinds of speculative behavior that is embedded in Wall Street's DNA. But Mr. DeLorenzo, a Massachusetts-born convert to Islam, is on a mission to meld centuries-old Islamic law with modern finance in the U.S.

Mr. Rickards's fund couldn't bet on currency futures or some of the shares in the Standard & Poor's 500 index, Mr. DeLorenzo said, if he wants observant Muslims to invest. But some alterations could earn the sheik's approval—such as holding currencies instead of futures, and buying only S&P 500 companies that aren't debt-heavy or dependent on profit from interest payments. "Music to my ears," Mr. Rickards said. "It sounds like I can still get the effect I'm looking for."

With the Middle Eastern economy booming, partly thanks to soaring oil wealth, the Islamic financial industry has been expanding at a clip of about 15% a year, according to accounting firm KPMG, and is on pace to reach $1 trillion in two years. The money is seeking new outlets and Western financial institutions are seeking new clients—opening the door for more aggressive methods to reconcile two worlds that don't easily mesh.

The issue of what's permissible has opened fault lines within Islamic finance. Malaysian adaptations of Western-style bonds, for instance, have been condemned, then copied, in Muslim countries in the Middle East. Scholars consulting for Western financial institutions are criticized for bending religious laws to serve financial ends—the "rent-a-sheik" argument, says one U.S. bank official. Vendors profit by "capitalizing on people's religious insecurities," says Mahmoud El-Gamal, a professor of economics who holds a chair in Islamic finance at Rice University. "Don't take my duck, sprinkle holy water on it, and say it's a chicken."

Islamic law, or Shariah, stems from the Quran and subsequent interpretations by scholars. In the economic realm, commerce receives divine approval but several verses speak of a prohibition on interest, a practice viewed as exploiting the borrower. An association in Bahrain is the informal authority on Shariah compliance for Islamic financial institutions. But its standards aren't mandatory and don't govern the offerings of Western firms, which retain their own Shariah boards to advise them and issue their own rulings, or *fatwas*. Top scholars can serve on dozens of boards, earning retainers of up to $20,000–$40,000 a year per client. Scholars who give their seal of approval sometimes receive a percentage of assets invested.

Mr. DeLorenzo says it's rare to get a percentage of assets, but that one time he accepted such compensation. Among his other clients is Dow Jones & Co., parent company of The Wall Street Journal, which retains him and five other scholars to consult on its indexes of Shariah-compliant companies. Mr. DeLorenzo receives an annual retainer of $5000 plus stipends for attending two to three meetings a year.

(Continued)

Exhibit 6.3   (Continued)

Western banks say they make more than cosmetic changes to create shariah-compliant financial products. London-based Barclays Bank PLC, which worked with Mr. DeLorenzo and a firm called Shariah Capital Inc. on a platform for hedge funds to trade without violating Islamic requirements, had to rewrite a 20-odd-page brokerage contract. The concept of short-selling—using borrowed shares to bet on a stock's decline—was replaced with an Islamic down-payment structure known as an *arboon*. Any reference to a "guarantee" was replaced, for instance by a pledge of collateral, because Islamic rules require shared risk by all parties.

New Options

- *The Issue*: Hedge funds and financial services companies are seeking to create new products that can meet Islamic religious requirements.
- *The Incentive*: The Middle East's economy is booming, creating demand for new investment options, and Western firms are looking for new clients.
- *The Challenge*: Firms are adapting offerings to avoid prohibitions such as charging interest, while religious scholars decide how freely they can interpret Islamic Law.

"There were definitely a few firsts," says Kieran McCann, a director in Barclays Capital's prime-brokerage group.

The gap between Wall Street and Islamic financial law can be uncomfortably wide, especially amid lingering distrust on both sides after the 2001 terrorist attacks on the United States. But the United States also is home to several million middle-class Muslims, one of the largest markets in the West. A 2004 Zogby poll for Georgetown University found a majority have college educations and earn $50,000 or more a year. Some early steps in providing Islamic alternatives have exposed pent-up demand.

Vetting Services

Once word began to spread that Devon Bank in Chicago was exploring Islamic financial products in 2002, there was an immediate response from the local Muslim community, says bank vice president David Loundy. "People said, 'Can you do houses, cars, lines of credit, and how about my sister in Connecticut?" Some customers went as far as calling scholars in Pakistan to vet the acceptability of Devon's services, he said.

One Devon customer, Ahmed Khan, a technology executive at Dutch-based bank ABN Amro Holding NV, says he owned a home in the late 1980s but was "very uncomfortable" paying conventional mortgage interest and went back to renting. In 2005 he took out a Devon:

> "Shariah-compliant" mortgage using a method called *ijara*: The bank bought Mr. Khan's condominium and he pays a monthly sum to buy it from the bank over time, plus a lease payment for using the property.

(Continued)

Exhibit 6.3   (Continued)

In the first five years his cost of financing is about 7%, he says, and he paid some fees beyond normal closing costs for the specialized legal structure. Mr. Khan had to fill out a standard mortgage application, but says it's important for U.S. Muslims to accept such compromises to encourage banks' efforts. "If you don't show that demand, there will never be any supply," he says. The bank also converts the arrangement to a conventional mortgage for its regulators and the Internal Revenue Service, and advises customers to seek tax advice on whether it's deductible. Mr. Khan takes the deduction.

He began to establish his reputation as an expert in the late 1990s, after publishing a collection of English translations of the Islamic banking fatwas. In 2000 he began working with what would become Guidance Financial Group, a company founded by Mohamad Hammour, a former economics professor at Columbia University. The goal: to offer U.S. Muslims a competitively priced Islamic mortgage.

It took a year and a half to hammer out a solution that they believed could not only comply with Shariah, but also clear the various home-finance regulations of individual states. It also needed to be eligible for financing by mortgage giant Freddie Mac. "We had to essentially reinvent the entire mortgage process—from the day you talk to the consumer, to the day the mortgage gets sold on Wall Street," says Dr. Hammour.

Guidance offers a co-ownership agreement known as a *musharaka*, a slightly different strategy than that of Devon Bank. The customer and Guidance jointly form a new corporation to own the home. Part of the customer's monthly payment goes toward buying out Guidance's share and part is a "utility fee," which the home buyer pays in exchange for using the asset. Guidance says it keeps the fees roughly competitive with the market in 30-year mortgage interest rates, though there are added fees connected with the co-ownership venture. By the end of the term, the home buyer has completely bought out Guidance's stake and wholly owns the house. Guidance reports the transaction to the IRS as a conventional mortgage, like Devon Bank, and says its customers generally take a regular deduction.

Guidance says it reached $1 billion in such financing in June, and is now operating in 21 states and Washington, DC. The firm contends the market for Shariah-compliant mortgages in the U.S. could top $10 billion a year.

Mr. DeLorenzo is pushing the envelope with an even more complex product, the Islamic trading system for hedge funds he helped develop with Barclays and Greenwich, Conn.-based Shariah Capital. In the summer of 2001, Shariah's CEO Eric Meyer was a hedge-fund manager looking for a new venture. He was impressed by Mr. DeLorenzo's writing on Islamic finance. He sought him out and the two men talked for more than five hours about how to create an Islamic hedge fund.

Mr. DeLorenzo had his doubts. Hedge funds' variety of complex investment strategies—including "short selling" stocks by selling borrowed shares to bet their price will drop—poses a problem. In Islamic finance, investors aren't allowed to sell what they don't own because it represents an unacceptable form of speculation.

(Continued)

Exhibit 6.3   (Continued)

There are other prohibitions, too. Because of the ban on interest payments, investors must avoid companies like banks that rely on interest for their income. For the same reason, they are required to steer clear of firms that carry high levels of debt—defined in different rulings as around one-third of either market capitalization or assets—and thus pay a significant amount of interest.

Those are obstacles that would stop some experts. Monzer Kahf, an economist and consultant in Islamic finance who lives near Los Angeles, says he generally supports Islamic finance efforts, but draws the line at trying to make hedge funds Shariah-compliant: "What are hedge funds other than advanced forms of speculation?"

Source: Adapted from and permission granted. *Islamic Finance, Joanna Slater, Wall Street Journal*, August 9, 2007, p. A1.

Case Perspective: Contrasts Applied

This case of Islamic finance highlights the difference between Western and Middle Eastern comfort levels with risk, uncertainty avoidance, and future orientation. In Islamic culture, speculation is not valued in the same way it is in Western financial institutions. In Islamic systems, all parties involved must have equally shared risk. From our perspective with an intercultural competence lens, the Western financial institutions highlighted in this case example and, in particular, the profiled individuals, have achieved a high level of intercultural maturity. They have worked through the ambiguity and contrasts of two cultures (Western secular and Islamic) to build a bridge and create relationships for mutual benefit, not just for themselves but also for many people who can and will follow in their footsteps.

The Bottom Line

Changes, transitions, differing contexts, and novel situations all require that leaders possess the requisite skills to negotiate the inherent ambiguity. Intercultural leaders must be able to do this with the added layers of complexity associated with intercultural contexts. In all organizations, there are particular areas where ambiguity occurs.

Leaders in intercultural contexts must develop the requisite awareness, knowledge, and skills. Awareness of self and others enables leaders to appreciate difference and similarity toward creating mutually acceptable agreements and relationships. Knowledge of a leader's own cultural bias and a willing and active pursuit of knowledge of other cultures are necessary. Language skills and cultural practices allow leaders to optimize and set goals and objectives mutually. Four essential practices can enable leaders to prepare and navigate the terrain of intercultural relations:

1. Actively considering and adjusting to the thoughts and emotions of one's self as well as with the person(s) one is communicating.
2. Actively considering and then comparing and contrasting beliefs (e.g. religious, political, and cultural) of one's self as well as with the person(s) one is communicating.
3. Actively considering and then adjusting one's message given the prior knowledge or experiences of one's peers, customers, and employees.
4. Actively considering and then adjusting given the motives and intentions of one's self and/or their communicative partner.

7

The Principle of "Context"

It is of interest to note that while some dolphins are reported to have learned English—up to fifty words used in correct context—no human being has been reported to have learned dolphinese.

—Carl Sagan

Normally, humans are effective at conveying ideas to each other and responding fittingly. This is due to many factors: the richness of the *language they share*, the *common understanding* of how the world works, and an *implicit understanding* of everyday situations. When humans interact within cultures, they enjoy a higher degree, or capability, to use implicit situational information (context) to increase the level of comprehension. However, this ability to interact becomes complicated when humans interact across cultures. In such intercultural circumstances, social actors endeavor interactive exchanges with a lack of common understanding. Consequently, individuals from differing cultures, trying to interact are unable to use context as an expedient channel to comprehension. By increasing each person's understanding of the other's cultural context (language, norms, rules, etc.), in other words increasing their access to context. They increase the richness of communication interaction and enable mutual success.

Context Defined

Context means the surrounding circumstances and conditions in which something unfolds. It can be understood as the frame within which phenomena exist. It provides the staging, the backdrop, the props, and the script with which we interpret and derive meaning. In other words, we use context to make sense of what we observe happening around, or to, us. For example, normally we understand birds flying as belonging to the context of air, and fish swimming as belonging to the context of some body of water. However, as convenient as contexts are to us, human social contexts can be complex.

Not only are contexts complex; but they emerge, evolve, dissipate, develop, and change. While context may influence, it does not necessarily determine decisions and action. We argue that humans and context interact. Contexts exist within the minds and memories of people, and they consist in the external world of culture, nation-states, regions, the geopolitical climate (government, religion, war, agreements, and law), technology, resources, and naturally occurring phenomena in the biological world.

Effectively, "a context" has three essential aspects: (1) the objective reality—that which is created in form; (2) the relational—the exchange of energy between individuals and other entities; and (3) the transcendent—the individual's essence or group essence, which is always in a state of creativity. What this means is that context, as does "reality," exists in multiple dimensions, simultaneously. Context may be unambiguous, or it may be veiled.

Clear contexts need little explanation. For example, an email coming from your manager communicates a request for your attention, superficially. However, veiled contextual clues are those either which we must already know or which we must have trained ourselves to identify. Often, such training is made difficult because we commonly do not recognize that we have missed something. Veiled contexts, such as when cultural cues are sent, may be almost impossible to perceive, and are generally the most essential for us to perceive for mutual understanding between individuals (or groups). Frequently, deeper contexts will carry the most important clues to understanding what we are to do. For example, an email from a manager may just be intended to indicate that the company's CEO will be in for a visit on Friday. The meaning you take from this information, as an American engineer working in a high tech company in Silicon Valley, however, includes understanding that the project you were going to finish over the weekend must be ready by Friday morning and that the usual "casual Friday" blue jeans will be frowned upon. The manager's goal of gaining more resources for the department and your desire to exude professionalism are two contexts with which you interpreted the manager's email. In such ways, our success is often directly related to how well we learn to understand our organizations and ourselves. Understanding how to perceive contextual clues is the difference between understanding and confusion.

Contexts, which are unclear to us, present challenges. What happens if you miss the subtle or unspoken cultural-bound social cues in a message? For example, what if you, as an Indian engineer, are a relatively recent arrival to the United States, now working in the Silicon Valley high tech industry, and receive the same memo (as we described above) that your American engineer colleague received. What if you had been told, just the day before in a team orientation, that it was company policy and the "way we do things around here on Friday" to dress yourself in blue jeans to come to work? Further, what if you had been told that on the second Friday of the month, the team comes to work an hour later and gathers for a relaxing "team-building" activity? The salient point about context is that it is inseparable from those who constructed it. Unless you participate or are somehow privy, or made aware of constructed context, how would you know the essential information? How would you know how to behave?

The Intersection of Culture and Context

At its best, culture (with its elements of language, norms, artifacts, practices, and beliefs) is something humans use to make sense of the evolving world around them. At its worst, culture is something humans use to habituate decisions and actions based on outdated information. In other words, both culture and context have dual qualities of stasis and motion given by their creators. Here again, we emphasize the relational dimension between culture and context and between the creators of culture and context. We know and acknowledge of course that both culture and context have certain stabilizing characteristics also given by their creators. The point is that leaders, as users and creators of culture and context, must account for both the stability and the motion of culture and context, with the primary focus being on the relationship between the two in the immediate moment. By focusing on the immediate relationship between culture and context, between stasis and motion, the leader (along with others) is constructing context, what can be thought of as the enactment of context. In this relationship, we can perceive that context exists in the internal, as personal thoughts and feelings, and in the external as other people, objects, artifacts, and settings. What happens when the focus is not on the relationship between culture and context in the immediate present?

Cultural Misunderstandings vis-à-vis
The Intersection of Culture and Context

The following factual stories provide the reader with clear examples of how misunderstandings at the intersection of culture and context occur. Each story involves leadership failures not at top levels, but at all levels, where real-life action takes place where leadership competence is most necessary.

Armed with Guns Rather than Understanding

In the memoir of his distinguished career with the United Nations, Sir Brian Urquhart tells the story of the first night in 1957 when a contingent of the United Nations Emergency Force (UNEF) was deployed to Gaza. That evening, hearing from the minarets the muezzin's call to prayers, but not understanding Arabic or the meaning of this as a religious act, the UN troops thought it was a call to civil disorder and they fired in panic on the mosque (Urquhart, 1987). Through this tragic story of meaning lost, we can visualize the intersection of culture and context at play. Freshly deployed UNEF troops never before exposed to Arab or Muslim custom, in keeping with their internalized role context, behaved lawfully. By lawfully we mean they behaved in a manner congruent with their training, having internalized the role of the UNEF in entering Gaza as a "conflictual context." The failure to perceive, interpret, and discern the distinction between the "context of religious practice" and the "context of geo-political conflict" caused irrevocable harm. At a base level, in this example, we can perceive the failure to focus on the relationship between culture and context in the immediate moment. Fittingly, perhaps are the words of Aga Khan, a Muslim spiritual leader, who recently said, "the supposed 'clash of cultures' is in reality nothing more than a manifestation of mutual ignorance."[208]

Yours, Mine, and Ours

Some years ago in Nigeria, in a Catholic seminary, letters written by or to the seminarians were always opened and read by appointed priests before the letters were delivered to the seminarians or sent out to their friends and relatives. On one particular occasion, a letter arrived for a young Seminarian (who was preparing to be a priest and as is custom should have been celibate). The letter was sent from his village and was written in the Yoruba language. The Priest in charge of the Seminary at the time was a European Missionary who could not read the letter in the native language of Yoruba, so he called someone else who read the letter to his exact understanding. One passage of the letter said, "Your wife has just given birth to a child." The Priest in charge on hearing this news summoned the young Seminarian and sent him away from the seminary, unceremoniously. The Seminarian arrived home and learnt that his elder brother's wife had just given birth and that a letter had been sent to inform him, which was the reason he was sent away. A delegate had to be sent down to see the Priest in charge and explain to him that in the Yoruba culture (actually most Nigerian cultures) your brother's wife is called your wife. It turned out that it was the young Seminarian's elder brother who had a wife, who had just given birth to a child, and that the Seminarian did not have a wife, but as was the custom, the letter was addressing the brother's wife as his wife. The Priest understood his mistake and misunderstanding, in which case if he was right the expulsion would have been justified, but since he was not right, his action was based on a misunderstanding of the culture of the people. The Seminarian was rightfully restored to the Seminary and today he is a Bishop in Nigeria. In this example, we can see clearly the effect of context on understanding.

Hearing is Not Necessarily Believing

Several years ago, a British manager was in China for the signing of an important railway contract. The details and pricing had all been finalized and the manager only needed to endorse the contract with one of the Chinese ministers. The business location was in a small town in the northern part of China where people, by custom, speak loudly. Their business culture norm also is not to negotiate business deals on the first day they meet; instead, they first have a casual meeting followed by dinner and karaoke. On the following day, business deals are closed and then contracts are signed. The British manager being quite new to Asia (only five months into his assignment) and not knowing the Chinese culture, let alone specific regional cultures within China, *mis*understood that his Chinese counterparts were not happy when they first meet because they spoke quite loudly and dismissed his attempts to engage in signing the contract. Feeling frustrated, annoyed, confused, and bewildered, the British manager returned the following day without a signed contract and with having left without what the Chinese businessmen believed was the cementing of their working relationship. Because of the British manager's abrupt and perceived rude departure, another manager, familiar with the Chinese customs, was sent to salvage and close the deal.

Durable Structures at the Intersection of Culture and Context

When leaders focus on the immediate moment and relational motion between culture and context, they should not exclude attention to the durable structures of culture and context. Durable structures are the artifacts, institutions, and values existing within constructed reality.

"Learning Culture" is Different from "Learning *about* Culture"

How do we learn culture? Learning *about* a culture often means learning facts about its history, art, government, taking language instruction, learning what social scientists (sociologists, anthropologists, folklorists, etc.) report about them, and learning a few obligatory "dos and don't." Most often, however, such superficiality will serve you only if you plan a typical weeklong tourist trip. While our understanding of ways to learn about cultures improves, we are still trying to understand culture through cross-cultural comparisons and reductionistic methods. The truth is that such superficiality ignores important considerations and can actually cause more harm than good for everyone involved. The point is that if you are a Caucasian European-American, can you ever expect to "know" the experience of an African Kenyan by taking two courses in language and customs of West African countries? The answer is, no, you cannot, not even if you took 10 courses.

With the realization that both context and culture are inseparable from those who constructed them, the problem becomes how to know which culture one should learn. We will reframe this last statement just a little to ensure your comprehension because we do not mean, should you learn about German culture or should you learn about Thai culture. We mean that one important consideration concerns the tendency to "stereotype" cultures. While we have discussed stereotyping previously, here we mean the tendency to assume that because one studies a culture generally, one can know the culture. When we identify and categorize general tendencies in efforts to compare and contrast cultures, we reduce and oversimplify. The problem being, that within cultures, we also find significant variation. What is important to remember is that while one can draw certain generalizations, which can be helpful, since generalization includes flexibility for variation and evolution, stereotypes enforce rigidity. We recommend keeping three concepts in mind: (1) Context and culture are processes, (2) Learning culture as context means understanding the intersections and variability, (3) Learning culture as context means constructing an intercultural sphere. It is especially important that those in technical occupations, such as engineering or information technology, learn more about the behavioral science approach to management, such as culture.

Leadership and the Intersection of Context and Culture

Leadership, *the action of leading a group of people or organization*,[209] is a social construct. We construct leader and follower relationships as we interact with each other and the environment to create our future through our visioning and actions in the present. The truth is, everyone is born with potential to lead, and everyone must choose when and where s/he will take the initiative, step forward, and lead. Human activity and social interaction creates choice points for the people involved. Social interaction creates relationships between the involved parties. The choices individuals make create the potential of leader–follower relationships. In this way, social interaction creates context. In other words, and most relevant to our discussion, the leader–follower relationship creates context. This reality renders the longstanding debate about whether leaders are *born* or *made* moot.

The residual of human social interactions, beyond the immediate circumstance, is what we call culture. More importantly, reality is perceptually based and constantly in a state of flux. This means that leaders and followers are always in the position to effect and change their circumstances. Some of what we perceive as reality is actually residual from our former experiences. Experience can be beneficial or deleterious. Experience influences how leaders make decisions and how followers react to leader-initiated decisions. Outcomes depend largely on how effectively leaders and followers can create clear expectations. Expectations can be problematic however, when either the leader or follower create expectations based upon inaccurately anticipating certain behavior.

Currently, organizational leadership is influenced notably by two interrelated social phenomena, globalization, and the resultant, diversity. The leader's challenge is the competing tug between global standardization and local differentiation. As we have said previously, a leader's experience is vital to outcomes and performance. However, here, we are not speaking about leaders' *experiences* from the past. Here, we are speaking of the leader's ability to be fully present in all situations and in his or her ability to draw upon current experience to co-create and co-construct a workable, emerging reality for all stakeholders.

The Age-Old Debate: Are Leaders Born or Made?

The following is a little story about such a relationship: the leader–follower relationship and the interaction between humans and context. It is also a story of how leadership potential can emerge when the time, the place, the situation, and the person all gel.

In a suburb of Washington DC a group of teenagers took part in a community-sponsored leadership summer camp. Participants were required to submit essays and letters of reference along with their applications. Eleven 16-year-olds were eventually accepted into the program. The counselors in charge put the youths through a ROPES course among other team building activities during the first weekend so that the group could form as a team prior to the actual camp activities associated with learning leadership. The camp counselors were, as it turned out, most surprised by a seemingly awkward, gangly teen previously identified as being autistic, who emerged as a leader while on the ROPES course and other analytical problem-solving challenges.

The group of teens included a member of the high-school tennis team, a cheerleader, a basketball player, a softball player, a track star, a soccer star, two dancers, and a young man we will call Jesse. It is noteworthy also that Jesse was the only Hispanic-American person among a group dominated by African-Americans, with only two European-Americans. It seems that all the teens found the ROPES course and other simulated activities difficult, except Jesse. This fact was not lost on the group of teens and soon all of them began listening to Jesse once they realized that they kept falling, drowning, etc., whatever the simulation result proved. Jesse, who gently and confidently began making objective observations and suggestions, suddenly had a following. It turns out that he was able to size up the situations and for each, offer an effective sequential idea. By the end of day two, each of the teens went across the high log, after each one had refused to on day one. The turnaround in the perception and treatment of Jesse by the other teens was remarkable to the counselors by their reports. Counselors reported that several of the teens spoke to Jesse about the events and of his leadership. One teen was overheard to say to Jesse, "You probably don't remember that we were in the fourth grade together. I want to apologize for being such a jerk to you back then!"

Here was a circumstance where a person who showed his leadership, even when the team was at first reluctant, but with his calm gentle persistence at guiding was soon embraced by everyone. The circumstance, conditions, and composition of that particular group provided the necessary ground for Jesse to step forward, to shine such that others could see his leadership qualities. This same young man is awkward in many social situations. While he may not have all the skills necessary to be a superior leader in all contexts if matched in a job that requires his talents and skills, he will be a leader.

This fabulous example is one of *emergent leadership*, situated in a context. Jesse's ability to size up the situation and give sequential advice, where the other folks missed the mark, may have been because he was the only "sequential" thinker among a group of "global" thinkers. Sometimes, this is how a leader is "born," which makes a stellar point. That when we have the age-old debate about leaders being "made" or "born," we assume that by "born" we mean that leaders are taking charge and directing traffic straight out of the womb! When, in fact, what we mean by the statement "great leaders are born," is that at some critical juncture, perhaps early in life, perhaps not, the leader emerges, in part, because of context and circumstances, but also in part, because the person, for whatever reason, suddenly draws the strength and courage to step forward. The leader emerges because she or he is at the right time, in the right place, with the right group of people, and history is made. It is entirely possible that through this situation, this teenager, through reflecting on his experience at summer leadership camp and what was created in the context, namely, the "leader–follower" relationship, will have discovered something important about himself and will go on to do great things.

The Principle of "Context" in Practice

A Geoleader™ can negotiate the principle of Context through the following practices and behaviors:

- Practice setting intentions for all your actions.
- Practice asking other people with who you interact for their understanding and interpretation of your meaning and your intention.
- Practice evaluating your motives for your actions to see whether they are outdated or important for your future.
- Practice evaluating your "mental models" for their appropriateness to your "now" actions.

Case Presentation: Mark Shuttleworth

In Exhibit 7.1 is the story of an entrepreneur who has constructed context, by enacting a vision that permeates the boundaries of established context in multiple arenas. We perceive in the Shuttleworth story a person focused on the *relationship* between culture and context.

Exhibit 7.1

Bringing Free Software Down to Earth

As he lays out his vision for the future of open-source software, Mark Shuttleworth is enthusiastic, but he looks tired. He has been up late negotiating yet another deal as part of his mission to bring open source to a wider audience. A successful South African entrepreneur during the dotcom era, he wants open-source zealots to lose their religion and concentrate on ease-of-use instead. And he is putting his money where his mouth is. Since 2004, he has been using his fortune to fund the Ubuntu project, which makes a user-friendly version of Linux, the open-source operating system. Ubuntu is a Zulu and Xhosa term that roughly means "universal bond of sharing between humans." Ubuntu's slogan is "Linux for human beings," and it is aimed at mainstream computer users. Although Linux is popular on servers, it is not, so far, used on many desktops.

(Continued)

Exhibit 7.1   (Continued)

In part, that is because open-source software tends to polarize opinion. It has vociferous critics who suspect that software written by idealistic nerds, and made available free to anyone who wants to download it, must be some kind of communist plot.

Zealous believers, meanwhile, long for open source to triumph over the evil empires of commercial software. This clash is often depicted as an epic struggle for supremacy between Linux and Microsoft's proprietary Windows operating system. But the truth is that most computer users do not know or care about the politics of open-source software. Mr Shuttleworth says most people simply want to read their e-mail, browse the web and so on.

"It's very easy to declare victory," says Mr. Shuttleworth, describing the smug attitude of some open-source supporters. "There are big chunks of the software world that depend on free software." But Ubuntu's aim is not to conquer the software establishment and replace its products. Rather than seeing open-source software as one of two competing ideologies and focusing on the struggle, Ubuntu thinks about the user. Ubuntu is a complete bundle of software, from operating system to applications and programming tools, that is updated every six months and will always be free. Taking the hassle out of open source is intended to move adoption beyond politically motivated enthusiasts and encourage mass adoption of the software on its merits.

In his home country Mr. Shuttleworth is most famous for becoming the first African in space, and the world's second space tourist, in 2002. This involved a gruelling eight-month training regime in Russia's Star City, so that Mr. Shuttleworth could accompany cosmonauts on a Soyuz mission to the International Space Station. "Because of the changes that were happening in Russia there was a unique opportunity in changing the way people think about space," he says. This change is still under way, he says, and the growth of space tourism means that in the coming years, "we'll all have members of our family who will have been there and had their thinking changed by that experience."

Mr. Shuttleworth believes that open-source software can bring about a similar change in the way people think about computers. To achieve this goal he is relying on business acumen, rather than on the quasi-religious faith that permeates much of the open-source movement.

Ultimately, though Mr. Shuttleworth's ambitions stretch far beyond just providing the world with a cheap and friendly operating system. "The accusation of proprietary providers is that free software is just copying what's been done before, rather than innovating," he says. "I don't believe that. The collaborative approach of the open-source community is the richest model for stimulating innovation." In some areas, he insists, open-source software is not seeking to catch up, because it is in the lead.

One is localisation, or the translation of software into foreign languages. This can take open-source software into parts of the world where it makes little immediate commercial sense to go. "There are some 350 languages in the world with more than a million speakers," says Mr. Shuttleworth.

(Continued)

Exhibit 7.1   (Continued)

"Free software is only translated in a significant way into about 20 of those, although this is already a lot greater penetration than proprietary software." With a huge group of volunteer translators to draw upon, open-source programmers ought to be able to make software in other languages far more widely available.

But Mr Shuttleworth is most excited about free software's potential to open up the third dimension in the display and navigation of information. "In the space station there was no sensation of up or down," he recalls. "Yet if it was even slightly obvious which direction Earth was, everyone would point their feet in that direction. Our brain cannot reconfigure itself in a rational way. So we should exploit the irrationality to be productive."

Despite some problems, Mr Shuttleworth is confident that open-source software can help to make computing and Internet access more widely available. He is driven by a desire for greater digital inclusiveness, rather than knee-jerk anti-commercialism. "To me, open source is about making sure that everyone has access to the next wave of thinking," he says. In 2001 he set up the Shuttleworth Foundation, a non-profit organisation dedicated to educational and open-source projects in South Africa. It has launched innovative projects such as the Freedom Toaster, a machine for copying free software onto CDs in remote regions, where lack of bandwidth makes downloading software impractical.

Source: Adapted from and permission granted. *The Deliberate Tourist*, June 7, 2007, from The Economist print edition.

Case Perspective: "Context" Applied

In the Mark Shuttleworth case, we perceive a global leader who is focused on the immediate relationship between culture and context. Through his decisions and actions, Shuttleworth is not disregarding the durable structures in place within the information technology, software and Internet space. He is interacting with the context as both durable structure and as evolving structure. He has invited the world into a conversation, a co-creative construction of context, where the focus is not on the creators of software empires, or the anti-creators of counter-culture software. But on the *other essential* subject, rather than as *object*, namely the user of software across cultures that seemingly have been left out of the conversation previously.

At this point, it makes sense to revisit our discourse concerning definitions of the term *context* in order to bring up an important point, which is lost in much of what we read in terms of understanding what is meant by context. It is often instructive to review etymology of words for a greater understanding of their meaning compared with current usage and popular meaning. Context is taken from the Latin word *texere* (verb) whose meaning is "to weave." Interestingly, its cousin, *contexere*, means "to weave together," or, "to compose." To linguists, this latter meaning is familiar, for context is generally thought of as the territory of language. The Latin prefix "con" added to any other root term means "to join."

Case Presentation: Renewing Relations

In our discussion of context and leadership, we have observed that context is both stable and evolving. Context is dynamic and socially constructed, living in human minds and manifest in form as, for example, culture. Culture exists on multiple levels, such as national cultures, ethnic cultures, religious cultures, professional cultures, and organizational cultures. In the case we present next, one executive is challenging and reconstructing context on multiple cultural levels. Cynthia Carroll (an American, who has already lived abroad), is the new CEO of a company within the mining industry; a company with a long history and an entrenched organizational culture that operates in countries around the world, most of which are old, entrenched cultures.

Exhibit 7.2

Anglo American Company Profile

Anglo is the British company that originated from the 1999 merger between the companies Anglo American Corporation of South Africa and Minorco and is a genuine expert in gathering treasures. The company owns 51% of AngloGold Ashanti, one of the very first producers of gold in the world, 75% of Anglo Platinum, the global leader in the production of platinum, and 45% of De Beers, the world's leading company in diamond production and trade. These are strong, emblematic holdings that makes one almost forget the 5 divisions it owns outright, divisions not quite as graceful as the aforementioned gems and nuggets. These less noble productions include coal via Anglo Coal, non-ferrous metal with Anglo Base Metals, ferrous metals (iron ore, chromium, steel) via Anglo Ferrous Metals and Industries, industrial minerals for construction mainly through Anglo Mineral Industrials and finally packaging and paper with the division Anglo Paper and Packaging operating under the brand Bondi.

Exhibit 7.3

Cynthia Carroll hopes to extract greater riches from the dusty terrain of Anglo American

THE world of mining is in flux. Most firms in the business are flush with cash, thanks to high metals prices, and are buying one another up with gay abandon. Upstarts from Russia and Brazil are challenging more established Western rivals. Even the biggest firms are said to be plausible targets for takeovers.

The world of Cynthia Carroll is in flux too. Recently, she moved from Montreal to London, to become boss of Anglo American, the world's second-biggest mining conglomerate. Her husband and four children are waiting until the end of the Canadian school year to join her in London. Meanwhile, she has spent much of the past six months on planes, touring Anglo's operations around the world, peering into shafts and smelters, and chatting to managers and minions alike.

Anglo American is not used to such turmoil. Mrs Carroll, an American, is the first non-South African to head the firm. She is also the first external candidate (her previous job was at Alcan, a big Canadian aluminium firm). Her predecessor at Anglo, Tony Trahar, had spent 33 years at the firm. When she was appointed, Sir Mark Moody-Stuart, who chairs Anglo American's board of directors, explained that the new boss should be someone who could lead a change of culture at the firm. So Mrs Carroll, in other words, is supposed to breathe some fresh air into the $87 billion mammoth, whose reputation is rather staid, male, and much more old-school Anglo than cutting-edge American.

To be fair, that reputation is a little out of date. The 90-year-old Anglo American has branched out far and wide from its South African roots. It now employs 190,000 people in 65 countries. In 2005 the group decided to focus on mining, and embarked on an ambitious restructuring, which was well under way by the time Mrs Carroll took the reins. Mondi, its paper and packaging business, is being demerged and is due to list in London and Johannesburg on July 3rd. Anglo American has also shed its underperforming steel business and plans to sell its remaining stake in AngloGold Ashanti, since investors value free-standing gold-mining operations more highly than those that are part of conglomerates. All this has helped improve Anglo's margins and returns—and its share price, which outperformed its competitors' last year.

But there is plenty more to do. Anglo's two main rivals, BHP Billiton and Rio Tinto, seem to offer better margins and returns. Daniel Fairclough of Merrill Lynch points out that the pair are the products of block-busting (and cost-cutting) mergers—the sort of upheaval that Anglo American has never undergone.

Can Mrs Carroll burnish the firm's performance? She is no miner, but speaks the language thanks to a degree in geology. She has spent her career in similar industries, first at Amoco, an oil company, and then at Alcan, where she ran the core metal-making business. Under her supervision, its productivity improved dramatically. She also presided over the successful integration of a rival firm, Pechiney, into Alcan, reaping large savings.

(Continued)

Exhibit 7.3   (Continued)

Mrs Carroll would like to make acquisitions at Anglo too. In fact, the firm has already started shopping. So far this year, it has bought a share in an iron-ore project in Brazil and the Michiquillay copper deposit in Peru. It will also be growing organically, with $7 billion of new projects already approved, and another $10 billion to $15 billion under consideration.

The new boss also hopes to bring her knack for improving productivity to bear. She has already started thinning out layers of management and cutting red tape. She wants Anglo's many divisions to pool functions such as procurement so as to create economies of scale and to share practices that might cut costs or improve output. She promises to encourage innovation, to set ambitious targets, especially on safety, over which Anglo has suffered some recent lapses, and to judge managers by their performance. Such shared standards, she hopes, might imbue the firm with a sense of common purpose.

A new face might also help with public relations. Mrs Carroll admits that the firm's relations with the South African government have been prickly in the past. When Mr Trahar implied in an interview a few years ago that South Africa still carried a degree of political risk, President Thabo Mbeki was outraged. The authorities have berated the firm's platinum unit for its slow progress in meeting targets on black economic empowerment, a process meant to redress the economic injustices of apartheid. As a result, the government has not yet granted it the permits it needs to keep mining after 2009.

Mrs. Carroll says she intends to improve ties with governments, as well as customers, suppliers and local communities. "I think we're a very good partner," she says, mentioning the group's initiatives on HIV/AIDS and efforts to help small entrepreneurs in Africa. She co-chaired this year's World Economic Forum on Africa earlier this month, rubbing shoulders with politicians and businesspeople from around the region. "We've learnt to engage with governments in a constructive and co-operative way."

All these changes are needed if Anglo American is to get on top of its game—and out of its competitors' reach. Rumour persistently paints the firm as the object of an imminent takeover bid, although nothing tangible has materialised so far. But as long as Anglo American is thought to be underperforming its potential, it is at risk.

The firm's employees must be conscious of the threat. At any rate, Mrs Carroll says they are hungry for change and have welcomed her, despite the turmoil she brings. She could not have dreamt of a better reception, she says. "We came together at the right time.

Adapted from and permission granted: A New Broom, June 28, 2007, from The Economist print edition.

Case perspective: Context Applied

In the case of Cynthia Carroll, she is an American woman who has already lived in other countries and led major organizations, has become CEO of a large global organization in the mining industry. Mrs. Carroll's hiring already is challenging (cultural) stereotypes and paradigms being female and heading up a company in an industry normally thought of as male-dominated. Beyond this, however, Mrs. Carroll was engaged by Anglo American to re-envision and re-construct the company in more ways than just its image. This shift is how context is constructed and re-constructed by human actors.

Mrs. Carroll's task is monumental; there are the obvious challenges of restoring life in a staid organization, improving processes and financial performance. Beyond this, Mrs. Carroll has the task of refashioning the relationship between the larger corporate entity (Anglo American) and its local operations throughout the world including the contentious relationships with certain governments.

In this case, we see how context esists both in the minds of people as a static dimension and as an immediate construction of all parties involved in the creation of context.

The Bottom Line

In summary, we described context as being both helpful and a hindrance to us as leaders within intercultural situations. Every culture can and has been categorized as either high or low context. High context refers to societies or groups where people have close connections over a long period. Many aspects of cultural behavior are not made explicit because most members know what to do and what to think from years of interaction with each other. Countries like China, Japan, India, and some parts of Spain and Italy fall into this category. Inversely, low context refers to societies where people tend to have many connections but of shorter duration or for some specific reason. In these societies, cultural behavior and beliefs may need to be spelled out explicitly so that those coming into the cultural environment know how to behave. Countries like United States, United Kingdom, and some other western nations qualify as low-context cultures.

In China, communication tends to be very efficient because of their information-flow at work and in privacy. They discuss everything in advance and consider meetings as an official "ceremony" where the already commonly agreed decision will be announced. This is important in the way of "giving and keeping face." The Americans and Germans in contrast inform the participating attendants in a meeting about the hard and necessary facts. We have observed times when an American company hires employees from India or China; they tend to ask too many questions and are always inquisitive. Indians tend toward this and some have the habit of wanting to know it all before they commit to something. Americans might sometimes find that behavior intrusive and unnecessary; placing great importance on ambience, decorum, the relative status of the participants in a communication and the manner of message's delivery. In France, it might be hard to feel fully accepted for outsiders within their culture because of their big diffuse connections.

In comparison members of individualistic cultures using low-context communication like Germans, Americans, and Finns sometimes ignore those differences from high-context countries cultures.

In case of a meeting where those countries from low- and high-context cultures would have to work and discuss matters together, the French and especially the Chinese would not interact and express their disagreement or reservations. For Chinese issues, circumstances and relationships are as important as work so they would comment only in a more private or appropriate occasion. Additionally, people from high-context cultures (Indian, Chinese employees) tend to form min-groups at work where they would talk in their native tongue and discuss everything in detail. In contrast, the American employees would keep work and friendship away from each other as far as possible. Discussions at work in a professional environment would be to the point and concise. High-context cultures are often misunderstood as being too relationship oriented. The fact is that these cultures tend to value relationships more than the task. These differences in cultures create misunderstandings and miscommunication.

The Principle of "Change"

If you don't like change, you're going to like irrelevance even less.

—Eric Shinseki

Change has several meanings, the primary few being to become different or render something or someone different, to replace or substitute something for another, and to pass from one state of being to another.[210] It is cliché to say that the only constant is, change. However cliché, the fact remains that people working in global business contexts face an evolving state of affairs. Change requires that individuals remain flexible in adapting to dynamic cultural environments. We devoted several sections of Chapter 1 discussing the various challenges apparent at the time of this writing. Now, we address the effects of external change on the efforts of leaders and what change means to these individuals in terms of what is required of them.

A discussion about change commonly is paired with discourse on adaptation. In terms of adjusting foreign cultures, adaptation describes a person's response to a new social environment. Aggregate patterns of adaptation are called modes of incorporation. Whether as individuals or as members of social groups, people entering foreign cultures typically modify old behaviors and beliefs and learn new ones as they adjust to new institutions and new situations different from their native environment. A person's ability to participate fully and effectively in a "host society" is diminished until such adaptation occurs.

> ### "Change Defined"
>
> Postmodern organizations require having learning-agile leaders who demonstrate flexibility in adapting to dynamic cultural environments. Intercultural leaders must shift from the old mechanistic mindsets of the industrial era to the flexible adaptive perspective of organizational life as what it is, a complex socio-cultural system.

Prominent in adaptation literature are discussions on the theory and model of acculturation. Acculturation strategies refer to the planned methods that individuals use in responding to new stress-inducing cultural contexts.

According to several models, acculturation strategies can be categorized into a four classifications, which include "assimilation," "integration," "separation," and "marginalization." Assimilation strategy occurs when individuals decide not to maintain their cultural identities by seeking contact in their daily interactions with a dominant group. When the individuals from the non-dominant group "place a value on holding on to their original culture" and seek no contact with the dominant group, then these individuals are pursuing a separation strategy. When individuals express an interest in maintaining strong ties in their everyday life both with their ethnic group as well as with the dominant group, the strategy used is "integration." The fourth strategy is marginalization in which individuals "lose cultural and psychological contact with both their traditional culture and the larger society."

Integration implies both the preservation of the home culture and an active involvement with the host culture. Central to integration strategy is the assumption of universality. This perspective assumes that although there are substantial variations in the life circumstances of the cultural groups that experience acculturation, the psychological processes that operate during acculturation are essentially the same for all the groups. In other words, an individual's acculturation strategies reveal the underlying psychological processes that unfold during their adaptation to new cultural contexts. Other psychological processes such as "behavioral shifts" (changing behavior), "culture shedding" (eliminating traditions), "culture shock" (sudden exposure to an unfamiliar culture), and "acculturative stress" (stress related to adapting to different cultural expectations) are also experienced in varying degrees by an individual undergoing acculturation.

Another adaptation strategy, "segmented assimilation" describes three contrasting acculturation patterns characteristic of some individuals and groups as they cope with cultural shock. The first is linear acculturation and assimilation whereby the assimilating individual or group advances effectively and is integrated socially, culturally, and politically into the host culture. In other words, this is when an individual or group has been effective in their strategies to integrate and has been welcomed by the host group. The second pattern is selective assimilation where individuals and groups develop bonds with other expatriates and deliberately preserve their native culture behaviors. In this strategy, incoming individuals are less effective in being welcomed by a host culture. Conversely, the third pattern is descending assimilation where entire expatriate groups fail to adjust and disintegrate. Ostensibly, the acculturation process is highly influenced by structural and contextual factors in the host culture. In other words, some cultures, at certain times in their history, are more or less welcoming of strangers into their midst.

The Key is Learning Agility

We begin by stating that people when faced with change have choices. They can refuse to participate, they can resist and sabotage, they can blithely go their merry way and see how they will fare (letting events dictate their fate), they can stubbornly adapt, they can adapt fittingly, or they can lead the way by setting a shining example. We would posit that the latter two choices are the only choices for leaders, potential leaders, and nearly everyone else who envisions a satisfactory future. The question then, is not about shall we adapt, but how shall we adapt. The answer should come as no surprise. We must be *learning agile*.

Before we consider learning agility, though, we will first discuss the idea of learning about culture within culture. The nature of learning is culturally diverse, although learning is universal (found in all human cultures). The ways in which people learn to think, perceive, build beliefs, behave and feel, capture and comprehend, and derive and create meaning, have an intimate connection to their own cultural context. In other words, you cannot understand learning without considering the specific cultural terrain within which it occurs. Most of us tend to think about learning in ethnocentric ways, in accordance with our own cultural preferences; although there is, naturally, variation within cultures. The challenge is that we need to develop the capacity to stand outside our own cultural conditioning in order to appreciate and invite a variety of cultural perspectives into our own learning atmosphere.

The idea that people learn through the lens of the relationships between living things and their environment is relatively new. The time was that the words *learning* and *agility* seldom were found within the same sentence, let alone as its subject and predicate. In recent years however, and we agree, one contributory factor to business success for intercultural leaders and their organizations is building *learning agility*. To be agile, means to move quickly and easily. The inference here is that to be successful in a global economy, one must be agile at learning.

Research suggests that people who are quick learners, and therefore have a greater capacity to adapt, are not necessarily smarter than other people are. What they possess is superior (and quantifiably more) learning strategies. Exhibit 8.1 presents how individuals can build learning agility.

Exhibit 8.1

Building Learning Agility

- *Critical thinking skills*—a repertoire of thinking skills including analysis, synthesis, evaluative, etc.
- *Self-knowledge*—including awareness of one's own learning styles and building access and usage of alternative styles and under which circumstances each is best utilized
- *Comfort with ambiguity*—the ability to deal effectively under unclear circumstances
- *Comfort with taking risks and making mistakes*—including being willing to experiment in public forums.

Link Between Emotions and Learning

Have you ever been told not to let your emotions rule your thoughts and actions? If you are like many adults, the answer is yes. Throughout the history of Western civilization, people have been in conflict about the connection between emotion and thought. In general, the wisdom was not to allow emotion to rule the "rational" mind. Recent research conducted by neurologists and educators shows an inextricable, if not *healthy*, link between emotion and reason—perhaps finally putting to rest the maxim that emotion is the antagonist of reason. Neurologist, Antonio Damaino explains that,

> "Reason may not be as pure as most of us think it is or wish it were, emotions and feelings may not be intruders in the bastion of reason. They may be enmeshed in its networks, for worse and for better. Emotions are inseparable from the ideas of reward and punishment, pleasure and pain, approach and withdrawal, personal advantage and disadvantage. In organisms equipped to sense emotions—that is, to have feelings—emotions have an effect on the mind, as they occur, in the here and now. *Emotion is devoted to an organism's survival.*"

Learning is identical in process to any other cognitive brain function in that the circuits that control and link reason with memory connect emotion and decision processes as well.

Consider just the brain's process for digesting information First, everything is processed through a kind of switchboard called the thalamus, located at the base of the brain.

Second, the information is then routed automatically to different sections of the brain. Initially, the information goes through the brain's emotion-arousal systems for evaluation to determine whether the information is perceived as benign, beneficial, or threatening.

The evaluation involves a number of feedback loops originating in long-term memory. If we perceive the incoming stimuli as threatening, we automatically engage in a series of reactions, which sometimes remain unconscious, to help us process the information. This process illustration is the "flowchart" of *sense making*.

In other words, our brains must decide whether to admit or reject all incoming information (or stimuli). During this process, when unconscious emotional awakening reaches a certain point, it pushes into our conscious level and is experienced as *feelings*.

So, what do emotions have to do with learning? Memory and problem-solving processes that develop a solution to a situation are activated when we *attend* to risk and/or opportunity. Attention then locates the risk or opportunity and provides useful information about it to the person, who then acts on the information.

It turns out, that emotion activates attention, which is our focusing system and root of learning. Once again, emotion drives attention, which drives learning, memory, and problem-solving behavior.

In other words, it is an emotional structure that stimulates us, not a logical structure. Here we will apply this more explicitly to learning. Simply put, learning cannot take place when there is no emotional stimulation. Now let us also be clear that emotional stimulation does not necessarily result in learning! Here is why.

As a reminder, basic human emotions include just six: surprise, happiness, fear, anger, disgust, and sadness. No doubt, you noticed that the many of these basic human emotions represent, what is generally perceived as, negative experience. *However*, people do not always experience emotions in the purist form.

For example, a person who has just received a promotion to a challenging position may experience surprise, happiness, and fear all at once. This combination of emotion may create a sense of exhilaration and may be perceived as excitement and considered positive by the person. Another person, in the same situation experiencing the same combination of emotion may perceive the reaction as anxiety, and feel overwhelmed by all of the new things they will have to face. Global leaders need to be capable at both the cognitive and feeling levels of analysis. "I think" is not enough without "I feel." The blending of both leads to emotional maturity, and better use of "intuition."

At this point, we want to introduce the principle of *Learning Trajectory*. All learning has a trajectory. This means that may be learning occurs in *continuous motion*.

This motion sometimes follows a linear path in its progression, but more often occurs along a circuitous route. At times, it quite planned and structured, while at other times a learning trajectory can occur serendipitously, almost coincidentally.

Along all learning trajectories, there are moments when there are naturally occurring rewards. These types of rewards natively belong to the learner and are those special moments when there is a feeling of exhilaration on the learner's part at having achieved something he or she perceives as important. Other moments along the learning trajectory provide opportunity for managers (and organizations) to recognize and reward the result of individual learning. In Exhibit 8.2 below these opportunities are listed.

Exhibit 8.2

- At the moment the learner takes a risk to try something and makes a mistake and learns from that mistake
- When the learner is observed utilizing a learning for the first time
- At the time when a new skill is used to perform at a higher level
- When that same skill generates an innovation
- When a particular skill makes the individual an important resource
- When the individual attains a new level of certification
- At the time when the individual is perceived as an expert by others and becomes a mentor.

Ostensibly, the organization's executive leadership decides the compensation and benefits policies for the enterprise. Managers have the responsibility to support these policies within their units. However, managers can influence policy decisions as well as the espoused and practiced values of the enterprise.

Developing Learning Strategies

Have you ever observed an accomplishment of someone and wondered to yourself: How did s/he do that? Perhaps you have wondered the same thing about yourself and your own accomplishments. If so, you are in good company! Two theorists entered into answering this question several years ago and one said to the other: "If you teach me to do what you do, I'll tell you how you did it." In this way, the second theorist was providing a "model" for understanding the underlying patterns used by the first theorist to accomplish a task, expertly. Of course, most of you will recognize this as inductive reasoning—identifying and describing patterns from the behavior of something. This is one fundamental process for model building. Such an example is simply one way of codifying knowledge and competence so that it may be replicated at will. The result of these two theorists' work is one meta-model that allows people to find out *how* they do something so that they can repeat their successes and transfer their learning and doing process to other endeavors or communicate it to other people.

Therefore, what does this all have to do with Learning Strategy, you ask? To begin with, a learning strategy is the pattern and process people (unconsciously) use to learn. Everyone has a learning strategy. The question then, is not *whether* adults have learning strategies, so much as it is a question of how *effectively* a person's learning strategy is in meeting (their) objectives. Research indicates that some people develop very effective strategies while other folks, for various reasons, do not. The implication for modern global organizations is that to optimize intellectual capital, global workers must possess *both* content expertise as well as *learning agility*. Now, let us focus attention on the meta-model we discussed earlier and how managers can facilitate effective learning strategies.

To review, we said that a learning strategy consists of the patterns and process a person uses to learn. We also said that there is a way of modeling a person's expertise such that their knowledge and expertise is codified. What we are saying then, is that the modeling process is identical for describing patterns and processes someone uses for doing and learning. The objective of modeling is to identify outstanding patterns of doing and learning, which provides workers with the data they need in order to replicate their most effective learning and doing patterns. Next, we provide the simple steps to the basic modeling process applied to learning in Figure 8.3.

Implications of Learning Strategy for Intercultural Leaders

In modern global organizations, managers must first build their self-awareness related to their learning strategies. This process will include conducting modeling exercises like the one described above and by adapting and building *learning agility*. In this way, managers will increase their own capability and provide needed role modeling for associates. However, this is only part of the story.

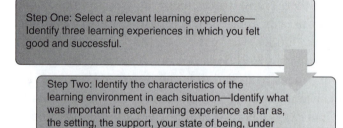

Step One: Select a relevant learning experience—Identify three learning experiences in which you felt good and successful.

Step Two: Identify the characteristics of the learning environment in each situation—Identify what was important in each learning experience as far as, the setting, the support, your state of being, under what conditions did each occur?

Step Three: Identify the steps you took—Describe the process, how did you begin? What did you do to motivate yourself? What kinds of things did you tell yourself about what you were doing and what you expected to do?

Step Four: Now, compare the process by identifying commonality in the patterns in the three situations.

Step Five: Identify one additional learning experience in which you felt weak and where you were not successful—Compare the two patterns to find what is missing in the unsuccessful experience.

Figure 8.3 The Five Basic Steps in the Modeling Process

Case Presentation: Building Learning Agility

There has been a tendency to distinguish between leaders and managers in our management development programs. Perhaps the reason for this is our Western tendency to analyze something in order to try to understand it. The process of analysis requires breaking things down into their component parts to distinguish one from the other. Nonetheless, the tendency to perceive leadership as being just the responsibility an occurrence belonging to the "top" of the organization is erroneous. The truth is that acts of leadership occur at all levels of organizations. Likewise, management occurs at all levels of an organization. What is important to realize is that everyone leads and manages, and they first begin with themselves. Every step in a person's career path is a progression of leading oneself from one stage of change to the next and managing the process along the way. In Exhibit 8.3, we present the case of Jan Trudeau. This is an actual case of real people in real organizations; however, the names have been changed.

Exhibit 8.3

The Case of Jan Trudeau

This case explores a Learning Project undertaken by a newly promoted manager who needed to learn quickly about global team management.

Jan Trudeau is a web infrastructure engineer for SoftTech a fortune 1000 company. She has been with the company for 5 years, having entered the organization after completing her college education. Jan is an excellent performer who identifies, evaluates, and integrates leading edge technology into the company's infrastructure. In this capacity she excels at all aspects of her job and is viewed by her peers as someone who has the ability to influence top management and who supports team efforts by always meeting or exceeding timelines. Jan has worked in a highly networked 10-person team and has responsibilities to three managers two of who actually work in partner organizations. Management and Human Resources has assessed Jan as a leader in the making because she possesses vision, is a clear communicator and can inspire her peers. Additionally, she is bilingual and relates well with diverse people and appears to have a high tolerance for ambiguity.

Jan's Opportunity

Increasingly, SoftTech's expansion strategy has placed a demand for people with Jan's technical expertise to develop new products for global markets. Jan's recent innovation has won enthusiastic support from top management who is driving to launch development within 45 days. With resources already stretched and given that, no one else has Jan's expertise; management has recommended promoting Jan into a global project management position. As a result, Jan would have to lead a seven-person development team (with cross-boundary authority). The team membership includes personnel from five different countries. This would be Jan's first time at managing people and projects and her excitement and anxiety about this prospect were observable when her manager extended the promotion offer.

Sanay Veech, Jan's group manager, had been thinking about how to support Jan in her new role. Therefore, when he received a phone message from Jan saying that she was happily accepting the promotion and had just submitted to him a Learning Plan for acquiring some key knowledge and skills, Sanjay was both relieved and impressed that Jan had acted so quickly.

He sent an e-card and arranged to have a little floral bouquet sent to her desk as a way of recognizing her courage and determination since Jan is an avid gardener. Then, he asked for a meeting between the two of them, so that they could discuss her resource needs.

Jan identified her most immediate needs as being project management, team transitions and start-ups, and coaching, in addition to learning company administrative policy. Her plan was comprehensive and integrated a variety of knowledge and skills acquisition strategies. She would complete the company's three online Orientation to Management modules, which would serve as a foundation to assist her administrative duties. Completion of these three modules would take her three hours.

(Continued)

Exhibit 8.3   (Continued)

In addition to the Orientation modules, Jan prepared herself to enroll in a self-paced online course on project management sponsored by the company that provided the learner with a situation-based format and an e-coach for the applied portion of the learning. Her biggest dilemma was to find an appropriate method to learn skills in team start-up. Jan was an active learner who was not at all comfortable with the idea of reading about or taking classes in interpersonal skills and group leadership. She really struggled between needing to grasp the "big picture" about teams, and wanting badly to know how and where to begin with a global group. To her relief, Sanjay had a suggestion that supported her desire to find an alternative learning source to build her team start-up skills.

Sanjay suggested that Jan could consider a structured mentorship. Jan was eager to hear more about this idea, since it meant joining a learning community, which was an approach she had used in the past and had found quite beneficial. Sanjay told her that the structured mentorship meant having a guide who would make contact with her quickly to establish goals, objectives, and a timeline for the life of the mentorship. The mentor would make suggestions about what resources Jan could utilize to learn quickly some key concepts and practices. Then they would plan Jan's first meetings with her team and debrief each meeting to capture Jan's learning and make adaptations when necessary. More importantly, Jan's mentor would be a person who had experienced working across international boundaries. Thuy Ngugen was such a person. Thuy, had worked as a manager in several international contexts in Asia and Europe. She spoke three languages had lived in several countries, and had successfully led small product design divisions. Thuy also had volunteered for SoftTech's leadership mentor program.

The Learning Project Begins

No sooner did Jan complete the administrative modules than one of her new global team members had a life event that required management assistance.

While Jan was experiencing a few anxious moments about juggling all the new tasks, and continuing work on the design aspects of the new product, she felt somehow comforted by the fact that she had her shadow mentor, Thuy Ngugen. Thuy assisted Jan in managing this first personnel issue since Thuy was familiar with how to involve the Human Resource department with employees from countries outside SoftTech U.S. headquarters.

Together, Jan and Thuy planned each step of the global team start-up process, and regularly reviewed Jan's progress. In her first few meetings with her team, Jan established herself quickly as the leader of the group. The members seemed to accept Jan probably due to their prior experience with her as a peer. Sanjay had even received unsolicited feedback from other managers who had heard from their staff members on Jan's team. All the feedback had been positive, although Jan was not privy to this feedback.

(Continued)

Exhibit 8.3 (Continued)

Rough Water Ahead

Jan's big test came after about four weeks in the position when her technical work and demand for her time was at its peak. When the team encountered an unexpected glitch in design process, a rift in the team occurred. In a particularly intense video-conference team meeting, it became clear that the team was in danger of losing its compass. The team became split into two camps with some members siding with Wilhelm Cout's (Germany) perspective, while others voiced support for an opposing perspective offered by Pauly Genge (United Kingdom). As the meeting uncharacteristically spilled over its scheduled time, and frustrations grew, Jan broke her long silence and abruptly declared the meeting over.

Dealing with conflict was not one of Jan's natural or prior learned strengths so her coping mechanism during the meeting had been to retreat into reflection about the design dilemma. Unfortunately, the team members perceived this as abdication of leadership on Jan's part, even though, it was the first time she had exhibited such behavior. Jan was confused about the argument between Wilhelm and Pauly, because it seemed to her to go deeper than a difference in design.

At the meeting's end, Jan retreated in frustration to her cubicle office and without hesitation placed a call to Thuy to get some insight into what had just happened. Jan was overwhelmed between the design problems and the team conflict; she did not know which to confront first.

Through her discussion with Thuy, Jan realized that in this situation, the design problem was hers to solve and it was her decision as to what to do. Individually, the team members could only propose hypothetical solutions to the problem. What was important was to ensure the team members had what they needed to function properly.

The question that Thuy posed to Jan was about what to do for the team, so that they would not "twist in the wind." Jan was uneasy about this question and Thuy knew it, so she proposed that Jan reflect on the situation overnight and get back with her in the morning. Thuy perceived that there were some cultural-based style differences between the engineers. Meanwhile, the pressure on Jan mounted because one of the team members mentioned the incident to Sanjay in an unrelated phone conversation, who after hearing about the conflict sent an (email) message of concern to Jan.

Insight to Action

Later that evening, Jan began thinking about her choices, what was best for the project, what was best for the team, and what was best for her own reputation as a fledgling manager. She pondered her options, the potential project delays, the morale of the team, and her own ego investment in her innovation. Clearly, indecisiveness was not an option; neither was abdicating to the team.

The next morning Jan arrived in her office to find one of her team members waiting for her. Juan Ortega had flown up to California from Guadalajara,

(Continued)

Exhibit 8.3   (Continued)

Mexico for a product specifications meeting. SoftTech is headquartered in California. Before Jan could get in a word, Juan started in right where the team debate had ended the day before. Instead of being flustered, Jan let Juan finish his thoughts and calmly told him that she understood his concerns and that she was prepared to send an immediate communiqué to the team explaining what their next steps would be to solve their situation. Juan seemed quite relieved with this news and left for his meeting.

While it had been easy for Jan to calm Juan's fears, convincing other team members would not be so quickly done, especially given the time and distance. Wilhelm and Pauly were both strongly in opposition to one another's perspectives and had become uneasy about Jan's leadership.

Jan punched the speaker button on her phone to call Thuy to report her decisions, and as she waited, she checked her morning email. To her amazement, there were already several messages that had gone back-and-forth between Wilhem and Pauly each outlining their own ideas about how to proceed and with each successive message sounding more and more like project decisions were being made outside of Jan's authority as project manager. Wilhelm and Pauly were at odds over production deadlines; Pauly was adamant about meeting deadlines, while Wilhelm was just as adamant about testing cycles for product quality.

Jan left a brief message for Thuy and hung-up so that she could concentrate on the flurry of email messages left by Wilhelm and Pauly. Overnight, it seemed that Jan's mistake had added complications to the project. Now, she wondered if this would escalate into a feud between two important team members.

Jan wasn't so sure that the decision and plan she developed was sufficient to address the team's problem. She had thought about sending a message to inform the team that she would develop a plan to address the design issue independent of them and that they were to focus their attention on the work that was not dependent on the design. Then, she thought, she would finish the design and in the next scheduled meeting announce her decision and work with the team to develop their plan. Instead, she wondered if she should call a quick teleconference to straighten out the situation and she wondered whether she should now involve them more in the solution. Certainly, it was a question of demonstrating leadership. She felt she had to get the team back working in cooperation and prevent the conflict from spreading. Right now, she had no idea how many others might have been blind-copied on Wilhelm and Pauly's messages, nor did she know how long she would have to wait before she heard back from her mentor.

Jan's decision was to act before she talked with Thuy, and to bring Sanjay in on the issue by copying him on all her messages and by sending him a message detailing her chosen course. Since, it was early morning in California, and therefore still during work hours in United Kingdom and Germany, Jan's action was to immediately call a teleconference between herself, Wilhelm and Pauly to discuss their concerns and to remind them of their agreed upon responsibilities as team members. Next, she would tell them about her plan and gain their commitment. Following this meeting,

(Continued)

Exhibit 8.3 (Continued)

she would send out a general communication to the entire team detailing next steps. Finally, she would send a message to other organizational members who needed to be informed about any project changes.

As Jan finished considering her plan, her mentor called. Jan outlined her plan to Thuy, who suggested that, while the plan should work in principle with a more culturally homogenous team, and that Jan needed to pay particular attention to the riff between Wilhem and Pauly. Since, in German culture, there is a strong value for quality and precision, and since in English culture there is a value for punctuality, Thuy suggested that Jan direct her conversation facilitation efforts on these cultural values. First, as Thuy pointed out to Jan, although all cultures have their own characteristics, within cultures, people vary. Therefore, it is important not to make broad assumptions about individuals.

Jan and Thuy decided that it may be fruitful if Thuy sat in on the teleconference and assisted Jan in facilitating discussion by making suggestions when and if appropriate. Prior to the meeting Thuy advised Jan that there were a few things to watch out for in the meeting. One having to do with any differences between Wilhelm and Pauly in future orientation, in the degree of demonstrated emotion, and where values seemed to be in conflict.

During the teleconference, Jan noted that Wilhelm seemed to be quite animated, while Pauly seemed to become even more dispassionate than usual. Jan decided to try out something and commented to Pauly that she imagined that he was very committed to the project and regarded it with great importance. Pauly responded in the affirmative. Wilhelm stated that he was gratified to know that finally and that he had been concerned about it. Then, he said that he was committed as well, and Pauly acknowledged that he could easily perceive that of Wilhelm. Jan was pleased with this level of cooperative discussion; however, she was not sure what to do next. Fortunately, Thuy politely asked if she could interrupt just to make the observation that both engineers seemed to be quite dedicated to the project and that both seemed to have strong values. She asked if the two were willing to share those and both replied affirmatively. It became clear quickly, what Jan had sensed, and Thuy had suspected from her experience working in both English and German businesses, that Wilhelm did not want to sacrifice quality for production deadlines, and Pauly did not want to sacrifice marketplace commitments. Once the two engineers realized that both values were important, they began backing off of their positional stances, and considered the problem from both perspectives. The meeting resulted in the successful cooperative effort by the three team members in creating a preliminary plan which they then agreed to take back to the larger team. Pauly and Wilhelm enthusiastically agreed to co-present the preliminary solution to the team, and also agreed, thanks to Thuy's suggestion that they bring back their preliminary plan keeping a flexible mindset, in order to be able to receive feedback from the other team members since each team member owned an important piece of the overall project and Pauly and Wilhelm could not know what the others knew relative to their domain.

(Continued)

Exhibit 8.3   (Continued)

The Results

With the design problem solved, the quality and production cycle issue settled, the team back on track, and another month gone by, Jan and Sanjay met to review Jan's progress. The project was on schedule and the product completion date was in sight. In three months, Jan had successfully, but not uneventfully, bridged the gap between individual contributor and project manager of a global product development team. Along the way, she had developed an ambitious Learning Plan, led the start-up of a new global team, produced an efficient project plan, negotiated her new administrative duties, and continued her design work on her innovation. She had also made a normal mistake of a new manager when she panicked and withdrew during a team conflict.

To her credit though, Jan had solved the conflict by acting swiftly to facilitate a resolution between two culturally diverse team members, had articulated and clearly communicated a plan, and by executing the plan. Through her plan, the team was able to contribute to the solution because each person knew his/her role and objectives. Moreover, each team member had been encouraged to participate fully and their values and approaches had been honored in the process. Jan wondered, though, about what she could do to avoid finding herself in a similar situation in the future. It seemed obvious to her that conflict is an inevitable part of global team and organizational life.

From a manager's perspective, Jan knew that she did not have the luxury of sitting back and letting conflict fester. Clearly, she would need to learn a way of acting in the moment, or at least to being able to recognize when it was time to act. She knew now that she could handle conflict when she was prepared for it and when she had the benefit of her mentor. She had been successful with turning around the conflict between Wilhelm and Pauly because she demonstrated her respect for both.

Seven months to the day of the project start, Jan's team successfully launched their product prototype for production. As the team and their guests celebrated their success, Jan looked back with pleasure on her journey and felt satisfaction that she had accepted the challenge of the position. She wondered now where this would lead her next.

Case Perspective: Change Applied

In the case of Jan Trudeau, a high performing individual contributor, with aspirations of ascending into management, made a successful transition between employee to manager with immediate personnel responsibilities. She and her manager attributed her success to her having a learning plan and the organization having embedded learning process in place to assist personnel in their development endeavors. In this successful global organization, intercultural teams are the reality of the work environment.

The organization (a Fortune 1000 corporation) espouses a respectful and diverse culture that promotes intercultural learning with systems and processes in place to support people in their efforts to understand and appreciate one another.

In this organization, when new intercultural teams are forming, the company wisely gathers all the team members together in one location to bond and establish their working agreements and processes. While some project teams come together with short life spans, other long-standing (intercultural) teams rotate their quarterly meetings so that team members have the opportunity to spend some time in all the countries from where members originate.

The Principle of "Change in Practice"

A Geoleader recognizes opportunities for learning and change within differing cultural comfort-zones including:

- Accepting that certain changes cannot be co ntrolled
- Identifying those variables that can be controlled and acting upon them accordingly
- Recognizing one own reasons for fealing fearful or angry at changes to be imposed
- Looking for the positive benefits of te change rather than concentrating on the negative implications'
- Remembering that change will occur whether one embrace it or not

Case Presentation: Sun Microsystems

The current opinion held in many companies is that the U.S. segment of most industries is saturated. Consequently, corporations are turning to emerging markets such as China, India, and Latin America for revenue expansion and cost reduction, and are as well increasing focus on existing European and Asia-Pacific operations. For many corporations, concentrating on the global customer experience is critical for sustaining business. The case we profile next is Sun Microsystems (Exhibit 8.4) and its commitment to achieving excellence in global expansion. The company achieved impressive results by viewing globalization as an enterprise-wide business practice and unifying content and translation business processes and technologies. Through presenting the Sun case, we highlight the principle of "Change," specifically learning taking place, individually, at all levels of the organization, which of course does add up to learning at an organizational level (discussed in the next chapter on Capability).

Exhibit 8.4

Sun Microsystems Company Profile

Sun Microsystems, Inc. supplies network computing solutions, including servers, storage, software, and services worldwide. The company's computer systems product and technology offerings include a range of workgroup and enterprise servers, desktop systems, UltraSPARC microprocessors, and software that are used as integrated systems for network computing environments; software products, comprising enterprise infrastructure software systems, software desktop systems, developer software, and infrastructure management software; and storage systems, including storage, storage components, and software. It also deploys and maintains network computing environments through a range of services comprising support services for hardware and software, client solutions, and educational services. Sun Microsystems's products and services are used in a range of technical/scientific, business, and engineering applications in industries, such as telecommunications, government, financial services, manufacturing, education, retail, life sciences, media and entertainment, transportation, energy/utilities, and healthcare. The company markets its networking architecture platform solutions through direct and indirect channels worldwide. It also offers component products, such as central processing unit chips and embedded boards on an original equipment manufacturer basis to other hardware manufacturers; and supplies after-market and peripheral products to their end-user installed base directly, as well as through independent distributors and value added resellers. The company has strategic alliances with AMD, Fujitsu, Google, Microsoft, Oracle, and SAP, as well as with Laszlo Systems, Inc. Sun Microsystems was founded in 1982 and is based in Santa Clara, California.

**The Global Customer Experience: Sun Microsystems'
Vision for the Participation Age**

In Their Own Words: The Sun Microsystems Perspective

How Does Sun Define the Participation Age?
"In the Participation Age, the network connects not only the computing power of each node, but also all the humans behind the power."

"It's important to understand open source as just one facet of the social change the global network has brought about. In this Participation Age, the move from closed to open affects security, software deployment and pricing and *customer engagement* as profoundly as it affects software development."
Simon Phipps, Chief Open Source Officer, Sun Microsystems

What were the symptoms in the organization that brought the need for an intensified global customer experience to attention?
"The disparity across our processes was too wide; we needed to close the gap."
William Snow, Senior Director of Sun Engineering

(Continued)

"It is no secret that cost control and operating efficiency are factors in any company's long-term success on the Web. Along those lines, for Sun, scalability and optimization of Web resources were paramount to ensuring the ability to sustain growth and meet our business' rapidly changing needs over time. We had to put the right solutions in place fast to support those factors, or we knew we'd always be playing catch-up." *Kristen Harris, .Sun Content Management Engineering Manager*

The Problem: Intensify the Global Customer Experience

"Sun views our global web experience as core to our doing business and views this practice as the standard way we do business. We strive to achieve the best possible web experiences for our customers as critical to achieving our company's goals for brand management, continued customer reach around the world, and overall customer satisfaction." Curtis Sasaki, Vice President, Sun Web Properties

Sun consistently demonstrates its commitment to the Participation Age. A key part of the vision focuses on ongoing, two-way global communications with consumers. Hence, it is critical for the company to intensify the impact of the global customer experience for prospects, customers, partners, and developers.

Fostering interest, participation, and loyalty requires a corporate focus on three strategic areas:

1. Information management infrastructure
2. Globalization and localization process management
3. Content distribution lifecycles.

A global customer experience requires a 360-degree view of the customer lifecycle, from prospecting to retention to up-sell opportunities (Figure 8.2).

Within each lifecycle segment, there is opportunity for attracting new customers, building and strengthening customer relationships, and enhancing individual loyalty. Opportunity however, is directly dependent on *how* the target audience experiences the human and information-driven interactions that take

Figure 8.2 The Customer Lifecycle

(Continued)

place within them. In essence: How does the prospect or customer feel about what they saw, read, or heard? Was the experience personal enough to make a strong impression? Did they perceive it as genuine and compelling?

Sun's global customer experience strategy is highly focused on consistently gaining insight from the answers to these questions through a strong customer loyalty research program. In addition, the company maintains over 100 "targeted gateways" based on vertical industry and business requirements.

To its credit, Sun views globalization as an enterprise-wide business practice as part of its commitment to a worldwide customer base. The company also had the foresight to renew focus on the global customer experience based on increasing revenues in international markets as opposed to reacting to the common pitfalls of large global companies—brand mismanagement, customer retention issues, and inconsistent product availability. Still, even Sun was challenged to strategically evaluate, reengineer, and optimize the cross-departmental and external business processes required to ensure brand consistency across multiple vertical markets, geographies, and cultures, increase the availability and distribution of localized content, and align globalization and localization business processes with product launches.

A team led by Will Snow, Sun's Senior Director of .Sun Engineering and Kristen Harris, Content Management Engineering Manager, set out to tackle these challenges head-on by focusing on key Web access points to Sun's technology, product, and training resources.

Assisted by Youngmin Radochonski, Globalization Program Manager, Jed Michnowicz, Engineering Lead and other key players in the publishing and engineering groups, the team included the range of skills needed to design Sun's Global Customer Experience platform.

The Need: Eliminate Content Mismanagement and Disparate Business Processes

Like many large organizations, the evolution in the volume and number of content-centric processes within Sun had resulted in divisional, departmental, and individual silos.

Mismanagement creates obvious risk for redundancy, errors, and inefficiency. Without project controls for content and translation management, Sun experienced cost control issues, project delays, and in the words of team members Jed Michnowicz and Youngmin Radochonski, "undesired repetition and unpredictable outcomes." Because translation processes were not effectively shared, it was not uncommon for one source file to be translated multiple times—and in different ways—by different groups. Clearly, this would not be the path to a consistent, global user experience.

First and foremost on the agenda for the Global Customer Experience team was to unify and automate the global information lifecycle—from authoring and management to localization and publishing. The team's analysis, combined with surveys and interviews with content authors, country-specific business owners, and Sun's Global Services group, quickly revealed a set of requirements with "unified infrastructure" written all over them.

(Continued)

The Need: Increase the Volume of Relevant, Localized Content

Getting the right content to the right individual at the right time is imperative for all organizations. A global customer experience raises the bar for this mandate by stressing the need to respect cultural nuances and sensitivities when delivering localized content.

With an annual translation throughput larger than most companies can imagine, Sun's challenge to increase the volume, availability, applicability, and quality of localized content would seem insurmountable. However, the team understood the core principle for success: balance brand management and operational efficiency with customer-driven, geographic, and culture-specific expectations.

For example, operational efficiency would require that process owners, authors, and translators have a unified view of previously translated content versus new localization requirements. This would enable more collaborative decision-making within operational areas such as technical support, sales, and training. In addition, this same audience would need to understand the requirements for "corporate" versus "region-specific" content as well as have the flexibility to accommodate cultural nuances by intertwining the two content types.

The Need: Simultaneous Global Product Shipments with Localized Content

Market researchers in the customer loyalty arena agree that about 70–80% of all products are perceived as commodities. Given Sun's competitive arena, this makes product marketing a formidable challenge in terms of "standing above the rest."

Catalogs, long a staple in marketing broad product offerings, have become even more important in an Internet-enabled world. Standard customer expectations include the availability of electronic and print catalogs, and depending on the product, customers often prefer the former.

Sun's focus on catalogue.sun.com was a critical piece of delivering a global customer experience. It was also one of the more challenging, as the company releases a new product approximately every two weeks. The "negative buying experience" was simply not in the global customer experience team's vocabulary. The goal was not to meet customer expectations, but to exceed them.

Source: Adapted from The Gilbane Group (Leonor Ciarlone) (December 2006). The Global Customer Experience: Sun Microsystems' Vision for the Participation Age.

Case Perspective: Change Applied

Sun Microsystems' Participation Age vision is clearly aligned with the goals of a global customer experience. The company's investment in customer loyalty research, technology innovation, and contextual customer communications embodies an organization that understands that the experience *is* the product. Through all levels of the organization, learning has been embedded in order to engage with the organization's many global locations. We also see that the organization has made decisions about the degree to which they are willing to localize and not. Such decisions should be made by all organizations with the realization that the decision will affect the interface with the local culture. Only time can inform us the degree of success of these decisions. As recent history has shown (e.g. Wal-Mart's failures in Germany and Korea), the consumer, no matter where on Earth they are, will determine the extent of an organization's success in their attempts to operate in another culture.

The Bottom Line

Rarely do current business management textbooks prioritize "learning agility" at the top of their list of leadership skills required today." The truth is, in order for a leader to be a brilliant visionary and an adroit communicator, that leader must be able to scan and interpret what is going on in the world, and imagine a compelling future. The undergirding cognitive structure in all of this is the capability to learn. All people must and do learn, or they experience the consequences of not evolving.

Encountering a new culture is a learning experience, one that can be rich and rewarding. When that encounter is an integral aspect of our work life, especially as leaders and managers, our approach often dictates the quality or our experience and the quality of that encounter by the other parties involved. Our suggestion throughout this book has been that to enhance the experience one must have honorable intentions, a well-prepared and integrated strategy, a sense of adventure, courage, and determination.

9

The Principle of "Capability"

If we prove capable of showing a pioneering commitment, we shall create a community listened to around the world.

—Jacques Chirac

By now, the concepts of "learning organization" and "organizational learning" are becoming commonplace. There is, however, still a tendency to confuse these terms. For our purposes here, it is important to clarify the difference between these two related but distinct concepts since our discussion will focus on one more than the other. "Learning organization" is a concept of an organization in which humans cooperate in dynamic systems to continuously learn and adapt using particular processes and systems. Organizational learning, which is our interest in this chapter, refers to the natural process through which an organization acquires new knowledge and adjusts in order to adapt successfully to external and internal environmental changes and to maintain sustainable existence and development. Implicit in this definition is that organizational learning consists of two dimensions (individual and social), and occurs at three levels of functioning: cognitive (acquiring new knowledge), behavioral (adjusting to change), and system (cultural and structural). While there is much debate about what constitutes a "learning organization," it is not our interest here.

All organizations, to some degree, engage in learning, or they do not survive. Arguably, organizations that become proficient at learning have a greater chance of not only surviving, but thriving in their environments. Some gifted theorists such as Argyris and Schon[211] have speculated that the reason why organizations overall have such difficulties learning is simply that they still behave in ways that obstruct learning (e.g. stifling communication patterns and power-politics).

"Capability" Defined

In order for a leader to be effective in intercultural situations, there must be development of sufficient personal and organization capability. Intercultural competence requires leaders to assess their own and others' capability and build it where it is deficit. Organizational learning agility and understanding of how modern organizations operate are essential for intercultural leaders and managers.

The good news is that neither the organization theorists nor organizations have given up. Each year we see more efforts to address this problem and we may be making progress. In Exhibit 9.1 we trace the historical development of organizational learning in Western thought. As is shown, the origins of what we now refer to as organizational learning (and to an extent "learning organization") predate the work of Argyris and Senge. In fact, it is John Dewey's work in the previous century that began the conversation. The concept of "mental models" can be traced to a Scottish psychologist in the early 1940s. You may rightfully inquire why there is such interest in how and why organizations learn; however, the importance of learning to an organizations survival is critical. How else does an organization know what consumers want? How else do organizations track their competitors? How do organizations attract and secure top talent? How do organizations develop new products and services? The answer is that *they learn*.

Exhibit 9.1

Learning Organization Milestones

1938—In his book Experience and Education, John Dewey publicizes the concept of experiential learning as an ongoing cycle of activity.

1940s—The Macy Conferences—featuring Margaret Mead, Gregory Bateson, and Lawrence Kubie—introduce "systems thinking" to a cross-disciplinary group.

1940s—Scottish psychologist Kenneth Craig coins the term "mental models," which later makes its way to MIT through Marvin Minsky and Seymour Papert.

1946—Kurt Lewin, founding theorist of National Training Laboratories, proposes the idea of a "creative tension" between personal vision and a sense of reality.

1979—Consultant Charlie Kiefer, Forrester student Peter Senge, and researcher–artist Robert Fritz design the *Leadership and Mastery* seminar and offer it for the first time.

(Continued)

Exhibit 9.1 (Continued)

1984 to 1985—While on sabbatical at Harvard Business School, Pierre Wack, of Royal Dutch/Shell, writes two articles about scenario planning as a learning activity.

1989—The Center for Organizational Learning is formed at MIT, with Senge as director and with Ed Schein, Chris Argyris, Arie de Geus, Ray Stata, and Bill O'Brien as key advisers.

1990—*The Fifth Discipline* is published. The book draws on many influences: system dynamics, "personal mastery," mental models, shared vision, and team learning.

1994—*The Fifth Discipline Fieldbook* is published. Its authors include Charlotte Roberts, Rick Ross, Bryan Smith, and Art Kleiner (who serves as editorial director).

1995—Working with Dee Hock, the Organizational Learning Center begins a two-year process of building a consortium called the Society for Organizational Learning, which leads to the birth of The Society for Organizational Learning.

1999—*The Dance of Change,* the second book in the *The Fifth Discipline Fieldbook* series, is published.

2004—*Presence: Human Purpose and the Field of the Future*, by Peter Senge, C. Otto Scharmer, Joseph Jaworkshi, and Betty Sue Flowers is published in a private edition by SoL, introducing "Theory U," and sells over 15,000 copies.

2005—*Presence: An Exploration of Profound Change in People, Organizations, and Society* is published in conjunction with Doubleday and is distributed worldwide.

Source: Adapted in part from and permission granted. *Learning Organization Milestones.* Alan Webber, Fast Company, April 1999, p. 178.

The truth is, all organizations learn and have distinct patterns and strategies of learning. The most agile companies are sensitive to various levels of emerging changes internally and externally. They are sensitive to internal shifts and evolution as the organization as a whole and as a collective of individuals develops. Whether the organization builds its wealth and capability on knowledge (e.g. technological innovations) or on natural resources (e.g. lumber and oil), an agile organization thrives in harmony with its environment, and/or response synergistically with its milieu. Take for some examples how global organizations have done this successfully in their expansions into regions of China. Procter & Gamble sends employees to live with average Chinese families to acquire information on their laundering behavior. McDonalds is investigating the shifts in Chinese food culture to adapt its services to the needs and tastes of Chinese consumers. On the other side of the same intercultural engagement, China's Legend Computer

Company assigns certain employees to research the Internet for data and other benchmarks that may influence the development of the company.

General Electric is famous for having established a learning culture called "learning from your employees." However, Jack Welch was well known for fostering an organizational culture that learned the technologies of other organizations for the intentional purpose of improving technology and advancing into the competitor's market. Organizations now in a highly competitive global marketplace face both tremendous opportunity and temptation and must make decisions agilely to avoid costly mistakes. In other words, it is not enough just to figure out what other companies are doing. It is not enough to amass a group of brilliant innovative employees. Organizations must become capable. Figure 9.1 depicts the characteristics of agile organizational learning.

Capability is a person or group's core competence and potential <u>plus</u> the ability to learn and adapt to the changing environment.

Core competence is the essence of an organization. In a sense, it is organizational DNA. In effect, it is what distinguishes one company from any other. If you are a software company your core competence is probably the invention, development, and distribution of proprietary software (programs) that serves some specific purpose (i.e. financial software). However, even within this identity, there is a lot of room for differentiation. For example, you may really be specialists in R&D and not really focused on manufacturing nor marketing and distribution. In this case, your organization may

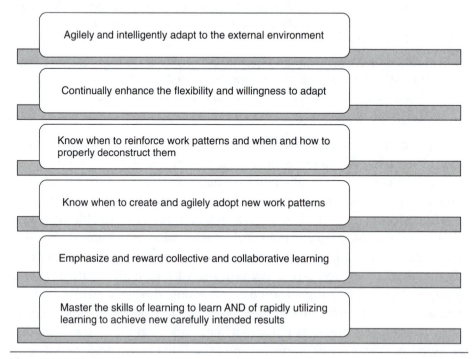

Figure 9.1 Skill Attributes of Organizational Learning

have built alliances with other organizations that have become part of your value network (similar to value chain).

As with domestic organizations, all global organizations must continually question their business and their place within that business in the larger market and industry contexts. Answering these questions require that global organizations go about the process differently than their domestic cousins. In a world before globalization, an automaker that developed a new model vehicle, for example of a type that they had not previously built, would likely re-tool a local factory. Now, in a global and highly competitive economy, where brand name is not synonymous with products being exclusively homegrown, an automaker wishing to enter a new-to-them market may acquire that segment of a foreign owned automaker's firm, and place their brand on a product which is made in another part of the world. In the case of a global software company that needs to expand its strategic position by development of a new software product, it is not about re-tooling factories. Rather, that company may choose to invest in the acquisition of an organization that has already developed the software, acquire additional intellectual capital and cut costs in the bargain by acquiring a small designer firm in another country, where innovation is high and labor cost is low. In any case, building organizational capability is a new game compared to decades past and organization-level learning agility is requisite.

The keys to building core competence and branding organizational DNA (at the strategic level) are: valuing and measuring intangible assets (intellectual capital); developing capability acquisition strategies; creating a tangible knowledge base and knowledge centers; creating intercultural collaborative cultures; and building or purchasing supportive collaborative infrastructures.

Optimizing Structure

If you take a moment to reflect on what it means to be a global organization operating in a highly dynamic global environment, and on what it means to be learning-agile, a picture should emerge of a very different looking structure than an industrial era organization. In the last decade, we have seen the organizations constitute themselves into new architectures. Some of the more notable designs include the network, the web, the lattice, and the holonic.

Does this mean that bureaucratic designs are dead? No, not entirely. It does mean shifts in how we grant authority, how we integrate units, how flexibly we construct boundaries, and how we view social work units. The benefits of designing these new types of structures are that they enable innovation, inherently demand resilience, and foster autonomy. The drawbacks of such structures *when* they are poorly constructed and/or mismanaged are confusion (about vision or standards), lack of boundary integrity (disembodiment), breakdowns in resource control, and instability. Although these drawbacks may seem formidable, they are manageable and no more a challenge than are the drawbacks of hierarchical bureaucracies.

The key principles of new organization designs are establishing flexible boundaries and interdependencies; constructing to the velocity of the business, creating renewable social agreements, and imbedding learning in work.

Optimizing Organizational Renewal Systems (Learning)

Various models have been postulated for building and maintaining learning agility. We favor models that include the following important processes of building agility and maintaining capability: discovery, reflection, selection, mining, transfer, execution, innovation, contribution, and memory. When studying these systems and processes, it is important to keep in mind the various culture dimensions we discussed in our chapter on contrasts and context (i.e. power distance, uncertainty avoidance, gender egalitarianism, performance orientation, future orientation, collective versus individualist orientation, social orientation, and ambiguity tolerance).

Discovery processes system that enables it to sense and monitor changes, problems, challenges, and opportunities in its internal and external environment, and that provides early warning signals to shifting trends. Through conscious and systematic monitoring and analysis and sense-making, the organization can maintain its engagement with its environment. This is particularly important when an organization embarks on global expansion. It will require establishing local relationships in the foreign countries.

Reflective processes facilitate the organization's ability to learn from its experience. The reflective process is perhaps the most challenging for organizations because there can be the tendency to reflect upon one's successes, learn from them, and assume that through precise replication, one can achieve the identical results. The fundamental problem with this type of thinking is that nothing in our environment actually stays the same through time. Therefore, the prevailing conditions of the past do not necessarily portend the same results in the future. Numerous theorists have given attention to this problem and none more astutely than Argyris and Schon, whose single-loop and double-loop learning theories and Issacs' triple-loop learning have provided viable means for organizations to avoid the classic mistake of assuming that past success is the best council for decisions in the future. Single-loop learning occurs when the problem is corrected by altering behavior or actions to meet organizational norms, goals, values, and assumptions. It involves detecting problems without questioning underlying policies and methods. Double-loop learning occurs when the underlying values are changed and new actions follow. It involves questioning and changing governing conditions or values and testing the assumptions underlying what is being done. Goals, norms, and assumptions are also changeable. Isaacs introduced triple-loop learning refers to examining the way in which one learns.

One practical example is a model called After Action Review (AAR), which is used to analyze the result of every action. In certain situations, reflecting and reviewing can lead to improvement for next time. A typical discussion during an AAR process revolves around four questions: What did we plan to do? What actually happened? Why did it happen? How might we use this knowledge again? Additionally, these processes can be used to reflect on the successes and mistakes of other organizations, which is particularly important in global ventures. Benchmarking results of other organizations should be part of the reflection processes.

Selection processes allow an organization to make the right choices about innovative ideas or external intelligence that is mined. An organization must develop a variety of selection and decision methodologies, processes, and activities, so that optimal business decisions can be achieved. Selection methodologies include both accepting in and starting new, as well as unlearning old habits and practices. Only when there is an internal selection system for optimization, can an organization build the capacity to adapt to external environmental selection and maintain competitive advantage. In a global organization, selection methods must be congruent with local customs, laws, and needs.

Mining processes allow an organization to remain open as a system with a continuous exchange of energy as well as information and knowledge between it and its environment. This acquisition system is crucial for an organization's ability to learn faster and build competitive advantage, especially in a new environment. The acquisition system should provide channels for the recruitment of people, foster social networks of employees (localized to the area/areas in which an organization has operations), and cooperative interactions with other institutions. We emphasize the importance of not only getting information and knowledge from outside, but also the organizations ability to assimilate and apply learning for intended purposes.

Transfer processes allow the organization to harness individual and team learning so that it can be transferred and utilized throughout the organization. Best ideas, practices, and experience obtained by individuals, teams, or departments should be transferred to the rest of the organization. This area is one of those that Argyris proposed is likely to cause problems because of the human tendency for turf and politics. In order for learning to be shared in an organization, its people must develop and foster trust and psychological safety. It has been suggested that processes that foster dialog between individuals and teams provides the requisite assistance for transfer of learning to occur. In a global organization, the interface between "global" structures and "localized" structures is one critical element for success.

Execution processes allow the organization to move, that which is incorporated cognitively, into behavior. In other words, learning about something intellectually is only productive if it can be translated into manifest form. Organizational learning not only includes changes of perception and thinking (such as discovering, innovating and selecting), but also changes of behavior. No action means no real learning. Transferring knowledge into action is sometimes a challenge for people and without processes, intentionality, motivation and courage, knowledge typically becomes shelved. However, leaders and managers must be aware of the cultural differences in their particular locales to make the proper tactical plan.

Innovation processes allow an organization to renew and maintain its core competence, even if that core competence shifts over the organization's lifespan. It is not enough for an organization to discover various kinds of changes: it has to find new ways to deal with them. It is not enough to perceive opportunities and envision brilliant ideas; the organization must continually recreate itself from concept to manifest form. Adjustments must be made, of course, based on local customs, since, for example, people's future orientation can effect how they go about innovative thinking. Future orientation (the extent to which a person perceives the horizon in imagining and envisioning the future) can change the types of innovations people generate.

Contribution processes enable an organization to participate in the circulation of life by putting back into the environment. Not only should organizations acquire knowledge from outside, but also they should contribute to the outside. For some organizations, such as universities, schools, consulting companies, and so on, providing knowledge service is the reason for their existence. Other organizations such as manufacturing firms do this too. Contributing knowledge can improve an organization's reputation, and, from the perspective of learning, can give the organization chance to receive feedback from outside about its own management and performance. An organization will never be a real learning organization unless it can contribute learning and knowledge to society. However, few Western literatures address how an organization can enhance its learning capability through contributing knowledge to environment. Chinese traditional philosophy, however, emphasizes that one must first contribute something (including knowledge) to other people before taking it from them. Therefore, if an organization wants to acquire knowledge from outside continuously, it should have the willingness and ability to contribute. Although the subject of corporate social responsibility is beyond the scope of this book, we do believe that it is an even more important consideration for global organizations, particularly in terms of maintaining caring and conscious relationships with local cultures.

Memory processes facilitate an important organizational function, knowledge management. There are two kinds of knowledge management methods. One is codification, which means knowledge is carefully codified and stored in a database, where it can be accessed and used easily by anyone in the company. The other is personalization in which knowledge is closely tied to the person who developed it and is shared mainly through person-to-person contacts. Just as a computer cannot solve complicated problems without a memory, a person cannot absorb intricate knowledge without a brain (memory). Similarly, with the growing complexity of the environment, organizational memory increasingly is needed for continuous learning. While knowledge generated by the eight subsystems is stored in organizational memory, the stored knowledge will also affect the eight subsystems. If an organization fails to establish organizational memory to retain knowledge, the loss is great—organizational learning cannot be a constantly upgraded and further learning cannot occur. Good experience cannot be exploited and failure may be repeated. Future orientation and uncertainty avoidance are two cultural dimensions that will weigh heavily in a global organization.

Leading Collectives

Over the past several decades in Western business cultures we have observed the rise of the team as a focal point of people management. The movement toward embracing the team concept, once fueled by the influence of Japanese management practices and later with flattening of hierarchies, continues. Much has been written about what constitutes an effective, high-performing team. Globalization has again brought attention to team performance, given the increase in diversity and in geographically dispersed membership. In Exhibit 9.2 we overview the four types of collectives leaders and managers encounter.

Exhibit 9.2

The Four Types Of *Social Units* Managers Encounter

- The *workgroup*, people working interdependently on a variety of loosely related objectives.
- The *team*, people charged with specific objectives related to the same result, sometimes time-bound and having the same reporting relationship.
- The *network team*, people working across internal and/or organizational boundaries working on related objectives, sometimes time-bound.
- The *community*, people either formally or informally organized around non-task related objectives, sometimes time-bound (e.g. communities of practice or communities of learning).

There are some important differences and similarities between teams and collectives for a global organization. A collective by its nature is a group, as is a team. It has been argued that teams are more effective than workgroups. However, for the global organization, especially those that are highly networked, teams can be problematic without some redefinition. The conventional wisdom, espoused in management literature, has urged managers to transform their workgroups into teams. The reasons for this are that while groups are loosely bound aggregates of people interacting during the course of their work, teams consist of members who influence one another, after having forged certain agreements, toward the accomplishment of organizational objectives.

The field of Organizational Development (OD) has influenced management practice by having introduced the concept of team building, a process whereby team members diagnose their effectiveness and plan changes to improve. In-and-of-itself this is not bad practice. What can become problematic is that teams can develop such a state of cohesiveness that their effectiveness is diminished. In these situations, the over-cohesive team may develop goals, which are in conflict with the organization's goals.

One of the major contributors to team effectiveness is team membership. In order for a group to become first a team, second an effective team, and potentially over time a cohesive team, the members must have certain attributes (based on several tangible and intangible elements) and must have relative stability (of members and environment).

Alternatively, the team must be constituted with the explicit understanding that its membership will be ever changing and that its environment will be unstable and that, more than likely, it will have a brief lifespan. The global economy demands that leaders and managers have a keen awareness of and skill at organizing and/or facilitating the work or purpose of collectives. Specifically, managers must know the different types of collectives and for what each is best suited.

Team Effectiveness and the Intercultural Leader

We observe that many specialists in intercultural team effectiveness preface their work with the disclaimer that intercultural teams begin with an inherent disadvantage by virtue of the cultural differences between members. We have worked on intercultural teams, consulted to intercultural teams, composed and lead intercultural teams, and in our opinion, cultural difference is neither advantageous nor disadvantageous. Legitimately, you may ask why we make this statement. The answer is simple. We have observed intercultural teams over the past 20 years, and find that such teams are no more or less likely to be effective than their culturally homogeneous cousins. Having said this, we recognized that intercultural teams require additional assistance and different base of approach. Whereas standard practices could/can be used when constituting and developing teams with less differentiation among the membership, intercultural teams require more tailored approaches depending on the membership and context.

However, our experience is that when people can focus on the universal similarities across human cultures there is a great potential for building strong working relationships. The truth is there are three levels of relationship between human beings. We are all individuals and completely unique—there simply are no nor have there ever been two human beings alike. As individuals, we all have our unique personalities, experience, and perspective. At the next level, we all share some common experience, perspectives, and behaviors with particular others—that which links us together in social groups and subgroups through culture (language, ethnicity, etc.). At the most fundamental level, all humans share the presence of the identical life force, or manna. Although, at the two lesser levels, we find wide variance, we also find similarities and universal characteristics. At our most fundamental level, we are all identical, as living human life forms.

While there is no "one best way" to build intercultural teams, there are some important considerations. In Exhibit 9.3, linguist Cornelia Schultheiss provides leaders with some wisdom about working with intercultural teams.

Exhibit 9.3

"We Need Courage and a Positive Attitude to People"

Cornelia Schultheiss is a theoretical linguist and has been assisting interculturally staffed teams at DaimlerChrysler in Berlin, Germany since 2001. In the "Software Technology" division she has been providing support for German and Indian employees working on projects to develop software-based systems. In this interview with Mondialogo, she talks about the advantages and difficulties of Indo-German cooperation and explains how employees are prepared for work in intercultural teams. Mondialogo (aka MM) reflects a partnership initiated by DaimlerChrysler and the United Nations Educational, Scientific, and Cultural Organization (UNESCO). Mondialogo is an intercultural initiative promoting worldwide dialog and exchange.

MM: Ms. Schultheiss, for some years now you have been working together with a department in Bangalore, India. What are the pros and cons of working in intercultural teams?
Schultheiss: One important asset is the different approaches to thinking that play a role in intercultural teams. We can find solutions faster and develop "more original" ideas. Every team member brings along their own expertise in a special area, which all combines to create great synergies. Added to that, the team members are forced to adjust to people with a different way of thinking. That creates flexibility and expands their horizons.

(Continued)

Exhibit 9.3   (Continued)

One of the drawbacks you can see is that this makes work more complex. It calls for a higher degree of flexibility. You also have to clearly recognize that intercultural cooperation means a lot of time and money has to be invested in the formation of teams and in building up confidence.

MM: How can we picture this cooperation?
Schultheiss: In most cases the colleagues from Germany and India are working on the same projects simultaneously. Particularly at the beginning of a project, the teams will be working together on one site. They stay abroad for between two weeks and one year. Later, when the teams have gelled together nicely, the employees can continue working on the project in their own countries. During this phase, the team members communicate regularly by email and phone or perhaps set up phone and video conferences.

MM: Are there any differences in the form of communication?
Schultheiss: Yes, most certainly. This is definitely where most problems arise. Mainly this is due to different basic communication needs. Germans, for example, communicate in a very direct way whereas Indians tend to use an indirect approach. As well as this, the German teams are used to an impersonal form of communication. Indians, on the other hand, talk far more often, in greater depth, for a longer time but then also more personally with each other. This comes from the fact that Indian colleagues have a greater need for communication and it's tremendously important for them to establish a personal level. A personal level like this helps develop trust and paves the way for a good working relationship.

MM: What role does an understanding of hierarchies play in this context?
Schultheiss: Hierarchies are much more important in India than in Germany. You can observe this particularly clearly in meetings. In Germany you may well find in a meeting chaired by a person with a democratic leadership style that the conversation tends to be fairly spontaneous and comes from all directions. When Indian workers are in a meeting attended by their supervisor, they will generally wait until their supervisor has finished speaking. Yet for us Germans, this taking it in turns to talk according to the hierarchy is not always visible at first sight.

MM: Are there any other cultural differences that affect the cooperation?
Schultheiss: The feeling for time! The German sense of time has a linear nature. We work on a time line where all the different events are defined as fixed points. Indians, on the other hand, have a circular conception of time. The idea of cycles, whether for the day, year of life cycle, is a very strong feature among Indians. Indian people therefore tend to think of phases within these cycles rather than of fixed points in time. It is also matters more to Indians whether the person they're talking to is young or old, whether the appointment is taking place in the morning, evening, or at a particular time of year. The exact date or the precise time of the meeting is less important to them.

(Continued)

Exhibit 9.3   (Continued)

MM: In your opinion how important is the awareness of these intercultural differences for collaboration in international teams?
Schultheiss: I regard an awareness of intercultural differences as being extremely important. After all, this awareness has a direct influence on the efficiency, performance, target achievement, and also the type of conflict-solving going on within the team.

MM: So how do the cultural differences show up in the daily work of your teams?
Schultheiss: There are a lot of these situations: Indian people care a lot for courtesy and good manners. Because of this they don't wish to disturb in any way if they appear in a meeting too late for reasons beyond their control. For Germans, however, this comes across as very rude if a colleague slinks into his seat as quietly as possible, without offering an apology. In a case such as this, you have to create an environment within which understanding can be reached on both sides for which a change in behavior from both can be achieved. In terms of language there are differences too. Intercultural teams can find solutions faster and develop more original ideas.
At the start we thought that everybody spoke English well and used the same terminology. However, English is not the mother tongue of German engineers. They didn't have that much practice in English and no particular self-confidence either, as far as language went. On top of this came the fact that many Indian colleagues speak English with a strong accent. On the other hand, the Indians had no idea that English was not the teaching language at German universities. This caused a great deal of astonishment among the Indian contingent and the German employees were very quickly branded as uneducated. Clichés like this are very difficult to dispel afterwards.

MM: In recent years you've set up measures intended to create awareness of the problems in intercultural collaboration. What are you doing specifically for the Indian employees?
Schultheiss: In Germany we run an intercultural training session once a year. All employees who work in intercultural teams can take part in the courses, ideally Indians and Germans together. We cover each of the specific problems areas in communication or collaboration between Germans and Indians. As well as this, there are German courses in Bangalore with the focus on "Business German." Indian colleagues who are just starting in Germany or have found out that they are going to be cooperating with Germany are also given our booklet "Fit for Germany." This brochure tackles situations from everyday life in Germany in a very pragmatic way and serves as a fast track to prepare Indian colleagues for life in the new country.

MM: You also regularly train German colleagues for cooperation with India. What do course in Germany look like?
Schultheiss: In Germany we offer intercultural training courses several times a year, always with mixed groups of German and Indian colleagues. Once a year a workshop takes place as well. The key topics are intercultural communication, working techniques, and trust. I run these seminars jointly with an

(Continued)

Exhibit 9.3   (Continued)

Indian co-facilitator. We give the participants theoretical input and work out the topics together in a plenary session through discussions and in group work.

MM: Problems of intercultural cooperation can in fact arise every day in very ordinary working processes. Are there any ways of reacting spontaneously to these situations?
Schultheiss: We offer a small form of mediation. If colleagues notice any intercultural problems within a project, they can approach us or their team leader. We then try to initiate a conversation, run a workshop, hold briefings, or even organize a role play.

MM: Can you estimate to what extent the training sessions have already paid off?
Schultheiss: We want to analyze the project results in the future. The question that concerns us here is how cooperation has taken place in the intercultural team. To answer the question, we look at the level of confidence achieved in the team, synergetic effects, the level of target achievement, and the time scheduling. Of course the assessment also considers whether any mediation or conciliation talks were necessary during the project work.

MM: What would be the ideal starting conditions for someone joining an interculturally staffed team?
Schultheiss: Employees in intercultural teams have to be very open and inquisitive. They have to enjoy developing new stimuli and ideas. Flexibility is another important requirement for successful cooperation. But courage and a positive attitude to people are important too.

Source: Adapted from We Need Courage and a Positive Attitude to People, from Mondialogo.com. News: 03. Working Together: http://www.mondialogo.org/16.html?&L=0

In our experience, there is a relationship between intercultural teams and the performance of a global organization. Intercultural teams develop intercultural competencies in order to perform. They then contribute to the organization's performance and capability because the organization's ability to learn and achieve is enhanced. Intercultural communication among the intercultural team membership through interaction, care and resolved conflict characterize global teams, which builds capability within the organization.

Managing the Organizational Culture

Organizations all have a culture. Culture reveals itself through the language, customs, and traditions of the individuals within the organization. The culture also finds realization through the standards and normsthat the group demonstrates on a daily basis. Culture arises from the shared history of a group of individuals placed together for a specific mission.

This integration of shared beliefs serves to lessen the ambiguity of the organizational environment in order for goals to reach fruition. Each culture features its own unique substance and form. An organization's ideologies create the substance of the decision-making process for the group in question. These ideologies are emotionalized, shared sets of beliefs, values, and norms that both impel people to action and justify their actions to themselves and others. Once the ideologies become an ingrained part of the group's activities, these thought patterns morph to form to create the organization's culture. Each new member who joins the organization learns how the organization operates based upon this intangible entity known as the culture's substance.

The cultural forms of an organization seek to give credibility to its substance. Examples of cultural forms include metaphors, myths, and symbols. Every organization must survive, and often strength derives from the usage of such metaphors. Metaphors find basis in experience and usually include personal elements. An example of an organizational metaphor arises when a group's formation and activities receive comparison to a team and a game. The cultural forms resident within an organization allow for greater simplification of concepts often too complex to understand. The role of a leader remains to recognize and leverage the organization's cultural substance and forms for the benefit of everyone.

An effective leader distinguishes between the various cultures and even subcultures existent within the organization. A leader must manage the culture efficiently or risk being managed by the culture itself. A leader conscious of the organization's structure grasps the various levels of culture that require management. Anyone involved with the organization, whether new or old, insider or outsider adapts to the culture as it directly receives direction from the leader. Three levels of culture that occur within any organization include artifacts, espoused values, and basic assumptions.

Attempting to decipher the espoused values of an organization can be challenging. The learning of a group mirrors individual values. When a leader emerges in the group, the values of the leadership prevail among the group itself. Over time, these shared values evolve into shared assumptions. As group values appear more regularly, the members of the group seek to validate these values within the social context of the organization. The original values of the leader thus grow into the culture of the organization itself and members of the group gradually become acclimated to this shared set of values. The key point to remember here remains that individuals possibly espouse certain values, however their actions sometimes demonstrate the antithesis of these values. Individuals desire to know that identical actions provide identical results. Theory evolves into practice. Assumptions serve to attach rationality to different situations. For example, if an individual fails to be a "team player" within a group culture, then the leadership of the group may relegate this individual to outside of the sphere of information. Individuals require a consistent pattern of decisions and results in order to function effectively within an organization. Acting only upon one's own assumptions, and not those of the group, distances an individual from the organization as a whole.

A cohesive strategy and common mission remain two characteristics important to an effective organization. Individuals require a road map to follow in order to act accordingly within the culture of this organization. These individuals also provide the willingness to contribute their individual efforts to the cooperative system.[212] Culture simply exists when a shared identity emerges that all individuals embrace. This sharing then provides for the goal-setting atmosphere necessary in an organized venture.

Goal-setting most effectively occurs when the organizational culture provides for shared language and shared assumptions. The mission of the organization (i.e. sell the best widgets in the world) needs continuous acceptance. However, the goals of the organization (i.e. reach $1 million sales in current year) must exist for a specific time. This idea of goal-directed, rational decision-making exemplifies more closely the mechanistic metaphor of the organization. The culture of the group defines the path to reach such goals and characterizes such variables as the division of labor and the bonus system.

The Management of Results

Reaching goals entails the measurement of results. Does the organizational culture possess a system whereby evaluation appears fair and impartial? If errors occur in the measurement process, what mechanisms exist to correct these problems? When change takes place within the culture, there exists the opportunity for growth. The culture of the organization survives as the group's experience in learning to cope with change.

The internal dimensions of culture face similar analysis. Such internal issues include shared language, power distribution, and reward incentives. How do the members of the culture communicate? Does a common vocabulary exist, either relevant to the organization or to the industry? An inclusive organization is one in which communication and information flow from all directions, in all directions and across all levels of responsibility. Once the group members possess a similar vocabulary, what decisions receive acceptance in terms of influence and authority?

The organization functions according to the power plays acted upon by the leadership. Does the power structure receive acceptance by the members of the group? Comparably, does the power granted appear valid and actionable by the group's members?

Any organization desires to reach certain goals. Rewarding accomplishment remains a major issue among the group's members and determines the cultural undertones of daily decisions. A clear path to performance and punishment motivates the individual to seek the most effective manner in which to succeed within the organization and accomplish common goals. The reward system perhaps appears logical only to an insider. However, each organization and its relevant members understand how success finds measurement in their own environment.

Intangible Entities: Reality, Truth, Time, Space, Human Nature, and Relationships

An organizational culture finds basis in how its members view the intangible aspects of their environment. For example, how does the organization determine what reality to believe? A fundamental part of every culture is a set of assumptions about what is real and how one determines or discovers what is real. Each aspect of reality appears influenced by external, social, and individual factors that remain difficult to manage, particularly in a cross-cultural scenario. Combining these cross-cultural influences within the relevant context demonstrates more clearly the organization's words and actions.

Once the sphere of reality appears understood, the quest for the truth ensues. Truth is impossible to represent as an absolute. Does the culture recognize the truth purely as dogma, rational thought, or the result of continuous debate? The scientific analysis and acceptance of the truth appears similar to dogma. The group must agree upon what constitutes information and then derive the truth accordingly.

The value of time within an organization determines the importance of past, present, and future activities. Do monochromic or polychromic time intervals prevail within the organization? The author knows of a firm that allows workers only one piece of paper on their desks at a time. The management believes that a worker can only concentrate on one matter at a time. Each organization perceives time differently also according to their industry (i.e. sales cycles). The function of time imbues a certain type of order to the organizational culture.

In conjunction with the value of time, how does the organization view spatial concepts? For example, how closely aligned do cubicles reside within the office landscape? Does the corporate culture call for management to dwell on a separate floor than the regular workers? We choose and operate in environmental domains according to how we construct conceptions of who we are and what we are trying to do. An organization's attitude toward space often symbolizes more than just a design sensibility.

Individuals may prescribe to Maslow's hierarchy of needs; however, leadership normally does not appear within this structure. Does the organization's culture evolve to recognize that the leadership individuals require at one point in their lives does not remain static as time passes? Leaders who give credence to the Being Orientation model of human activity state that humanity remains subservient. The individual may then choose to adapt to the organizational culture, or decide to leave it.

Individuals rarely act within a vacuum. Individuals within an organization interact with others within a dynamic environment. Does the organizational culture then stress the role of the individual or the group as more important? Do organizational relationships function more for utilitarian or moral purposes? The manner in which the organization recognizes its relationships signifies its value system.

Every variable that influences an organization's culture directly relates to its leadership foundation. The assumptions, beliefs, and values of the leader set the original tone for the organization's intangible culture. As more members join the group, the culture adjusts. When the original leader leaves the organization, then the culture also morphs into a different entity. For example, Wal-Mart today does not promote the same exact culture as when Sam Walton directly managed the corporation.

Leaders such as Sam Walton and others lend their own ideas to the organization, and thereby teach their followers. The acceptance of these ideas derives from such variables as charisma and socialization. Would the Rainbow Coalition still be as successful if Jesse Jackson stepped down from power? The leader creates an environment wherein the values of the leader remain paramount. Myths and stories abound then about the leadership as time passes. The effective leader realizes that the organizational culture changes according to the mechanisms implemented by the leader.

Every organization passes through a life cycle on its way toward fulfilling its mission. The leader of the organization both consciously and unconsciously shapes the culture of the group by instilling personal assumptions, beliefs, and values. Critics often suggest, "Money is culture." However, culture seemingly finds foundation also in such variables as geographical, industrial, and strategic differentiations. In addition, the existence of organizational subcultures greatly commands attention. Every organization undergoes dynamic changes throughout its existence. The most natural reaction to change is to challenge its validity, particularly if we are unable to explain the change. An effective leader efficiently manages organizational change and the relevant cultural paradigm shifts that ensue.

The assessment tool (see Table 9.1) seeks to outline a checklist of variables useful to any individual questioning the culture of a prospective (or even current) organization. The assessment allows an individual and the organization to match each other in terms of assumptions, beliefs, and values. As each individual completes this assessment, the higher percentage of affirmative responses reflects more of a cultural fit between the individual and the organization.

Table 9.1 Cultural Inquiry

Cultural inquiry	Yes	No
Do you perceive agreement between your assumptions, beliefs, and values and those apparent in the overall mission of the organization?		
Do you require the organization to match closely your own idea of what makes an effective organizational environment?		
Do you agree with the espoused values and practices of the organization's culture?		
Would you be (are you) comfortable working according to the various cultural norms of the organization?		
Do you understand how the various levels of culture operate?		
Are you willing to accept a greater sense of cultural ambiguity in return for higher rewards?		
Are your personal and professional goals in line with the organization's culture and structure?		
Are your perceptions of the variables such as reality, truth, time, space, human nature, and relationships in line with the organization's espoused and perceivable culture?		
Does the perceivable leadership culture match with your own cultural value system?		
Are you willing to accept less of a personal cultural fit in return for a stable position within the organization?		

The Changing Practice of Management

Review any basic textbook on management and you will notice that the body of knowledge about this profession has been divided into four functions, known as planning, organizing, leading, and monitoring. Within these four functions, there are essential responsibilities that fall into either strategic or tactical tasks and that occur at differing levels of management. In our opinion, management and leadership are much more than these four functions reveal. For convenience sake, though, we have employed the four-function rubric and have described the changes that are evolving or need to evolve within the profession of management to accommodate the demands of an increasingly global economy. However, before we begin to discuss the changes relative to each function of management one important preamble must be stated first.

As we have indicated in previous chapters, our belief is that there is no such animal as the "global leader." In our experience, no business leader has the universal capacity and capability required for the job because of the sheer complexity, scope, and magnitude. Rather, global organizations need to develop skilled leaders and managers with highly specialized skill sets, some of which are focused on "localization" and some of which are focused on "globalization" of strategy and operations. Arguably, this replicates a pattern of organizational structure from the past. The difference is that the requirements and the skill sets have changed dramatically. It is also our experience that great leaders and managers develop over time, and with time, after having developed through successive and increasingly more demanding roles from the bottom, up.

Planning

The traditional management function of *planning* has included the tasks and responsibilities associated with the strategic and tactical preparations of the normal business cycle. Such responsibilities as analysis of physical and material assets and forecasting of sales, profit, and capital expenditures based on business strategy occupied a significant portion of management time. Presently, we see the need for management and leadership specialties at global, regional, country, business, and functional (Marketing, Accounting, Human Resources, Legal, Information Technology, etc.) levels.

Increasingly though, managers now have to refocus their analysis and forecasting activities based on new requirements, not the least of which is the sourcing and allocation of resources. Chief among those resources is skill and knowledge. Now, organizations are no longer in competition with the factory down the lane; they are in competition with companies and countries all over the planet. Nowadays, when companies are begun they are often already multinational or global. Some of this is due to the types of business, such as information, knowledge, or creative based; and the other factor is because some businesses begun from third world, developing or small countries cannot find enough market base in their home regions. The solution to this is to compete in the global economy.

Commonly, Human Resources (HR) was called upon—in some organizations relied upon—to provide projections of "people needs" based on the headcount needed to, for example, work on an assembly line. Now, HR has shifted from being focused on enterprise talent management to global workforce planning and talent sourcing.

While the HR function will always have a role in people development, in a high-velocity, networked, multination or global organization, it is "local" business managers who assume a major role in determining people needs within their regions. Localized business managers must coordinate efforts with localized HR staff because they have the knowledge of local law. HR will assume the role of asset procurement and disillusionment based on their expertise in hiring, personnel law, etc., and will share a greater link with the accounting function whose role it is to "valuate" the organization's intellectual capital. HR is now seen as a collaborator with business and functions.

However, it is localized business and regionalized functional managers (Marketing, Accounting, Legal, etc.) who will analyze, determine capability needs for local Business Managers. Business Managers continually will be focused on building the capability to achieve organizational objectives. Building capability means managers will be ever focused on learning and the link between learning and performance.

A high-velocity global economy will operate with a smaller number of metrics than do more traditional economies; although a strong argument can be made for traditional organizations to do the same. Global companies operate in dynamic environments where it is necessary to establish the "critical few" measurements that will ensure that the company is on track to meet its business objectives. However, having said all of that, increasingly in our opinion, there is a need to remove the institutionalized greed that has taken hold of American business. Business performance metrics must be properly and ethically balanced in accommodation of all stakeholder needs, not just shareholders.

Never before has there been such a need to insure a strong infrastructure than there is now in the global economy. In order to optimize technology, other resources and intellectual capital, organizations need to prepare, maintain, and upgrade infrastructure. Over the last few years we have witnessed a significant shift from information processing to knowledge processing, which includes the concepts of learning tools, intelligent electronic coaching, decision-making systems, and collaboration tools. Tools such as these are vital to the successful global organization. As the marketplace becomes more dynamic, organizations become more networked, people become more autonomous, and processes become seamless, these same organizations will become more reliant upon the infrastructure that supports them.

Infrastructure and technology augment intellectual endeavors at different stages of information flow. For instance, they can support human thinking, facilitate information access, help the human interpretation of complex data, and provide decision-support.

We all bear witness to the rapid evolution of incredibly sophisticated new technologies. For example, we have seen the advance of data warehousing; discovery tools such as data mining and parallel processing systems; knowledge-gathering tools such as intelligent agents and text retrieval; guidance systems such as case-based reasoning and business simulators; thinking aids and collaborative technologies. This of course is in addition to the World Wide Web and Internet. The problem is that all of this is wasted unless it actually serves business goals, through human endeavors. Technology is marvelous when it supports people; otherwise, it is but a nuisance or a nightmare.

Modern technological advances are employed to optimize the flow and exchange of energy through the enterprise infrastructure. These processing systems accelerate the development exchange and application of useful knowledge required for distributed social interaction. They also integrate all business strategies, plans, and operations into a coherent assessment of situational positioning at any point in time.

At the beginning of this section, we stated that management specialties in global organizations should probably be global, functional, regional, country, and business levels. Those leaders at the global level are the few and are at the top of the organization. These specialist must be the most strategic and be the most synergistic, synthesizing, forward thinking of the organization. The functional specialists will have the most integrative role of all the management groups because their reach will cover the enterprise. The regional manager specialist must own the best collaborative and analytical skills among the group to maximize the organization's strategic potential in the marketplace, and with the keenest eye on allocation of resources. The country management group will be the true local specialist who can truly translate between the local culture and the organizational culture. These leaders must know their consumer and employee pool base intimately; however, they must be able to manage the ambiguity and tension between competing needs between local and global stakeholders. The business manager's role has the most balanced between strategic and tactical foci. Chief among the strategic roles of localized business managers will be tracking market trends designing market strategy focused on both the country, regional managers, and in coordination with functional roles.

Organizing

The organizing function of management has traditionally included the task of structuring the organization in a way that facilitates the accomplishment of strategy and objectives. This process occurs at the executive level of the organization first and then cascades through each region, country, business unit, and function.

One of the basic rules of design is that form follows function. To operate in a high-velocity environment organizations need flexibility to adapt quickly to change. Therefore boundaries and resource allocation will be primary elements to give due attention along with creating and managing alliances and partnerships with other organizations. The essential element is coordination, rather than centralization.

Working relationships between organizational members (employees and managers) as well as contractors and allied organizations must be built upon mutual respect, responsibility, and commitment rather than following orders. To build collaborative and respectful relationships, politics and turf wars must end. Politics and turf wars are built on an antiquated mental model of lack and limitation. In our experience, politicking and turf battles demonstrate a failure of imagination.

Whereas traditional organizations relied upon formal communication and information structures, global companies must support the use of both formal and informal channels—even strengthening and emphasizing the informal communication and social network—in order to provide the latitude people need to succeed at the appropriate pace.

Perhaps the slowest transformation, and the one most needed, is toward building structures that enable what we refer to as "imbedded learning." It must be a required element in all organization designs. There must be time allotted to and processes and systems developed for both individual and collective learning occurring on a daily basis. In a global organization, understanding how people of local cultures live, learn, communicate, consume, and make decisions is imperative.

Monitoring

It makes sense that an economy that has shifted from domestic, to international, to global requires new ways of measuring and monitoring progress. The field of accounting has undergone a period of renewal as it has redefined the new appropriate methods to assign value to and measure intangibles such as patents, copyrights, trademarks, licenses, and intellectual property. Within the management function of monitoring, there are new metrics and standards such as the balanced scorecard to use to measure organizational and individual performance. There are new and appropriate classifications for dividing intellectual capital.

These categories divide intellectual capital into four categories consisting of the following elements:

1. Human capital—The minds of individuals employed or allied with the organization including their competence, knowledge, experience, and know-how.
2. Structural capital—All of the infrastructure left once the human capital is removed, such as databases, knowledge centers, processes, and repositories.
3. Intellectual property—Your patents, copyrights, trademarks, and licenses.
4. Customer capital—The relationships and contracts with customers, brands, and trademarks.

Increasingly, global organizations have begun to develop a greater awareness and understanding of the nature of intellectual assets and the role of knowledge in their strategic portfolio. Managers within globalized industries must operate with a common framework and language to bring meaning and clarity to an already high ambiguity economy. This meaning and clarity must extend to the development of coherent measurement models and systems with matching reward systems all of which must be congruent with the local cultures of countries in which a business operates.

More importantly though, is the change in how businesses monitor performance. To begin with, and as we have already stated in multiple ways, it is time to move away from the tendency of leaders and managers, on behalf of businesses, of hyper-focusing on profit above all else. Business leaders and managers must care about the ultimate well-being of all stakeholders. The implication of holding this intention in a global business requires leaders and managers to understand their local culture's customers and norms related to performance and to their ethical practices.

On a practical level, monitoring and leading (discussed next) are management aspects that directly involve working with people. In our Capability in Practice section, we provide some suggestions for managers working in intercultural situations related to understanding the employee's perspective and related to motivation, reward, and performance. Motivation is closely related to the performance of human resources in modern organizations. When considering motivation in the context of intercultural work contexts, management must remember that although the motivation process may be similar across cultures, what motivates people often is culturally based. What motivates employees in the United States may be only moderately effective in Japan, France, or Nigeria. Therefore, although motivation is the concept of choice for analyzing employee performance, an international context requires country-by-country, or at least regional, examination of differences in motivation. Even more importantly, motivation, while influenced by culture, is also influenced by age, health, and differs based on personality. However, some solid research has found that, as they approach their goals in life, people apparently take into consideration their psychological needs (intrinsic), their physical survival and pleasure (physical), their desires for rewards and praise (extrinsic), and their existential quest to have a meaningful place in the broader world (self-transcendence). These influences on goals might be considered as four occasionally overlapping but sometimes conflictual motivational systems that people must negotiate as they make their way through life.[213]

Culture and national laws will affect the management not only of people but also of processes. Some processes that work in some regions in the United States may not work internationally. Cultural awareness can facilitate the translation of management of people and processes and there are many questions to ask. For example, is time perceived differently in the production environment? In many Latin American countries, for example, promptness is not normally practiced. Is work ethic driven or more casual? In Japan typically, the work ethic is stricter than in many European countries. What are the attitudes toward risk?

The stage of technology in a country also affects culture. Where technology is limited, product demand and production capabilities are limited. Greater technology exposes people to greater products made and consumed. Greater technology increases educational opportunities, and thus the skill level of the labor force. This affects culture as we have mentioned previously because more material possessions are available and sought in the culture. Consider the effect of increasing materialism on the cultural values of the United States.

Principle of "Capability" in Practice

- Identify multiple but conflicting culturally learned viewpoints in the employee's context
- Identify multiple but conflicting culturally learned viewpoints within the individual employee
- Explain the actions of employees from their own cultural perspectives
- Listen for information about cultural patterns that leaders can share with the employee at an appropriate time
- Learn to shift topics in culturally appropriate ways
- Reflect culturally appropriate feelings in specific and accurate feedback
- Identify culturally defined multiple support systems for the employee
- Identify alternative solutions and anticipate the consequences for each cultural context
- Identify culturally learned criteria being used by the employee to evaluate alternative solutions
- Generate accurate explanations for the employee's behavior from the employees' cultural context.

Leading

In this knowledge culture, the managerial responsibility of leadership has and will undergo the most significant change in its history. A global economy based on knowledge, creativity, technology, and information requires that organizations possess a level of leadership and management sophistication far above anything previously seen. Old practices like "supervision" and "training" will be transformed into practices like "facilitation" and "imbedded learning." Managers will now need to be competent in both their "technical" profession, in performance learning and in building proper social relationships. Leaders and managers must now know (1) how to learn; (2) how they, themselves, learn; (2) how to teach others how to learn; and (3) to teach others to know how they learn. Opportunities for learning must be imbedded in every work practice. Leaders and managers must possess emotional, social, and cultural intelligence in order to establish strong long-term and short-term relationships with a variety of people.

Global organizations cannot afford to have work cultures burdened with politics and power conflicts where learning is obstructed and where managers have no idea about social organization. Since intelligence, knowledge and expertise resides within the minds of individuals, it is incumbent upon managers to accept that their primary role is to cultivate a learning-rich intercultural work environment in which social interaction is optimized and where people flourish. Managers need help in this because they need the tangible support of their companies who must provide appropriate compensation and reward systems that reward the right behaviors and that is anchored and based in local customs, which have been coordinated with the organization's strategic objectives. Lastly, it is incumbent upon the leaders within global organizations to set new and high standards of ethics, which truly are congruent with local cultures.

In summary, leading and managing global organizations is different in many ways from how domestic organizations are operated as we have detailed. In one very important way, successfully operating a global organization is precisely the same as successfully operating a domestic operation. Aside from e-business and a few business types, all successful businesses rely on establishing and caring for customer, employee, and partner relationships. Doing so is a localized effort. Global businesses rely on localized efforts.

The way we think about leading and managing has changed, or at least, it should change. For a number of decades we have put too much energy and effort into perceiving and treating management as a "science" when it is actually a "science" and a "social art" of and within specialized domains. By this, we mean the following about these three management and leadership dimensions. First, leading and managing are inseparable, you simply cannot do one without the other. Second, there are methods for accomplishing many management and leadership tasks; this is the science dimension. Third, leading and managing require knowledge, skill, and expertise in social relationships, what we call the social art dimension. Fourth, all business and organizational pursuits fall within some domain or profession, therefore leading and managing within a domain area requires skill and expertise in that domain, this we call the "technical" dimension. Now, when we add global marketplace intentions to business endeavors, we add layers of complexity within all three of the leading and managing dimensions.

Arguably, how we develop leaders and managers should have changed long ago. However, we are now in the place in our history as humans that our ways must change to avert potentially dire results. We now shift the reader's attention to Exhibit 9.4 (Mintzberg interview). We have included this particular interview of Henry Mintzberg because we believe he has captured several important points that we have woven throughout this book.

Exhibit 9.4

Mintzberg on Management and Management Education

Managerial Correctness

MBA programs, says Henry Mintzberg, are producing not managers but functionaries. That doesn't bode well for either business or society.

Listen to enough academics and gurus in the field, read enough books and articles about the way we work now, and you might conclude that an MBA degree is absolutely essential to becoming a successful manager—indeed, that it's the fast pass to the top tier of top-tier companies. Henry Mintzberg probably wouldn't disagree with that conclusion, but he would also say that it's all wrong that it is concocted of distortions, shortsightedness, and lazy thinking.

The criticism is especially telling because Mintzberg belongs to the very establishment that he so vigorously decries. He is Cleghorn Professor of Management Studies at McGill University in Montreal and one of the world's best-known management scholars. So when he says, "The MBA trains the wrong people in the wrong way for the wrong reasons," one cannot dismiss his words as the rant of a know-nothing. His just-published *Managers Not MBAs: A Hard Look at the Soft Practice of Managing and Management Development* (Berrett-Koehler) is his thirteenth book and probably his most sweeping in its scope and, in its language, as biting as anything he's ever written.

That bite was readily apparent when *Across the Board* editor A.J. Vogl interviewed Mintzberg by telephone during the professor's vacation sojourn in Provence.

Your publisher describes your new book as "the most extensive and far-reaching critique that has ever been produced about how managers are educated today and the consequences of that education for managerial practice, corporations, and society." Even allowing for hyperbole, that's quite a statement. Would you call Managers Not MBAs your magnum opus?
My inadvertent magnum opus. I set out to write about management education, both the negative and the positive, but I think the most important part of the book may be its critique of management itself, the questioning of so much that's going on in management today. It's not solely attributable to MBA programs, but they are part of that syndrome and contribute significantly to it.

How do they do that?
By pretending to create managers out of people who have never managed. As I say in the book, trying to teach management to someone who has never managed is like trying to teach psychology to someone who has never met another human being. Leadership and management are part of life, and education cannot teach life experience to those who haven't acquired it. You cannot learn how to lead an organization from a classroom.

It's interesting that you don't make a distinction between leadership and management. Others do in fact, consultants have made a good living by belaboring the distinction.

(Continued)

Exhibit 9.4   (Continued)

I think that's part of the problem. The more we train for leadership independent of management, the more we get hubris the idea that the leader is somebody big and important, separate from someone who has to deal with the
daily nitty-gritty of running an organization. That's a dangerous distinction.

Why dangerous?
Because when you're connected and have a deep, tacit understanding of
the issues, you do things more effectively. So a leader has to be a manager,
and a manager has to be a leader—somebody who knows what's going on,
what's happening in the business. Look at Kofi Annan, who gets involved
in so many issues; think of the nuance involved in dealing with a Cyprus,
for instance, or Iraq. You can't do this by remote control. You have a president who does it by remote control, and look what's happening: "Give me a
20-page report and I'll give you a war."

*While you exalt true management, you also say what it is not—neither a sci-
ence nor a profession.*
A profession has a codified body of knowledge, and to practice a profession
you need to be trained and certified. Look at medicine, for instance, where
we know which surgical procedure works best in which circumstances; or
engineering, where we know which material holds best in a bridge. These
things can be taught in advance of practice.

But we don't have much codified knowledge in management, and we certainly have no accreditation that ensures people are good managers; in fact,
the most common accreditation—the MBA—is exactly the opposite. We have
great managers who have never spent a day in a management program. We
don't have great surgeons who never spent a day in medical school, or great
engineers who never studied physics. So the idea of management as a profession doesn't hold up at all. There's no aspect of management that conforms to professional qualifications.

As far as being a science, physics is a science; chemistry and biology are sciences. Management isn't a science; it isn't about finding truth. Management
isn't even an *applied* science, because that's still a science. Management is
the *application* of science, among many other things. Managers use whatever they can in a practical way to get things done or to encourage other
people to get things done.

Most management is a craft—that is, it relies on experience, on-the-job
learning. I put it this way: It's as much about doing in order to think as
thinking in order to do.

*And by your reckoning, business schools are not up to the task. What exactly
are they doing wrong?*
The typical business school today is concerned with business functions,
not management. Certainly managers have to understand business functions—marketing, accounting, sales, and so on—but the practice of business
is not the same as the practice of management. Mixing all these functions
together in a person is not going to produce a manager.

(Continued)

Exhibit 9.4   (Continued)

Now, while business schools have been successful in *analyzing* things, in separating all these specialized functions, they have not been successful in putting them together, in synthesizing them into a coherent vision or integrated system. That's the difficult—and the interesting—part of management. In the book, I compare two ways of looking at this synthesis. The first is the Ikea model: The schools supply the parts, and the students do the assembly. Unfortunately, there is no instruction book, and the pieces, although they look neatly cut to size, don't all fit together. Management in the real world is more like playing with Lego blocks: There's no one way of assembling the pieces, and it takes time to build the more interesting structures.

The trouble with business schools' emphasis on analysis is that it leads to an emphasis on technique or formula thinking. I define technique as something that can be used in place of a brain, and management schools have made a specialty of offering courses in techniques—empowerment techniques for human resources or portfolio models for financial resources.

I'm not saying that technique doesn't have a place in management, but it must be used carefully and in context, not generically by people on the fast track who see technique as a way of compensating for a lack of experience. You've heard of the so-called rule of the tool: Give somebody a hammer and everything looks like a nail. Well, MBA programs have given their graduates so many hammers that many organizations look like smashed-up beds of nails.

Let's talk about the people whom MBA programs attract. Are they the right people? The right people at the wrong time? Or are these programs attempting to teach the wrong people?
First, there's not much evidence that these people have managerial skills or even that they truly want to be managers. Some do, obviously, and some have those skills, but the selection process using GMAT scores and the like doesn't necessarily sort out those people who really have it. In my book, I refer to David Ewing's 1990 book *Inside the Harvard Business School*, in which he had a list of 19 of Harvard Business School's best alumni—the superstars of that time. When I saw people like Frank Lorenzo on that list, I thought, there's something funny here. So we tracked those people from 1990 to 2003. We found that ten were total failures, four were very questionable in their performance, and only five—Lou Gerstner was one—had clean records. Somebody like Lorenzo, who had major failures with three airlines and continuing problems with employees, shouldn't have been allowed to run anything because he didn't have true managerial skills—although he *did* have a lot of manipulative financial skills.

So some people are the wrong people to begin with. MBA programs seem to attract more than their share of people whom I characterize as impatient, aggressive, and self-serving. Not all of them, of course, but a noticeable number. It doesn't take that many because they're the ones who are grabbing all the attention. Those characteristics in turn are reflected in their management style.

That's one problem; the other is that even if they're the right people, it may not be the right time, because they are trained to be managers when

(Continued)

Exhibit 9.4   (Continued)

they know nothing about management. The consequence is that they get a distorted view of management and so become the wrong people.

You also make a distinction between some people's "zest for business" and their lack of "will to manage." Isn't this a distinction without a difference?
I think they're quite different. One is talking about interest in business and business dealings, and there are lots of people—like Warren Buffett—who are driven by love of the game of business rather than the need to be in charge of thousands of people trying to get things done. Tom Peters is another example of somebody who has a great zest for business but hasn't shown a great will to manage a business. I'm sure they don't mind making tons of money, but I would guess they are driven more by the game.

In your book, you say, "The zest for business means getting the most out of resources, while the will to manage is about tapping into the energy of people." Aren't people also resources?
No. Absolutely not. Viewing them as resources is deadly. It turns them into robots. And you can't possibly get them enthusiastic about their jobs when you're treating them that way. It's not coincidental that the rise of the term *human resources* coincided with a wave of downsizing. You can fire resources, but you can't fire human beings very easily.

Before HR, there were personnel departments. Didn't that term also objectify people?
Not as much. That's a fairly neutral term.

Now, despite having the will to manage, many MBA graduates take up jobs in consulting and investment banking, rather than with companies that make things and sell things. Why?
They're in a hurry to make money, and both investment banking and consulting pay well. Those fields also are very much like school in the sense of offering case studies: Every day a new challenge, every day a new business, which doesn't get them deeply into anything, and they don't have to bear the consequences of their advice or implement it.

In this context, I was struck by a quote in your book, an observation by a business-strategy professor. If you know how to design a great motorcycle engine, he said, he could teach you all you need to know about strategy in a few days. But even if you have a Ph.D. in strategy, years of labor would not be enough to enable you to design a great motorcycle engine.
Yes, I say business is about motorcycle engines. Conventional MBA programs are about strategy in the absence of motorcycles.

But aren't you also saying that for a business to be successful it must have a good product to start with?
Yeah, and to have a good product, you have to know products. We get so-called managers flitting into industries without any understanding of the

(Continued)

Exhibit 9.4   (Continued)

industry. In fast-moving consumer-goods industries—the model for most MBA cases—you can flit from pens to bottled water to potato chips, because you can carry marketing skills with you. But "fast-moving" is really a synonym for "new and improved." In these industries, change comes slowly. Exploiting the brand is what's important.

I'd guess that most of the people who build better motorcycle engines—if I can use that product as a metaphor—are entrepreneurs. How do MBA graduates fare as entrepreneurs?
Look up rankings like the *Inc.* list of entrepreneurs, and you'll see that MBAs don't figure prominently on them. Harvard Business School claims that, after a certain number of years out, many of its graduates become entrepreneurs, but when you look at the data you see that most of them have small operations—as consultants, or running a little real-estate office.

We took the technology list from NASDAQ, selected out all the companies with more than $1 billion in market capitalization, and looked at how many MBAs there were who had founded and were running those companies. There wasn't a high percentage of founders, and they were mostly the smaller ones. More of the MBAs running those companies came in afterward—and I'm not sure they run them very well.

In your book, you don't really discuss women graduates of MBA programs. Is their orientation any different?
I think women who are attracted to MBA programs are a bit different from women in general: more aggressive, less apt to exhibit female characteristics in managing, and so on. I see a yin-and-yang approach to managing—a more masculine, macho view of management versus a more engaging style.

The MBA education is unbalanced by denigrating experience in favor of analysis, which in turn leads to two dysfunctional styles of management: the calculating and the heroic. The calculating manager, who was prevalent for many years in the automobile and telecommunications industries, is focused on so-called hard data. They were successful because conditions in these businesses sometimes tolerated mediocre quality and the absence of innovation. But then there arose a demand for better quality and innovation—think of competition from Japan. And then came the ascendancy of shareholder value, which has trumped quality and innovation and led to the rise of the heroic manager. Performance is no longer measured by improving product or service but, rather, by raising the stock price. Boards of directors decided that power had to be concentrated in one man, who would do whatever was necessary to improve the numbers. And so the CEO became king, and shareholder value became the standard of excellence.

These dysfunctional styles, you argue, have had a corrupting impact not only on management but on society at large: exaggerated compensation practices, firing people with impunity, and so on.

(Continued)

Exhibit 9.4   (Continued)

It's a syndrome of which the MBA is a significant part. It has to do with certain consulting practices, with the business press that builds up heroes and looks for short-term drama. Bold mergers and mass layoffs make good stories. It's a whole series of things of which the MBA is one component.

You're particularly harsh on the concept of shareholder value.
I call it corporate social *irresponsibility*, period. The argument that Milton Friedman and others use is that business has no business dealing with social issues—let them stick to business. It's a nice position for a conceptual ostrich who doesn't know what's going on in the world and is enamored with economic theory. Show me an economist who will argue that social decisions have no economic consequences! No economist will argue that, so how can anyone argue that economic decisions have no social consequences? And if we train managers to ignore the social consequences, what kind of a society do we end up with? According to Aleksandr Solzhenitsyn, whom I quote in the book, we end up with one that rests on the letter of the law, and that's a pretty deadly society. I'm not saying that businesspeople should take the place of politicians to decide social issues, but they have to be managing with a sensitivity to the social impact of their decisions.

You're saying, then, that MBA programs promote a narrow—indeed, a mercenary—view of management?
The short answer has to be yes, although there are all sorts of qualifications. Yes, because it promotes the idea that you can manage anything, and a mercenary literally is someone who's paid to fight *any* battle, regardless. I think there's a lot of that in management, and the idea of teaching management out of context, which MBA programs do, encourages that kind of behavior.

What do you think of the trend toward corporate social responsibility? Is that real? Or window dressing?
For a lot of people it's real, but the impact is largely window dressing.

For which people?
The people who promote it—they're serious about it; they believe honestly in it. But I don't think they get very far.

Why not?
Because of the era we live in—it's like teaching a course in ethics against eight courses in shareholder value. An uphill battle. It's sort of, "Be nice, please," while somebody else is offering you bribes. Social responsibility is important, but I don't think we're going to get anywhere by imploring managers to be socially responsible. This is a political battle right now because of the absolute control the financial community has—not only over business, which might be normal, but over all of society, including buying politicians outright—legally, through all the phony ways of donating money to the political process. What's going on is just obscene.

(Continued)

Exhibit 9.4   (Continued)

What you call legal corruption-behavior above the letter of the law?
Just above. Enron and the rest of them are the tip of the iceberg, and you can deal with the tip in courts of law. What worries me is the *legal* corruption below the surface. I'm talking here of the extremes in executive compensation and the casual firing of people, of professional managers who describe themselves as being so-called hired guns applying neutral techniques to whatever needs managing. But a technique is not neutral when it drives an organization to a greedy form of morality, when its goal is "lean and mean." Do we want to create a mean society?

And by your reckoning, B-schools are not up to the task of producing graduates who can make a positive change in society, in the sense of being effective in government or leading organizations in the non-profit sector. Indeed, you say, "Of all the distortions emanating from the business schools, none is more flagrant than the claim that this degree in business administration prepares people to manage any organization." A rather strong statement.
I don't think so. I think what business schools are doing is a strong statement. How can they educate people in business administration and just assume that these people can run other kinds of organizations? Their implicit assumption that *everything* should be run like a business has been incredibly destructive. To the MBA who wants to reinvent government, I would say, "I am a citizen, not a customer." As for one of them running a hospital, anybody who needs a mission statement to run a hospital should find a job somewhere else.

Believing you can run anything implies a certain arrogance, which in turn points to an insensitivity to people. Why don't B-schools teach soft skills?
Business schools make the biggest fuss about things that they are least able to teach, and the soft skills are one of those things. It's not a question of deciding what to teach and teaching it—that's a very American perspective on things, that as long as you covered it or teach it, you'll convert people. But you can't take people who've never managed or barely managed and give them the soft skills in a classroom. What you can do in a classroom is to take people who live with those soft skills and try to use them every day.

To expand the skills they already have?
Yeah, and to give them a chance to share and reflect upon the things they do as managers. But it's nonsense to take kids who've never managed and pretend you can teach them leadership or other soft skills.

All right, you've taken traditional MBA programs to task. Let's hear about your alternative.
The premise of McGill's International Masters in Practicing Management program is to do what I just said: to make better managers of people who already are managers. We want these people to be sent and sponsored by their companies. They come for only two weeks at a time in several modules,

(Continued)

so that they stay on the job; we want them on the job as managers, and then we can focus as much of the learning as possible on their reflections on their own managerial activities. We bring the concepts and ideas and cases and theories; they bring their experience. And the stew that we stir in the classroom is where those two meet, individually, in groups, or in plenary. The idea is to focus as much of the learning as possible on their own experience.

How long has the IMPM program been in existence?
It's been nine years; the ninth class is just about to start. We've graduated about 250 so far-there are about 30 to 35 per class. I'm talking here about executives from big, traditional companies, like Matsushita, Fujitsu, Lufthansa, Motorola.

There should be many such programs, and tens of thousands of people attending them. Our model works, clearly. Some other schools have adopted parts of what we're doing. And corporations have taken up the model in their own programs. British Aerospace, now called BAE Systems, has been running with it for about six years—they've had their entire senior management, about 150 people, through the program.

You describe this program in detail in your book, and it's an intriguing alternative to the traditional MBA.
I have nothing against the MBA so long as it's recognized for what it is, which is training in the business functions. There's nothing wrong with that, but it has nothing to do with management. People will pick up on my critique of the MBA because it's dramatic, but the real message of the book is its critique of management practice—the corruption of management practice—and the fact that there are other ways to manage and, correspondingly, other ways to develop managers.

Source: The Conference Board Review®, A.J. Vogl is editor of Across the Board, July–August 2004.

Analysis of the Mintzberg Interview

Leading and managing have changed, and how we prepare leaders and managers for their roles must change. In his interview (Exhibit 9.4), Mintzberg makes several important points that we find most relevant. Mintzberg makes the point, and we concur, that it is impossible to teach a person how to manage through simply classroom methods and expect excellence in actual management practice.

Mintzberg also decries the practice of MBA graduates taking roles in consulting firms; consulting firms whose chief practice is charging large sums of money to advise organizational leaders and managers. We concur with this opinion because we have witnessed the damage done to organizations to by people who have no practical expertise.

Combined, these two points (managers cannot acquire true skill at managing and leading through classroom education) and (consultants without experience advising organizational leaders and managers) suggest a perspective that mirrors our discussion thus far in this book. That perspective is that you cannot expect a person who has never had the experience of engaging with another culture, to be able to lead or manage an intercultural organization.

Another important point Mintzberg raises concerns the tendency to think of management as a profession in and of itself, as though it is divorced from any particular context. We believe that while it may be possible for a well-seasoned leader or manager to take on a role in a completely different arena or industry to perform marginally at many aspects of an organization, she or he will not readily and optimally succeed. Likewise, the tendency to think that because a leader or manager has built a solid "track record" at leading and managing in several U.S. operations, she or he will, without experience, be the answer to the question of who can pack up, move abroad and manage in Turkey, for example, has cost many organizations. You might as well ask that manager to perform heart surgery on your mother, the patient will have the same chances of survival.

A final point of Mintzberg on which we want to comment is his admonishment to everyone, that it is time we stop behaving as though there are no consequences to our decisions and actions. Ethics are important. In global business, ethics are more important as is the importance of the intentions of leaders and managers. Operating unethically in one's own country is disgraceful and harmful; operating unethically in someone else's home country can have even more far-reaching consequences. It is time that all leaders and managers behave as though they understand that everything they do has ramifications far beyond their perceptual horizon. It is helpful to think of the world as a system (including human society) and that what one does in one part of the system affects the other parts. In a sense, "fouling" someone else's nest, means fouling one's own.

It has taken academia, as witnessed by Mintzberg's latest efforts, an incredibly long time to conclude what some of us arrived at long ago, which is that true *skill* and expertise requires an integrated approach in which one acquires values, attitudes, knowledge, practice, and experience at "doing" any professional endeavor. In the same way that it takes this integrated approach over time to acquire ordinary management and leadership skill, so too, it takes an integrated approach to learning all of that which concerns leading and managing done in an intercultural context.

Case presentation: Ford in Australia

In our case presentation (Exhibit 9.5), Ford Motor Company and their Australian subsidiary are profiled for their approach to incorporating intercultural sensitivity with their efforts to increase their organizational learning capability and serving employees and consumers alike.

Exhibit 9.5

Ford Australia Limited Company Profile

Ford Motor Company and its subsidiaries design, develop, manufacture, and service cars, trucks, and parts worldwide. The company operates through two sectors: Automotive and Financial Services. The Automotive sector sells cars, trucks, and parts under Ford, Mercury, Lincoln, Volvo, Land Rover, Jaguar, and Aston Martin brand names. This sector markets its products through retail dealers in North America, and through distributors and dealers outside of North America. In addition, it sells cars and trucks to dealers for sale to fleet customers, including daily rental car companies, commercial fleet customers, leasing companies, and governments. This sector also provides a range of after-the-sale vehicle services and products, maintenance and light repair, heavy repair, collision, vehicle accessories, and extended service warranty. The Finance Services sector offers various automotive financing products to and through automotive dealers worldwide. It offers retail financing, wholesale financing, and other financing, such as making loans to dealers for working capital, improvements to dealership facilities, and the acquisition and refinancing of dealership real estate. This sector services the finance receivables and leases that it originates and purchases, makes loans to affiliates, purchases receivables, and provides insurance services related to its financing programs. The company was founded in 1903 and is based in Dearborn, Michigan.

Note: On July 18, 2007 Ford Motor Company reported that it was closing the smaller of its three Australian plants and is cutting 600 jobs. The action was taken in response to the Australian's decreasing interests in large automobiles.

The Importance of Diversity to Ford Australia

Ford Australia stands out as a true leader of diversity management in Australia. The company has a proud record of investing in their workforce and optimizing the benefits of diversity for their organization. Ford Australia has been a key partner in the Productive Diversity Partnerships Program of the Department of Immigration and Multicultural and Indigenous Affairs (DIMIA). Through their collaboration, Ford Australia and DIMIA have developed new ideas and useful tools for realizing the full benefits of a diverse workforce. At the 2001 Census, Australia had 18,769,074 people.
  Of this population:

- 43% were either born overseas or had at least one parent born overseas. This represents just over eight million Australian consumers.

(Continued)

- Over 200 languages were spoken, with the most common being English, Italian, Greek, Cantonese, Arabic, Vietnamese, and Mandarin.
- 23% of Australia's workers were born overseas, with 15% coming from non-English speaking countries.
- 29% of the total number of small businesses in Australia was operated by people who were born overseas.

How Does Ford Australia Champion Diversity?
Ford Australia optimizes the benefits of diversity by investing in their workforce. The Ford Australia leadership team believes that to have a relationship with your customers you have to understand their needs. A diverse workforce is one way of achieving this. Ford Australia:

- A diverse workforce that resembles recruits, understands their customers.
- Trains the workforce—through targeted diversity training initiatives for employees.
- Builds respect in the workforce—through celebration and acknowledgment.
- Uses surveys and other measurement tools to communicate the diversity message and track the effectiveness of their diversity programs.

One of Ford Australia's innovative strategies is to recruit diverse employees who mirror their customer base. They draw upon employees' knowledge and understanding of customers to design cars that are suited to a wide variety of buyers, maximizing their market share. As a result of their recruitment efforts, Ford Australia currently has over 68 nationalities represented in their Geelong and Broadmeadows plants.

A Woman's Touch Used in Car Design
A prime example of the benefits Ford Australia has gained from diversity is found in their customer clinics. These clinics assess each new Ford Australia launch and are made up of a diverse group of participants: engineers, volunteers from the Ford Australia workforce, and so on. Through comments and feedback received from women on these review committees, Ford Australia discovered they were looking for features that were not available in some of their car models. Employees identified that women needed more room for children's items, handbags, and groceries. A lower steering wheel with higher seat placement was also essential. Women also preferred a wider range of colors and options. In response, Ford Australia has incorporated these suggestions in some of their vehicles.

The Benefits of Recruiting a Diverse Workforce
As women become more closely matched to men in terms of careers and salaries—and as around 50% of the potential market—Ford Australia recognized that their ability to attract women as customers is imperative to their bottom line. Ford Australia has been recognized for their efforts. The Ford Escape, for example, was rated one of the Top Five Cars for Women by the on-line car magazine autobuy.com.au, in terms of practicality, style, driving ease, and price.

(Continued)

Recruiting Strategies to Optimize the Benefits of Women in the Workforce

Ford Australia has championed women in the workforce through their diversity programs, coming up with unique and innovative initiatives to encourage more women to work at Ford Australia. Since 2000, Ford Australia has funded the "Ford of Australia Women in Engineering Scholarship Program," an undergraduate scholarship program aimed at encouraging more women into the field of automotive engineering. Ford Australia offers flexible work options such as job sharing, telecommuting, childcare facilities, and work-life balance programs to attract and keep top talent in the organization. By investing in such programs, Ford Australia hopes to ensure that it remains an employer of choice for women. In 2002, women comprised 43% of Ford Australia's total university graduate intake.

Ford Australia has extensive training programs in place to ensure that its diversity mission is understood, supported and acted upon in every work site. Ford Australia and DIMIA decided to take Ford Australia's current training program one step further. Together they developed a training workshop to extend the skills, knowledge, and understanding of diversity management by their middle level managers. Ford Australia sees diversity training as an important way of achieving a more productive, innovative, creative and satisfied workforce.

The Training Workshop Partnership Project

Ford Australia provided DIMIA with input on key learning needs, case studies and skill practice scenarios based on actual situations that have occurred at Ford Australia. As a result of this input DIMIA then developed a training workshop. The modules contained in the workshop were designed to build on emotional intelligence, expression of empathy, and promoting inclusion. The workshop was developed in a flexible format that could be delivered by external trainers or trainers within Ford Australia, with minimal input from DIMIA.

Ford Australia recruited a small group of line managers, middle managers, and supervisors to trial the workshop and test the materials for relevance and application. The managers came from a variety of areas within Ford Australia and represented a wide range of skills and experience. The case studies were extremely valuable and provided managers with intervention strategies to better equip them when they are confronted with a real-life diversity issue in the workplace. The case studies also gave managers information on preventative measures and tools to use in their work areas.

Ford Australia learned from their collaboration with DIMIA that:

Their current diversity training is good, but only a starting point.

- Telling people what they should be doing and what they shouldn't be doing in relation to diversity management isn't enough. Managers need to be put into situations that are real and challenging.
- Facilitated diversity training makes managers confront their own stereotypes and apply appropriate management techniques.
- Diversity training using real-life case studies, which develop managers' skills, is the only option if you want to make positive changes in your workplace.

(Continued)

Building Mutual Respect

Ford Australia firmly believes that a workforce built on mutual respect increases opportunities for collaboration, idea generation, and innovation. For Ford Australia, innovation is key to being successful and profitable in a highly competitive car manufacturing industry. Ford Australia's primary goal for Harmony Day was to actively promote workforce diversity in a fun and celebratory way and to provide a day where employees could reflect on Ford Australia's success as a multicultural workplace. Ford Australia believes in constantly reinforcing the positive benefits of diversity. Harmony Day provided Ford Australia with an important opportunity to do this as well as providing a respectful and supportive workplace. Ford Australia's participation in Harmony Day included all staff, from the manufacturing line to the CEO.

The purpose of the day was communicated to employees several weeks in advance through a number of mediums such as mail outs to dealerships, messages on all employee computer screen savers, announcements on pay stubs, and through employee workgroups and weekly meetings. The day was launched at Ford Australia's Geelong facility by Ford Australia's CEO and the Minister for Citizenship and Multicultural Affairs, The Hon Gary Hardgrave MP. The on-site day care facility at Ford Australia was intimately involved in the celebrations. Children of employees marched into the production plant two-by-two, holding hands, and singing songs from around the world for the manufacturing line workers. The celebrations included international food, music, decorations, and dancing.

The Harmony Day materials of orange banners, pins and lollies provided a visual and clear message to the workforce. Ford Australia incorporated the Harmony Day motto, You + Me = Us into the celebrations by wrapping vehicles in banners with the motto and decorating the manufacturing plant.

For Ford Australia, Harmony Day was an enormous success, encouraging participation from a high percentage of the workforce. Ford will be involved again in Harmony Day in 2003, to reinforce their commitment to diversity.

Building Respect in the Workforce Through Acknowledgment

Ford Australia promotes respect in the workforce through a number of other initiatives as well as Harmony Day. A prime example is how Ford Australia structures its work calendar around religious and cultural events such as Christmas, Chinese New Year, and Orthodox Easter. Ford Australia believes that if you have a diverse workforce, employees must be allowed to observe celebrations of their choice whether it is a Christian holiday, a Muslim holiday, a Jewish holiday, and so on. It is simply the right thing to do. For Ford Australia, respecting religious practices makes good business sense. For example, Ford Australia would rather know in advance that members of the workforce need time with their families so they can plan their staffing needs more effectively at critical times of the year.

Ford Australia's Open Policy for Religious Holidays Is a Win-Win Situation

Consider the fact that Ford Australia makes approximately one car per minute. Without a policy that accommodates religious holidays, car production could be compromised by employees who feel obligated to take the time off, but don't feel comfortable asking for it. Ford Australia is able to maintain

(Continued)

efficient production schedules by better planning and anticipating staff down time through religious leave. Efficient production schedules are crucial in car manufacturing. For employees, they are able to spend time with their families knowing that they have their employer's support.

Communicating with the Workforce
Ford Australia continuously seeks feedback from their workforce to ensure that their diversity programs, facilities, and practices are working effectively and are communicated back to staff. Ford Australia views diversity as a long-term learning process.

Gaining Feedback from the Workforce
Ford Australia uses three key strategies to communicate with their workforce on diversity.

Focus Groups—Salaried members from all levels of the organization participate in focus groups to identify what diversity initiatives are working, where gaps may be, and what they feel the future "ideal" may be in terms of diversity.

The Pulse Survey—For 2002, the salaried workforce has been given a Pulse Survey, which assesses Ford Australia's commitment to and performance in achieving a diverse workforce. The Pulse Survey is an internationally recognized research tool designed for organizations that want to measure the effectiveness of certain parts of their business. Ford Australia uses this survey to focus on diversity.

Leadership behavior assessments for managers—As part of their performance review, all managers at Ford Australia are assessed against their ability to manage, support, and improve diversity initiatives within Ford Australia. The assessments give Ford Australia a way to hold managers accountable to their diversity policies.

Why make diversity your business?
Whether your business is a leader in diversity management or just starting out, Ford Australia is a prime example that diversity can give you a competitive edge in the marketplace. The benefits of diversity can be realized by all businesses, whether they be small, medium, or large. Like all other investments, diversity can yield a return that is commercially viable and sustainable over time. Demand for goods and services in the domestic market is not homogenous. The profitability and growth of any business depends on reaching the "whole market." To do this, businesses must understand and cater to the tastes and preferences of each segment in this market. Diversity is a reality in today's society, particularly language and cultural diversity. The statistics cited at the beginning of this case study indicate the magnitude of the purchasing power of people from different cultural and language backgrounds. Is your business making full use of this diversity? Are you reaching this important segment of the market? If not, then making effective use of the language and cultural diversity of your employees, as an integral part of your management and recruitment strategies, can help you. Competition to capture the business of consumers from linguistic and culturally diverse backgrounds is not only strong in the domestic market. In an increasingly globalized marketplace, competition from overseas is also growing. If your business is trading overseas, understanding and being able to serve a more diverse customer base can give you valuable knowledge that can

(Continued)

significantly add to your export capabilities. It can also substantially reduce your costs of market intelligence, research and testing. So, why make diversity your business? The cost of ignoring it could be significant.

Source: Adapted from The Commonwealth Department of Immigration and Multicultural and Indigenous Affairs as a joint initiative with Ford Motor Company of Australia Limited, March 2002.

Case Perspective: Capability Applied

Through its dedication to diversity, Ford Australia has not only shown care for employees and consumers, it has demonstrated learning agility in engaging in ongoing capability building with compassion, consciousness, and financial responsibility. Ford Australia has demonstrated that it is not only possible, but also profitable and preferable to function with all stakeholders in mind and in such a way that honors people in the local cultures within which it operates.

The Bottom Line

We began this chapter by suggesting that all organizations must learn and continually build capability in order to survive and thrive. Further, we stated that cultural intelligence is a prerequisite of global leadership and for global organizations. Global competition has intensified as new organizations enter into global expansion activities and as new globally birthed organizations arise. In such an environment, it is critical for organizations to establish strong intercultural relationships with culturally diverse groups of employees, interorganizational partners, and consumers in local contexts. In order to manage these relationships effectively, organizations need a means to understand and improve their capability. The complexity of intercultural business requires leaders and management to understand the nature of domains of global relationships and the level of complexity when attempting to communicate with multiple partners having unique national and organizational cultures. While organizations are gaining in expertise and cultural sensitivity, some initiatives flounder as people fail to consider fully culture's impact in context-specific situations. Understanding differences is important; however, we also state that focusing on similarities and universal human goals and needs is a powerful way of building bridges toward mutual benefit.

10

Geoleadership and the Community

Globalization has changed us into a company that searches the world, not just to sell or to source, but to find intellectual capital—the world's best talents and greatest ideas.

—Jack Welch

The sentiment expressed in the chapter lead quote by Jack Welch, former Chairman and CEO of General Electric (GE), sagely states the impact of globalization on a large U.S.-led firm. Globalization is not an option; it is an imperative. As the new millennium soon closes its first decade, U.S. business leaders no longer have the luxury of ignoring potential revenues from large markets such as China and India, as well as newly developing opportunities in countries in Africa, Asia, and South America. Outsourcing is only the tip of the iceberg. More and more skilled workers are immigrating to the United States, which makes cultural understanding a domestic, not just a global, agenda item.

The purpose of this book on Geoleadership has been to identify the vital intercultural competencies needed by U.S. business leaders working in global situations. Through the previous seven chapters, we presented each of the seven dimensions of the Geoleadership Model, explained their importance, and provided case examples to help readers to recognize various leadership skills being used in intercultural situations.

The seven chapters of the Geoleadership Model highlight how moving U.S. business leaders to a place of cultural competence is a several-tier process. A certain amount of energy, effort, and time are required to achieve such intercultural competence. The implication for U.S. leaders and organizations is that the process of internalization of the various components of intercultural competency requires a multi-faceted approach. However, Hofstede

(2004) asserted that the United States reflected a more short-term orientation in its business environment. Such short-term orientation appears antithetical to the longer-term personal investment by the U.S. business leader.

The tiered learning process was first explored in the first chapter of this book with an overview of the multitude of challenges in the global marketplace faced by leaders and organizations. Leadership emerged as a universal concept occurring in all contexts, yet it retained its own cultural perspective. The second chapter of this book highlighted that the concept of culture remains one of the most misunderstood constructs within organizations. A thorough overview of how culture and leadership are interconnected followed. The concept of care was discussed in the third chapter to show leaders who need to find value beyond economic indicators, meeting objectives, and spreading the *American Way*. Rather, caring about individuals in another culture and understanding how they view leadership emerged is critical. In terms of leading others, the book showed that those leaders who paid attention to the concerns of employees and looked at problems in new ways were more effective in their intercultural business dealings.

Chapter 4 discussed the importance of effective communication among diverse business constituencies. The unspoken ways of communication remain just as important as the spoken ones, and the written modes of communication are taking on vital significance due to the advent of online messaging systems on top of the already-entrenched practice of email. Chapter 5 discusses that if business leaders are not often able to communicate face-to-face with their colleagues, then such leaders must become self-aware of both their own and the other's cultural mindsets. Chapter 6 showed how contrasting approaches to leadership emerge when leaders hold differing expectations and values. Chapter 7 focused on the context of leading, which is similar to the idea of situational leadership.

Chapter 8 speaks to the dynamics of organizational change globally and how competent leaders must be adaptive to such opportunities. Chapter 9's central message was that an interculturally competent leader is capable of operating in a multitude of diverse situations for the benefit of an organization.

Two important questions remain and are the topics of this final chapter. The two questions relate to practical application and scholarship. First, how do we recognize intercultural leadership within our global and local communities? Second, what is the future for global leadership research?

To answer the first question, we present two excellent Exhibits that illustrate leaders who, in business vernacular, "walk the talk." In both cases, the leaders demonstrate a very important aspect of business that is often unattended to in most business courses and texts. Before terms like "corporate social responsibility" existed and before debates raged about which should take precedent, "stakeholders," or "shareholders," people in business, in most countries around the globe, understood that one of their essential success factors was something referred, or akin, to goodwill. When this writer, at age 18, embarked on an academic and professional career, on-the-job management training was a business basic. It was an integral aspect of taking care of the business. It meant, in tangible ways, building, and maintaining reciprocal relationships with the community and all of its members. Goodwill was predicated on the simple idea that when you take out resources from the community, you must put back something of value. This concept is easily understood by anyone who grasps the necessary principle that everything is connected in layers of systems and sub-systems. The roots of the goodwill concept can be found in all of the world's religions—it is, in truth, part of the general concept of the circulation of life. In the sale of any business, goodwill is calculated as an intangible asset. Goodwill in practice is the unconditional and freely given "good" of one person to another. It is a practice found in all European, Middle Eastern, and Asian cultures.

Goodwill, reciprocity, and the simple practice of giving and receiving is a fundamental principle of business—it is all about circulation and exchange. It works best when all parties are well intended and assume that all other parties are well intended.

Exhibit 10.1

The $100 laptop is fast becoming a reality

BACK at the dawn of the personal-computer era, in the late 1970s, millions of future programmers around the world got their first taste of writing software by using an ingenious little computer that cost less than $100 (about $240 in today's money).

For the vast majority of individuals who could not afford the $2500 (more than $6000 today) that IBM and others were about to start charging for their revolutionary PCs, the diminutive Sinclair ZX80 and its ZX81 successor were inspirations. If you didn't mind soldering the motherboard together yourself, the laptop-sized computer could be had in kit form for around $70. Your correspondent built two, one of each model. For a while Clive Sinclair, the innovative genius behind the ZX80/81 and much else, was the patron saint of schoolboys of all ages everywhere.

Sir Clive's current equivalent is Nicholas Negroponte, co-founder of the Media Laboratory at the Massachusetts Institute of Technology and the father of one of the worthiest causes in contemporary computing. In the sweep of its ambition, Mr. Negroponte's pet project, One Laptop Per Child (OLPC), is remarkably similar to the thinking behind the original ZX80—giving inquisitive but economically deprived children the chance to feel the exhilaration of computer-based learning.

(Continued)

Exhibit 10.1   (Continued)

This week sees the realization of Mr. Negroponte's five-year dream. After field-testing in Nigeria and Brazil, the OLPC project's first model, a rugged little green laptop called the XO that can run on batteries, solar power, a miniature windmill, or hand- or foot-crank, goes into mass production. Schoolchildren in developing countries will start receiving the remarkable computer from October onwards.

The first batch is being supplied to some 30 of the world's poorest countries for $176 apiece. As production builds up at Quanta, the huge Taiwanese laptop-maker that is producing the machine for OLPC, Mr. Negroponte hopes to drive the unit cost down to $100.

After more than a quarter century of progress, Moore's Law (chipmakers double the power of their semiconductors every 18 months or so) would suggest that the modern equivalent of the Sinclair machine should be about 20 times smarter. In reality, the XO is more like 1000 times better. That's because innovations in information technology are not just cumulative; in closely coupled fields, they can have powerful multiplier effects. Also, some very smart people have refused to accept the conventional wisdom about how personal computers should be designed.

Overall, the XO tips the scale at around half the weight of a comparable laptop, gets over twice the usual running time when operating on battery power and costs less than half the normal price of an entry-level computer. One of the tricks has been to make many of the XO's components serve at least two purposes.

EPAWonder Toy

To save power, for instance, the XO's liquid-crystal display (the biggest consumer of juice in a laptop) can be flipped from backlit color to self-reflecting monochrome. That not only saves electricity, but helps the screen to be seen better in bright sunlight, where many XOs are likely to be used.

The number crunching is done by an AMD Geode processor running at a modest 433 megahertz, compared with the 2–3 gigahertz of conventional laptops. This processor allows the XO to use less energy and therefore generate much less heat. Result: no power-consuming cooling fan.

Indeed, all rotating parts have been dispensed with—to make the XO rugged enough for the wild. Instead of a hard drive, for instance, the XO uses a one-gigabyte "flash" chip to store data even when the power is off. The keyboard has a waterproof rubber coating and the case is sealed to prevent dust from encroaching. A pair of wireless antennas swivel up from the screen's sides like rabbit ears, endowing the laptop with two to three times the normal Wi-Fi range. When folded down, the antennas not only lock the case and but also seal off its various ports.

Better still, the Wi-Fi circuitry makes every laptop not just a communications device, but also a router. In other words, each laptop is part of a wireless mesh that relays the broadband signal from laptop to laptop—so those out of direct range can still get a connection to the internet.

(Continued)

Exhibit 10.1   (Continued)

If the ingenuity of the XO's hardware is impressive, the machine's software is truly ground-breaking. Red Hat, the world's largest Linux distributor, has provided an extremely compact version of its Fedora operating system, called Sugar, that uses a mere 130 megabytes of the XO's flash memory. By comparison, Windows XP requires 1.65 gigabytes.

The XO comes with a word processor, PDF viewer, Firefox web browser, media player, drawing tools plus the usual set of utilities. But it is the way the Sugar operating system lets the user work that's so clever. Instead of the usual hierarchical view of a computer's applications and data, Sugar organizes everything around what has been used recently. Alternatively, it can group applications and files in terms of who is connected on the wireless mesh. As such, the mesh approach gives XO an array of collaborative tools that puts expensive business laptops to shame.

Clearly, trying to produce such an extraordinary product as a laptop that is kid-proof and capable of working in jungles, deserts or the bush, miles from the nearest grid connection, and all for the cheapest possible price, has concentrated minds remarkably. The XO offers a lesson for laptop-makers everywhere. In fact, quite a few have gone from ridiculing the OLPC project to trying to emulate or join it.

Most notable has been Intel. After first dismissing Mr. Negroponte's laptop as a toy, the chip making giant suddenly rushed out a spoiler design of its own for developing countries, fearing it was about to be left out of an emerging market. Called Classmate, Intel's $225 laptop has failed to impress. Last week Intel admitted defeat tacitly by asking to join the OLPC association.

Excerpted from and permission granted: A Computer in Every Pot, July 27, 2007, The Economist print edition.

Goodwill underlies the Geoleadership Model and provides an appropriately convenient organizing principle as we focus attention on the model as a whole and in practice. In Exhibit 10.1, we present the case of Mr. Negroponte and his vision and successful mission to bring the world of computing to children who otherwise may not have had the opportunity of such a learning experience. Mr. Negroponte is not out to "Americanize" children of other cultures, he is out to extend their possibilities, out of simple compassion and the notion that privilege does not belong to the only the rich. Mr. Negroponte's view is that much of learning occurs without, or beyond, teaching, through interaction with the world around us. He also beliefs learning should be egalitarian, should not be restricted and should be seamless.

Mr. Negroponte recognizes that learning, connecting with the world around and expressing ourselves are fundamental human needs. He also acknowledges that his project to put an inexpensive laptop in the hands of every child should be of interest to any global organization's shareholders. It makes good business sense, in keeping with the notion of reciprocity and circulation of resources, to enable young people to reach beyond their own boundaries. While it could be argued, that such a project to expose all children to the computer, and the Internet, is a mission to enculturation generations of new consumers, thus spreading capitalism globally. However, breeding consumerism is not the intention; learning, connecting, and enabling self-expression are the intentions. Many U.S. states and countries around the world have funded the project in their areas.

In Exhibit 10.2, we present the story of a community that has undertaken the mission of enhancing its intercultural competence and living the principle of reciprocity. The city of Louisville Kentucky, faced with a potentially crip-pling labor shortage and having observed the critical need of another, and foreign, community is demonstrating good will and nicely illustrates all of the principles of the Geoleadership Model. Led by Louisville's' Mayor and other citizens, the city is demonstrating how intercultural competence is developed.

Exhibit 10.2

Bourbon, Baseball Bats and Now the Bantu

LOUISVILLE, Ky.—In 2003, Mattie Cox read about the arrival here of Hussein Issack and other refugees from Somalia's long-persecuted Bantu minority. Mr. Issack came from a subsistence-farming family and had never set foot in a factory. Nonetheless, Ms. Cox's first thought was to put him to work at the trailer maker where she is a human-resources manager.

"He was a man with kids who was new here and needed work," she says. Four years later, Mr. Issack is still working at Kentucky Trailer, having learned on the job how to use industrial tools to make doors for Allied Van Lines Inc. and other moving companies. "Today, he's multiskilled," Ms. Cox says.

Louisville's past was built on racehorses, bourbon, and baseball bats, but the city is staking its future on Somali Bantu and other immigrants flocking here from across the globe. As neighbors like Nashville join a national wave of cities drafting ordinances designed to repel many foreigners, Louisville's business and political leadership is working aggressively to absorb immigrants.

In speeches, Louisville Mayor Jerry Abramson champions the city's immigrants, whom he calls "internationals." In each of the past four years, he has handed out "international awards" to individuals, companies, and organizations working to integrate and improve the lot of newcomers.

(Continued)

Exhibit 10.2   (Continued)

"Communities that embrace diversity are going to be the most successful," says the mayor, who has been at the city's helm for most of the past two decades and avoids distinguishing between legal and illegal immigrants.

The powerful mayor hasn't faced much opposition to his strategy, but at his monthly community forums, some city residents have questioned whether his policy might be robbing Americans of jobs.

Louisville hasn't actively recruited the immigrants: Many of them are refugees who were randomly assigned here. Others ended up in Louisville because they heard that the housing was affordable and jobs were abundant. But among the new arrivals are many foreigners who first settled elsewhere in the United States.

"It's not that the city has a 'Let's go and find immigrants' approach," says Randy Capps, a senior research associate at the independent Urban Institute in Washington, DC. "It hopes that by being a welcoming place, more immigrants will want to settle there."

There's a practical reason for the city's openness: Like many other U.S. cities, Louisville faces an aging population and falling birth rates that are shrinking its work force. United Parcel Service Inc., General Electric Co. and other major companies with operations in Louisville say they need immigrants to keep thriving.

"It's an economic imperative to attract immigrants at all levels, from factory workers to software engineers," says Omar Ayyash, a Palestinian from Jordan who runs the city's Office of International Affairs.

Louisville isn't the only place eager to attract immigrants. But these towns are swimming against the tide. After the recent failure of the federal government to enact immigration reform, states and towns across the country have begun drafting their own laws to tackle illegal immigration. "Many states and local governments are getting back into the immigrant-bashing mode," says Mr. Capps, the immigration researcher.

Mayor Abramson figures that immigrants are more likely to contribute to the community if they're integrated into it. "You can engage these folks or you can wait to deal with the liabilities," he says. "What I am trying to do aggressively is ensure they become assets."

Louisville's approach has changed the composition of a 700,000-person city, which was once mainly white and African American. From 1990 to 2004, the city's foreign-born population jumped 388%—far above the 73% increase in the national average—as it absorbed thousands of Asians, Eastern Europeans, Africans fleeing persecution and Latin Americans in search of opportunity. Some 80 languages are spoken in its schools, and one apartment complex—"Americana"—houses families from 42 countries.

All of the immigrant groups pose challenges and perhaps none more than the Somali Bantu. While the overwhelming majority of Bantu men have jobs, their large families, illiteracy and limited skills can make self-sufficiency an elusive goal.

Historically, the Bantu in Somalia have been treated as second-class citizens by the country's lighter-skinned dominant clan. When civil war erupted

(Continued)

Exhibit 10.2   (Continued)

in 1991, thousands of Bantu were enslaved, tortured and murdered. The lucky ones managed to flee to the relative safety of refugee camps in Kenya. The U.S. agreed to resettle about 13,500 Bantu, and starting in 2003, the refugees were scattered across the country, from upstate New York and Florida to Idaho and Oregon.

The first couple hundred Bantu arrived in Louisville in 2003 and 2004. But since then, the city has attracted hundreds more of the preliterate Muslim minority who were originally assigned to other U.S. cities. "People are nice, the rent is cheap and you don't need English to get a job," says Nahiyo Osman, a Bantu woman whose family moved to Louisville from Chicago six months ago.

"The Bantu have plenty of life skills. But they have to learn from scratch basic things that we take for granted," says Katie Carman, director of Arcadia Community Center, which is attached to a large apartment complex and offers Bantu children an array of free services.

A hive of Bantu-related activity, Arcadia relies on grants and volunteers to operate. In 2006, it got a $25,000 grant from the Louisville Community Foundation, a local non-profit, to fund Bantu cultural classes, after-school programs and a summer camp. In May, employees from GE, which makes appliances here, renovated the center with a $5000 grant from the company.

Charnley Conway, a vice president of human resources at UPS, which plans to add 5000 jobs at its Louisville hub over the next three years, says investing in immigrants like the Bantu is vital. He adds that UPS has enlisted mentors to work alongside Bantu and other foreign employees struggling with English. The company funds English-language programs and the work of resettlement agencies, such as Catholic Charities, which help new immigrants.

Hussein Issack and his family—two children at the time, but now four—were among the first Bantu families to land in Louisville. Kentucky Trailer, which hired him, had already developed expertise in immigrant labor. The closely held firm had turned around its business by hiring Bosnians and Latin Americans in the late 1990s and translating its instruction and safety manuals into their languages.

The Somali Bantu, who speak Maay Maay, have no written language. So Mr. Issack learned through observation how to drive screws and rivets, use an electric saw and mount doors on trucks.

Despite everyone's efforts, the immigrant population is sometimes a financial burden on the city. A year ago, Mr. Issack moved into public housing because he couldn't afford a bigger apartment after his fourth child was born.

But Tim Barry, the director of the Louisville Metro Housing Authority, says he isn't concerned. "This is the sacrificial generation," says Mr. Barry, who is convinced the next Bantu generation will be better off.

Excerpted from and permission granted: Louisville, Ky., Welcomes Immigrants to Bolster Its Shrinking Work Force, September 18, 2007.

Our second question to be addressed in this final chapter has to do with the future of global leadership and intercultural leadership research. We propose that there are several interesting areas to explore. Recommendations include exploring how cultural immersion and the *American Way* of conducting business can effectively coexist. In addition, a study highlighting how leaders understand the concept of caring for their global employees would further global leadership topics. Another proposed research study could include one that examines the concept of leadership (to lead) in other cultures and would prove valuable in determining situational leadership strategies on a select per country basis. Determining intercultural leadership competencies remains a situational and diverse endeavor.

In regards to diversity, many U.S. companies have designated training programs to teach employees and leaders about working with diverse colleagues in a company. Appendix C contains a recommended leadership training tool, *The Power of Leadership*. While diversity initiatives are to be applauded, they inherently begin a discussion on a negative note. I would propose that the opposite type of training begin to take place in order to build cultural synergy. This idea of *cultural similarity training* deals with what similarities have in common and starts interactions on a positive tone. To liken it to a colloquial idea, it is akin to dating. People want to know what they have in common with one another so that they can then build relationships from there based on like foundations.

When individuals realize that there are certain things everyone has in common, particularly not having any control over where, when or into which culture someone is born, then a dialogue can become more relevant. Companies who then deal internally and internally with diverse constituencies can start focusing on what values are similar and then leverage this information to bridge the differences. Cultural synergy is created when leaders realize that a particular mindset must be adapted to deal globally, however many inherent similarities exist among individuals which can serve to make cultural adaptation easier. In addition, according to the book *World on Fire* by Amy Chua, ethnic minorities are the market dominant majorities in many countries of the world. Leaders who step back and realize the cultural values and norms of such cultures and subcultures can then initiate effective strategies to take advantage of more global opportunities. This book by Chua also is highly recommended, as it is the first book of its kind that links culture to economics…it is a stupendous resource!

For me, the possibility of actualizing human potential so that leadership can be culturally relevant is the paramount issue for U.S. business leaders in this millennium. If I were to develop an action plan for U.S. leaders operating within the global arena moving forward, I would stress the following in Figure 10.1.

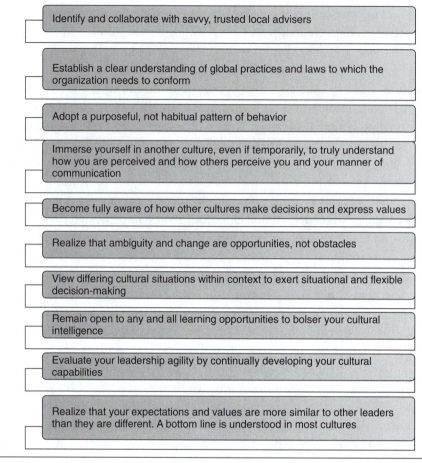

Identify and collaborate with savvy, trusted local advisers

Establish a clear understanding of global practices and laws to which the organization needs to conform

Adopt a purposeful, not habitual pattern of behavior

Immerse yourself in another culture, even if temporarily, to truly understand how you are perceived and how others perceive you and your manner of communication

Become fully aware of how other cultures make decisions and express values

Realize that ambiguity and change are opportunities, not obstacles

View differing cultural situations within context to exert situational and flexible decision-making

Remain open to any and all learning opportunities to bolser your cultural intelligence

Evaluate your leadership agility by continually developing your cultural capabilities

Realize that your expectations and values are more similar to other leaders than they are different. A bottom line is understood in most cultures

Figure 10.1 Action Plan for U.S. Leaders Operating in Global Business

Appendix A
The Research Behind the Geoleadership Model

The term "global leadership" has been variously defined as meaning the ability to work together effectively with other people anywhere in the world.[214] Although we have presented an argument that no individual can be fluent in the language, customs, laws, and ways of all cultures, we do believe that leaders who work within globalized organizations can become interculturally perceptive in multiple cultural contexts. We have also argued that there is no one best way of preparing leaders for intercultural work contexts; however, from our empirical research and experience in the field, we created a model that encompasses our best collective knowledge to date about what the important considerations are for such contexts. Through the preceding chapters, we presented what we call the Geoleadership Model consisting of seven dimensions found to be most important for leaders who work within intercultural contexts. The Geoleadership Model is the essential product of a yearlong study conducted with the participation of intercultural experts from around the world. In other words, this book reflects the collective effort of many people. In Chapter 10, we provide a detailed summation of the research study, which undergirds the Geoleadership Model. It is our hope that the information presented in the preceding chapters will assist leaders in developing intercultural leadership competencies.

Research Design

The purpose of the research study was to determine intercultural leadership competencies vital to U.S. business leaders. In the study, we gathered the authoritative feedback concerning needed intercultural competencies of U.S. business leaders from a diverse group of participating intercultural experts. Our approach was to maximize certain characteristics of both qualitative and quantitative methods, yet we required more than most common mixed method approaches afford. A qualitative research methodology, specifically a Delphi methodology using three sequential rounds of data gathering, provided the means to access, explore, capture, and analyze what ideas and approaches currently existed and/or potentially could be employed to assess intercultural competence in U.S. business, as well as the specific nature of intercultural competence. A Delphi study served as the means to gather expert opinions on cultural and social phenomena.[215]

Dalkey and Helmer pioneered the Delphi method at the RAND Corporation in the 1950s. The method is qualitative, exploratory, and utilized where high complexity and uniqueness prevent quantitative methods from being used.[216] Delphi methodology involves a series of focused and structured questionnaires that seek to reach agreement from a group of participating experts. The utility of Delphi methodology aided our efforts to explore and gather data from qualified participants over a global area because the method has been established previously as not requiring participating experts to interact in face-to-face communications.

The Delphi methodology also is a communication structure geared toward producing detailed critical examinations and discussions, rather than a simple compromise.[217] In addition to reaching group agreement, Delbecq, Van de Ven, and Gustafson found that the Delphi technique facilitates additional objectives.[218] Another of our objectives was to determine or develop a range of possible solution alternatives. A third objective was to explore and expose underlying assumptions or information leading to different judgments. A standard Delphi research study generally consists of three progressive rounds of data gathering.

Pilot Study

Before conducting the actual data gathering rounds with the selected panel of experts, we conducted the first round of the pilot study using the same Internet-based survey delivery service intended for use in the research. An advantage of conducting a pilot study is that it might give advance warning about where the main research project could fail, where research protocols may not exist, or whether proposed methods or instruments are inappropriate or too complicated. To avoid bias, the researcher utilized different pilot participants than actual study participants.

Participants enrolled in the pilot study via electronic mail invitations. Seven intercultural experts responded to the eight-item open-ended questionnaire. The questions posed were:

1. How can U.S. business leaders recognize the concept of culture?
2. How can U.S. business leaders utilize the concept of culture in understanding their own cultural background and bias?

3. How can U.S. business leaders analyze and evaluate intercultural situations?
4. How can U.S. business leaders negotiate and make decisions within intercultural situations?
5. How can U.S. business leaders communicate in intercultural situations?
6. How can U.S. business leaders motivate and lead in intercultural situations?
7. How can U.S. business leaders develop intercultural teams?
8. What intercultural competencies can U.S. business leaders learn to compete globally?

In addition to the theoretically based set of questions, the pilot participants commented on the delivery medium and question content and clarity. The feedback received from the first round of the pilot indicated themes and patterns, and although it was a small group, the answers provided sufficient data to formulate the questions for the second pilot round.

The second round utilized the same question set as Pilot Round 1; however, we then formulated a questionnaire using a five-point Likert-type scale and the analyzed data from Pilot Round 1. We asked the pilot participants to rate items for each question. The results of the second pilot yielded data related to the degree to which participants agreed or disagreed with factors associated with the posed question.

We analyzed data from the second pilot round and calculated the means and standard deviations for each item. We retained items that received a mean of 2.5 for the final pilot round and then eliminated data that did not for the third pilot round. Additionally, due to participant feedback, we made certain modifications in wording for clarity.

In the final pilot round, we asked participants to accept or reject each item for each question. The objective of this action was to discover areas of convergence and divergence.

Since the goal of our pilot study was to ensure that the data-gathering instrument or protocol was viable, it was important to test the delivery mechanism as well as to ensure that the questions were as free of bias as possible. Although the pilot study was small, it did allow for the rewording of some questions for more clarity in later rounds.

Rounds of the Actual Study

The first round took place to select and enroll the participating experts in the study. These participating experts received an invitation to participate based on their contributions in the intercultural leadership arena and their publication of relevant research in peer-reviewed and refereed journals. These participating experts also had worked in the field of global leadership for at least 10 years. We selected participants based on their publication history, education, and work experience.

Only those experts selected to participate and who agreed to participate took part in the study. Similar to the pilot study, the first round also involved sending out a structured questionnaire, already approved by the pilot participants, to the participating experts and asking for their opinion regarding future events. Participating experts received an invitation to speculate on the future of intercultural leadership. The participating experts returned the initial questionnaires, with the data consolidated into a summary document describing the participating experts' feedback.

The second round involved sending out a second questionnaire to the same participating experts and asking them to rank and comment on the priority issues that emerged from the initial feedback. The second questionnaire asked the participating experts to rank the probability and magnitude of effect of these issues. The participating experts then submitted their rankings to the second questionnaire with the rankings then measured using a Likert-type scale. Next, a document summarizing the rankings of the feedback statements emerged. This revised summary document went to the participating experts for the third round.

The third round involved a third questionnaire that focused on reranking feedback statements given the results from the second round. The participating experts reviewed their feedback from the second round and identified where they saw both convergence and divergence of opinion. A document emerged that compiled that highlighted the agreement, disagreement, and uncertainty. In a Delphi study, each subsequent questionnaire builds upon responses to the preceding questionnaire. The process normally stops after the specified three rounds when agreement occurs among the expert panel. Each panelist also had the opportunity to construct additional trends, events, and analysis for contribution to the study.

Research question

What intercultural leadership competencies are essential for U.S. business leaders to develop in the era of globalization?

Population

We selected our panelists based on whether they matched our established criteria and research intent. Each participant was a recognized and published expert in the intercultural leadership field and possessed a minimum of

10 years of experience in either university-level academics or the consulting industry. The participants did not fall under the federal guidelines for vulnerable subjects. They also had Internet access to participate since the rounds of data collection were delivered through a web-based platform. Lastly, the participants possessed written English fluency since the Delphi survey appeared in U.S. English.

Researchers have conducted Delphi studies with a range in the number of participants; however, the median group size is 15–20 participants. For our study, we determined that a sufficient number of participants would be between 20 and 50 participants since an international expert group was gathered from Africa, the Americas, Africa, Europe, and the Middle East. Although we contacted 50 potential participants, the eventual number of 26 experts took part in all three rounds of the study. We considered that adhering to a rigid group size was less of a determinant in conducting the study than participant expertise and response rate. Our sample proved to be large enough, yet not so overwhelming as to not allow us to perceive patterns in responses.

We conducted our study during the spring of 2005 over a period of eight weeks. This period included the initial contact of participating experts to the final feedback analysis. The survey utilized purposive sampling since the selected participants were representative of the intercultural studies field. Purposive sampling was non-probable in nature. The study participants received initial contact through personal networking and industry association memberships.

Geographic Location

The selected participants resided or worked in various countries, including nations in Africa, the Americas, Africa, Europe, and the Middle East. All participating experts accessed the survey electronically, which allowed individuals from geographically disperse locations to participate and interact without any required face-to-face communication. The Delphi method allowed for improved communications across geographies in an inexpensive and effective manner. The Internet served as the mechanism for this global interaction.

Instrumentation

We developed a questionnaire delivered through an Internet platform. The questionnaire posed questions based on our central research questions regarding the intercultural leadership competencies necessary for U.S. business leaders and inquired how these leaders could develop such skills. These questions remained open-ended for full and free comment by the Delphi participating experts. NVivo software (QSR International, 2005) provided further analytical analysis of the data results.

Each Delphi expert had Internet capability to access the questionnaires online. Each individual received a separate electronic mail invitation and feedback to protect anonymity. Participating experts received notification that the study data gathered remained confidential. Participants had a specific period in which to respond to each questionnaire in order. An advantage of the Delphi process included the logical progression of participating experts focusing on a selected topic, providing answers, and then viewing descriptive statistics from the group. This process in the Delphi study spanned three rounds after the pilot study was complete.

The first round consisted of exploration of the subject under discussion through open-ended questions. The questions generated data that received coding and categorization. The participants then received this edited data. The second round provided an opportunity to understand how the group viewed the initial issues. The participants provided data through closed-end questions in the second round, usually through a Likert-type scale via the website. The first round repeated the process to gather specific feedback on individual responses and rankings from Round 2.

Validity and Reliability

Researchers in several fields previously utilized the Delphi method to identify a variety of competencies such as computer competencies,[219] competencies for distance education professionals,[220] and international business skills[221]. The Delphi method focuses on how a researcher chose participants to provide their opinions and beliefs regarding a specific set of questions. In our study, data collection included rounds of questionnaires, compilations of data, tests of validity, and reports of participant feedback between successive rounds.

The development of methodologies and their subsequent legitimization in qualitative methods have resulted in a better-formed research practice. We relied on three categories to determine the effectiveness of our qualitative methodology: a focus on understanding the nature of a lived experience, cultural or social phenomena, and a language communication. The validity of qualitative methodologies such as Delphi is now well established. Our Delphi study consisted of quantifiable data as well as qualitative data collection and was valid in studying the phenomenon of intercultural leadership competencies.

The Delphi method utilizes the iterative process to produce a stronger result based on anonymous feedback. Typically, controlled statistical and aggregate commentary feedback to the participants and the results are statistical group responses. The stability of participants is critical in the value of the data collected and the ability to establish a summative knowledge base.

The effectiveness of the Delphi methodology lay in its manner to ensure anonymity, collect, and report accurate data, and allow for a flow of communication between participating experts to solve a particular problem. The reliability of the Delphi technique is unique when compared to experiments with traditional group discussions and other interactive activities to obtain knowledge from a group of individuals. In addition, a theoretical assumption by researchers remained that informed group judgments, achieved through controlled methodologies such as the Delphi method, are more reliable than individual judgments. Objectivity and truthfulness remained critical to the qualitative research method and particularly to the Delphi technique. Trustworthiness and verification signified the Delphi method more than the traditional validity and reliability methods. Our research project utilized the Delphi process within the confines of a descriptive research study.

Data Collection

Data collection involves boundary setting and collecting information from varied processes. The boundaries we set in our Delphi study through the questions and manner of data collection allowed feedback and controlled interaction among participating experts regarding the intercultural competencies necessary for U.S. business leaders. Through repeated interrogations, solicitations for feedback began with the first round of a set of open-ended questions. The second and third rounds focused on closed-ended questions derived from the data collected and analyzed from the previous rounds.

Data Analysis

Our data analysis was an ongoing activity of obtaining and organizing emerging themes from the data collection process through the three sequential rounds of questioning. Using inductive analysis, repeated Delphi data emerged allowing us to discover developing themes and patterns. We analyzed collective and individual data from each participant and across participants. We eliminated any response combined after its submission through the website report and duplicate responses from the first round's feedback.

A Likert-type scale of 1–5 made it possible to score the final list of specific second round rankings. A total score for each response ranking emerged from the statistical analysis we performed. The initial data report provided the responses and their occurrence percentage. Since the data may not have been continuous, the median emerged as a statistical indicator. We reserved only those responses receiving a median score of four or higher for the third round. NVivo software (QSR International, 2005) provided further analytical detail to this qualitative feedback.

Third-round rankings emerged in order of importance; numerically from 1 to n; n was equal to the total number or responses to that particular question. Round three data, analysis concentrated on the total score received for each response. The response to the original research question receiving the lowest score ranked as the most important intercultural competency of a U.S. business leader. The qualitative data lay in the descriptive statistics generated by this Delphi study. We employed descriptive statistics for demographic and frequency data.

We determined that consensus occurred when an interquartile range score of less than 1.2 existed. This process of analysis provided a rationale for strong similarities among the participants. A second component of analysis allowed us to evaluate the perceived importance of each item. To accomplish this, the five-point scale divided into different levels of importance or relevance. These items received categorization based on an analysis of feedback combined with importance. The five-point scale provided an equal interval between high, medium, and low importance of the items as scored by the participants.

Analysis, Results, and Findings

In this section, we present the data analysis approach used to evaluate the results and summarize the main themes discovered in our research. The themes were associated with the six areas of inquiry. The questions that guided this study included: (1) How can U.S. leaders utilize the concept of culture in understanding their own cultural background and bias? (2) How can U.S. business leaders can recognize the concept of culture? (3) How can U.S. business leaders can analyze and evaluate intercultural situations? (4) How can U.S. business leaders can negotiate and made decisions within intercultural situations? (5) How can U.S. business leaders can communicate in intercultural situations? (6) How can U.S. business leaders can motivate and lead in intercultural situations? and (7) How can U.S. business leaders can develop intercultural teams? These seven questions enabled the answer to the fundamental question of what intercultural competencies U.S. business leaders can learn and possess to compete in intercultural contexts of global economies.

In sum, in our study we utilized expert feedback using three sequential questionnaires to determine the intercultural leadership competencies deemed necessary for U.S. business leaders in the era of globalization. The Delphi approach served as a means to gather expert opinions on cultural and social phenomena. Through industry and professional networking, participants who fit the intent of the study emerged. Each participant was a recognized and published expert in the intercultural leadership field and possessed a minimum of 10 years of experience in either university-level academics or the consulting industry. These participants did not fall under the federal guidelines for vulnerable human subjects. The participants also had Internet access to participate in this Web-based Delphi study. In addition, the participants possessed written English fluency since the Delphi survey appeared in U.S. English.

To analyze the round one pilot data, we took the following steps to ensure proper rigor. First, from the database created containing all of the text from the panel participant's responses, segments of text that relate to single concepts received tagging. For example, in answering the question of "how U.S. business managers can become aware of the concept of culture," if a response repeated, creation of a new tag or "node" emerged. One such node was "training." Then, after this first procedure of categorization according to themes, the next phase was to reduce further the data by searching for cross themes. For example, under training, two categories emerged as "self-education" and the other was "formal training." This step led to creation of a hierarchy of categories.

The themes that emerged from the qualitative data provided content items for the question set prepared for the second round of data collection. Although the first round instrumentation presented open-ended questions to generate breadth and depth of input (divergence), the second round initiated the process of convergence.

The second round utilized the same question set as Pilot Round 1; however, a formula emerged of a fixed alternative questionnaire using a five-point Likert-type scale and the analyzed data from Pilot Round 1. Each pilot participant then rated items for each question. The results of the second pilot round yielded data related to the degree to which participants agreed or disagreed with factors associated with the posed question; factors that the panel members generated (see Table A.1).

We analyzed the data from the second pilot round and calculated means and standard deviation for each item. Items that received a mean of 2.5 were retained for the final pilot round; those that did not were eliminated for the third pilot round (see Table A.2). Additionally, we made some modifications in the wording of certain questions for clarity due to participant feedback. In the final pilot round, participants were asked to accept or reject each item for each question toward objective of discovering consensus.

Table A.1 Pilot Round 2 Question Data Tables

	Mean	Standard deviation
How can U.S. business leaders recognize the concept of culture?		
Through understanding its effect on profit and loss.	3.00	(0.82)
Through experiencing culture first-hand.	3.67	(0.82)
Through self-awareness and education.	4.33	(0.81)
Through seeing cultural differences in getting work done in organizations.	4.33	(0.81)
How can U.S. business leaders utilize this concept of culture in understanding their own cultural background and bias?		
Through the utilization of professional consultants, reading, viewing appropriate videos/films, and developing a heightened sense of self-awareness.	3.75	(0.81)
Through understanding what the concept of culture means. By defining culture, business leaders can understand their personal assumptions that may be completely different for people from outside the United States.	5.00	(1.63)
Through realizing that leaders are not interested in a concept of culture and do not care about understanding their own cultural background. They want to learn enough practical moves to avoid disasters and to propagate their own ideology.	2.00	(0.57)
Through seeing that leaders only understands one's culture better when it is reflected in the mirror of another culture.	4.50	(0)
How can U.S. business leaders analyze and evaluate intercultural situations?		
Through training that is pertinent to their perceived needs.	3.00	(0.81)
Through collecting information about their employees/partners/clients/etc. and understand their cultural background.	3.00	(0.57)
Through hiring someone who knows about these things and could listen to them. Mostly they will simply react to threats and conduct damage control.	3.00	(1.54)
Through being in the culture and by reading and studying and learning the language of the culture.	3.00	(0.57)

(Continued)

Table A.1 (Continued)

	Mean	Standard deviation
How can U.S. business leaders negotiate and make decisions within intercultural situations?		
Through utilizing cultural awareness and skill training.	3.00	(0.81)
Through realizing that leaders will function to the degree that they can conduct in their own language and in their own framework of what they believe a negotiation to be and what it should produce.	3.00	(0.57)
Through understanding the other culture and the ways contracts and issues are negotiated and the ways decisions are made	3.00	(1.54)
How can U.S. business leaders communicate in intercultural situations?		
Through realizing that no matter how different the cultures are, if communication is made in a respectful way bearing in mind that we are indeed different, negotiation can be successful.	5.00	(0)
Through realizing that largely from the CEO of the nation down to the corporate leaders, leaders do not and cannot communicate within intercultural situations. They are dependent on others to do this for them if they recognize a problem. Usually they do not communicate well enough to know that there is a problem. They see communication as selling, convincing and winning hearts and minds	2.25	(1.52)
Through communicating preferably in the language of the culture and by being aware of norms and mores associated with the host culture. For example, do not show the bottom of your shoe to another person when seated in Indonesia.	3.67	(0.57)
How can U.S. business leaders motivate and lead in intercultural situations?		
Through understanding that leading in an intercultural situation is more about knowing the differences of the participants than technical skills. Leaders can motivate others if leaders know what is important for a person and what makes that person to be willing to invest energy and time in a project.	3.50	(0.57)

(Continued)

Table A.1 (Continued)

	Mean	Standard deviation
Through seeking to understand the host culture. By behaving in ways that are acceptable in the other behavior as long as it does not break either the host country law or United States. For example you cannot use a bribe to motivate someone in order to get a contract.	4.25	(0.57)
How can U.S. business leaders develop intercultural teams?		
By staffing correctly and/or by the use of external professionals.	3.75	(0.57)
By giving people of a different background a chance to lead an intercultural team.	4.00	(0.57)
By sending leaders out of the country and make them answerable to someone not of their culture.	3.50	(1.73)
By ensuring that the modus operandi of the team is consistent with other cultural concepts or if the team is multicultural, then by putting into place a team philosophy that does not violate other cultural norms or values.	4.25	(.57)
What intercultural competencies can U.S. business leaders learn to compete globally?		
Knowledge of language	3.75	(0.57)
Knowledge of history	4.00	(0.57)
Knowledge of ethics	4.00	(0.57)
Patience	4.00	(0.57)
Ability to listen	4.00	(0.57)
Awareness of other culture's ability to solve problems	4.00	(0.57)
Host culture empathy	4.00	(0.57)
Negotiation skills	3.75	(0.57)
Debase the currency, exercise selective protectionism, make others see that their culture is best and enforce its adoption.	1.50	(1.53)

Note: Total respondents for each question are four.

Table A.2 Pilot 3 Results Tables

	Accept	Reject
How can U.S. business leaders recognize the concept of culture?		
Through self-awareness and education	100%	0%
Through seeing the cultural differences in behavior in getting work done in organization	100%	0%
How can U.S. business leaders utilize this concept of culture in understanding their own cultural background and bias?		
Through understanding what the concept of culture means and how to define it. By defining culture, business leaders can understand their personal assumptions that may be completely different for people from outside the United States.	75%	25%
How can U.S. business leaders analyze and evaluate intercultural situations?		
Through hiring someone who knows about these things and could listen to them. Mostly they will simply react to threats and conduct damage control.	50%	50%
How can U.S. business leaders negotiate and make decisions within intercultural situations?		
Through utilizing cultural awareness and skill training.	75%	25%
Through understanding the other culture and the ways contracts and issues are negotiated and the ways decisions are made.	100%	0%
How can U.S. business leaders communicate in intercultural situations?		
Through realizing that no matter how different the cultures are, if communication is made in a respectful way bearing in mind that we are indeed different, negotiation can be successful.	50%	50%
How can U.S. business leaders motivate and lead in intercultural situations?		
Through seeking to understand the host culture. By behaving in ways that are acceptable in the other behavior as long as it does not break either the host country law or United States. For example, you cannot use a bribe to motivate someone in order to get a contract.	75%	25%
How can U.S. business leaders develop intercultural teams?		
By giving people of a different background a chance to lead an intercultural team.	75%	25%

(Continued)

Table A.2 (Continued)

	Accept	Reject
By ensuring that the modus operandi of the team is consistent with other cultural concepts or if the team is multicultural, then by putting into place a team philosophy that does not violate other cultural norms or values.	100%	0%
What intercultural competencies can U.S. business leaders learn to compete globally?		
Knowledge of history	75%	25%
Knowledge of ethics	100%	0%
Patience	100%	0%
Ability to listen	100%	0%
Awareness of other culture's ability to solve problems	100%	0%
Host culture empathy.	100%	0%

Note: Number of respondents for each question was four.

Since the goal of a pilot study was to ensure that the data-gathering instrument or protocol was viable, it was important to test the delivery mechanism as well as to ensure that the questions were as free of bias as possible. Although the pilot group was small, it did yield interesting data considered important and incorporated in the administration of the actual Delphi Rounds with the expert panel.

Data Analysis and Results

This section presents answers to the above research and includes the results from data collection of the three-round Delphi study conducted over a four-week period from April to May 2005 to gain consensus among the intercultural experts.

Demographics of Delphi Study Participants

Questionnaires were sent to 40 intercultural experts who had been invited to participate in the study. Of those 40 experts, 37 participated in Round 1, a 95% response rate. Thirty-eight questionnaires were sent to those who participated in Round 1 and 31 (82%) responded for Round 2. Thirty-one questionnaires existed for Round 3, and 26 responded, for an 87% response rate (Table A.3).

Table A.3 Age of Round 1 Panel Participants

Age	Number of respondents
20–30	1
31–40	3
41–50	15
51–60	11
61–70	7

Of the experts who participated in the Delphi rounds, 62% were male and 48% were female, and all but one held advanced degrees. Twenty participants identified themselves as being from the United States, eight identified themselves as being from a European country, three identified as being from India, one reported being from China, one from Taiwan, one from Australia, and two identified themselves as being from countries on the African continent.

Questionnaire Data

The purpose of the questionnaire was to determine what competencies U.S. business leaders need to possess in order to compete in a global marketplace.

Rounds of the Delphi Study

Round 1 of the Delphi Study began by posing 13 open-ended questions to the participating intercultural experts:

1. How can U.S. business leaders become aware of culture as a factor in conducting their business?
2. Can you give an example of a business leader from any country that is truly conscious of the reality of culture? What did this leader do and what was the result?
3. How can U.S. business leaders utilize this concept of culture in understanding their own cultural background and bias?
4. What school of thought, paradigms, and tools can U.S. business leaders use to analyze and evaluate intercultural situations?
5. Can you give an example of how a U.S. business leader analyzed and evaluated an intercultural situation?
6. What school of thought, paradigms, and tools can U.S. business leaders use to negotiate and make decisions within intercultural situations?

7. Can you give an example of a U.S. business leader who negotiated successfully within an intercultural situation?
8. How can U.S. business leaders motivate and lead in intercultural situations?
9. Can you give an example of a leader in any country that motivated others and led successfully in an intercultural situation?
10. How can U.S. business leaders develop intercultural teams?
11. Can you give an example of a leader in any country that was successful in developing intercultural teams?
12. Please list and describe the three most important competencies that U.S. business leaders need to deal within intercultural situations.
13. Can you give an example of a leader in any country that was successful in learning and implementing these competencies globally?

Round 1 of the Delphi Study

Thirty pages of raw data emerged from the first round. We extracted data from the electronic delivery system, exported it to spreadsheets, then coded, and categorized using qualitative software according to the same procedure as the pilot round one. Next, text data from the panel participant's responses were tagged and nodes were created once a single idea was repeated. This step concluded once data saturation was reached, in other words, once there were no new themes.

In the coding and categorization process, common themes emerged through recurring terms, phrases, and words. From this analysis, we developed and prepared a seven-item questionnaire for delivery through the Internet.

Round 2 of the Delphi Study

In Round 2 of this study, participants rated all items on the Round 2 instrument, which was a reflection of the data collected in Round 1 and contained many of the recurrent words and phrases from the raw data. The Round 2 instrument consisted of seven items involving definitions and statements about intercultural competence, specific components of intercultural competence, assessment methods, and other issues raised by the participants about assessing intercultural competence. The rating process for the items in Round 2 used a Likert-type scale of 1–5 as follows: 1 = Most relevant/important, 2 = Relevant/important, 3 = Neutral, 4 = Somewhat relevant/important, 5 = Least relevant/important to intercultural leadership competence.

Participants had the opportunity to add items under each question, but formal modifications were not allowed. Ten participants added items under questions and several other participants made general comments; however, the nature of the comments was in support of the respondents' question response, rather than additional information. Appendix D contains the qualitative data from the 27 participants in Round 2. Data collection occurred through the Internet delivery system. Downloadable data assisted in creating reports and importing them into spreadsheets. The next step included determining the standard deviations (Tables A.4–A.12).

Five of the items from Round 2 had a mean of 2.5 or above or a standard deviation of 2.0 or below, which indicated items for which there was a lack of consensus. The participants judged the latter items and eliminated them from further consideration. Of the items eliminated, four had a mean above 2.5 and 1 had a standard deviation below 2.0. A list of the five eliminated items can be found in Table A.13.

Round 3 of the Delphi Study

Round 3, the final round of this Delphi study, consisted of a fixed-alternative instrument containing nine questions with 34 items from Round 2 that had received a mean score above the threshold. Given some of the comments from participants in Round 2, for example, slight modifications

Table A.4 Relative to How U.S. Leaders Can Become Aware of Culture as a Factor in Conducting Business, Rate Each of the Following for Its Importance

	1	2	3	4	5	Mean	Standard deviation
Formal training/education (Higher education and training programs)	19% (5)	37% (10)	19% (5)	22% (6)	4% (1)	2.56	(3.02)
Self-education (Reading, observation, research, language tapes, interviewing people)	26% (7)	41% (11)	26% (7)	0% (0)	7% (2)	2.22	(4.39)
Cultural immersion (Living in the culture)	59% (16)	22% (6)	15% (4)	4% (1)	0% (0)	1.63	(6.38)
Coach/consultant/mentor (Using the services of a person from other culture, or who has worked within another culture for some time)	41% (11)	48% (13)	7% (2)	4% (1)	0% (0)	1.74	(6.10)

Table A.5 Relative to How U.S. Business Leaders Can Utilize the Concept of Culture in Understanding Their Own Cultural Background and Bias, Rate the Following in Terms of Importance

	1	2	3	4	5	Mean	Standard deviation
Recognition (Awareness of own culture, perspectives, differences between cultures)	48% (13)	33% (9)	11% (3)	0% (0)	7% (2)	1.85	(5.41)
Engagement (Meaningfully interacting with other cultures)	59% (16)	30% (8)	7% (2)	0% (0)	4% (1)	1.59	(6.69)
Intentionality (Purposefully seeking to broaden perspective and knowledge)	67% (18)	22% (6)	7% (2)	0% (0)	4% (1)	1.52	(4.93)

Table A.6 Relative to Which Schools of Thought, Paradigms, and Tools* U.S. Business Leaders Can Use to Analyze and Evaluate Intercultural Situations, Rate the Following in Terms of Importance

	1	2	3	4	5	Mean	Standard deviation
The use of Intercultural assessments and inventories	22% (6)	48% (13)	22% (6)	4% (1)	4% (1)	2.19	(5.44)
The use of Intercultural Models	15% (4)	52% (14)	19% (5)	11% (3)	4% (1)	2.37	(5.03)
Adopting a "global–local" perspective	22% (6)	26% (7)	33% (9)	15% (4)	4% (1)	2.52	(3.05)
Using general communication and interpersonal relations models	19% (5)	30% (8)	33% (9)	4% (1)	15% (4)	2.67	(4.04)

*Paradigm refers to an example serving as a model; School of thought refers to a belief system; Tool refers to a product utilized to understand a certain concept.

emerged, specifically adding definitions. The modifications appear in Table A.14. Participants ranked each item in an effort to achieve full consensus on specific items. Only one open-ended question was included, which appeared at the end of the questionnaire.

We sent an electronic mail invitation to participate in the survey to all of our potential intercultural experts. Then, we sent participants the Round 3 instrument, which included the mean and standard deviation from each

Table A.7 Relative to Which Schools of Thought, Paradigms, and Tools U.S. Business Leaders Can Use to Negotiate and Make Decisions within Intercultural Situations, Rate the Following in Terms of Importance

	1	2	3	4	Mean	Standard deviation
Values-based perspective	52% (14)	26% (7)	19% (5)	4% (1)	1.74	(5.44)
Ethics-based perspective	30% (8)	19% (5)	30% (8)	22% (6)	2.44	(1.50)
Context-based perspective	59% (16)	26% (7)	11% (3)	4% (1)	1.59	(6.65)
Ambiguity tolerance	44% (12)	33% (9)	11% (3)	11% (3)	1.89	(4.50)

Table A.8 Relative to How U.S. Business Leaders Can Motivate and Lead in Intercultural Situations, Rate the Following in Terms of Importance

	1	2	3	4	5	Mean	Standard deviation
Engaging the culture and its people	52% (14)	33% (9)	7% (2)	4% (1)	4% (1)	1.74	(5.86)
"Self-other" awareness and appreciation	37% (10)	41% (11)	19% (5)	0% (0)	4% (1)	1.93	(5.03)
Global perspective	26% (7)	30% (8)	22% (6)	7% (2)	15% (4)	2.56	(2.40)
Build Intercultural understanding/sensitivity/ communication/effectiveness	56% (15)	33% (9)	7% (2)	0% (0)	4% (1)	1.63	(6.43)
Culture is integrated and part of business practices (Feedback/rewards/goal-setting)	41% (11)	48% (13)	7% (2)	4% (1)	0% (0)	1.74	(6.11)

item so that they could view the group's position on each item. Twenty-six of the 31 experts returned the completed instruments.

We performed analyses of the questionnaire data two ways. In the first method of analysis, we used relative ranking of the number of items accepted by the group, and the second method involved calculating standard deviation. Both methods assisted in determining the items for which the respondents reached consensus. In Delphi studies, an arbitrary consensus point is determined.

For the purposes of Round 3, a relative ranking process occurred to gain consensus for priority competencies. The average of the importance

Table A.9 Relative to How U.S. Business Leaders Can Develop Intercultural Teams, Rate Each of the Following for Its Importance

	1	2	3	4	5	Mean	Standard deviation
Shared or joint leadership	22% (6)	44% (12)	19% (5)	4% (1)	11% (3)	2.37	(4.16)
Cultural preparation prior to assignment	48% (13)	33% (9)	11% (3)	4% (1)	4% (1)	1.81	(5.36)
Select people with cultural understanding to staff the team	48% (13)	37% (10)	11% (3)	0% (0)	4% (1)	1.74	(5.77)
Use processes, systems, and business models that are appropriate to the culture	30% (8)	48% (13)	11% (3)	4% (1)	7% (2)	2.11	(5.02)

Table A.10 Relative to the Most Important Competencies That U.S. Business Leaders Need to Possess to Work within Intercultural Situations, Rate Each of the Following in Terms of Its Importance

	1	2	3	4	5	Mean	Standard deviation
Self-awareness (including knowing one's own biases)	74% (20)	19% (5)	4% (1)	0% (0)	4% (1)	1.41	(8.38)
Curiosity, learning	56% (15)	41% (11)	0% (0)	0% (0)	4% (1)	1.56	(7.09)
Flexibility & adaptability	81% (22)	15% (4)	0% (0)	0% (0)	4% (1)	1.30	(9.42)
Imagination/creativity	26% (7)	59% (16)	11% (3)	0% (0)	4% (1)	1.96	(6.50)
Tolerate ambiguity	44% (12)	44% (12)	7% (2)	0% (0)	4% (1)	1.74	(6.06)
Patience	63% (17)	22% (6)	11% (3)	0% (0)	4% (1)	1.59	(6.87)
Mindfulness	44% (12)	33% (9)	15% (4)	4% (1)	4% (1)	1.89	(4.93)

levels assigned by group participants to each category appeared, and we calculated the standard deviation. If the deviation of the individual preference values for a particular feature was small, effectively the group reached a consensus. If the deviation for a feature was large, effectively there was variability within the group. Relative ranking occurs extensively in the nominal group technique and Delphi processes to reach consensus (Tables A.15–A.23).

Table A.11 Relative to the Most Important Competencies That U.S. Business Leaders Need to Possess to Work within Intercultural Situations, Rate Each of the Following in Terms of Its Importance (Interpersonal Dimension)

	1	2	3	4	5	Mean	Standard deviation
Perspective taking	33% (9)	26% (7)	22% (6)	19% (5)	0% (0)	2.26	(3.36)
Nonjudgmental	15% (4)	44% (12)	26% (7)	15% (4)	0% (0)	2.41	(4.45)
Empathy/compassion	19% (5)	15% (4)	44% (12)	15% (4)	7% (2)	2.78	(3.85)
Bridging/synthesizing	30% (8)	15% (4)	7% (2)	48% (13)	0% (0)	2.74	(5.17)

Table A.12 Round 2, Question 9: Relative to the Most Important Competencies That U.S. Business Leaders Need to Possess to Work within Intercultural Situations, Rate Each of the Following in Terms of Its Importance (Cultural Dimension)

	1	2	3	4	5	Mean	Standard deviation
Sensitivity/appreciative of difference	67% (18)	26% (7)	4% (1)	0% (0)	4% (1)	1.48	(7.57)
Effective communication	70% (19)	15% (4)	7% (2)	4% (1)	4% (1)	1.56	(7.70)
Multilingual	26% (7)	37% (10)	37% (10)	0% (0)	0% (0)	2.11	(5.08)
Local–global perspective	22% (6)	33% (9)	19% (5)	22% (6)	4% (1)	2.52	(2.88)
Understanding of how leadership is conceptualized in other cultures	52% (14)	33% (9)	7% (2)	7% (2)	0% (0)	1.70	(5.90)

Summary of Findings

Twenty-six (of 27) panelists participated in Round 3 of the study by completing the 18-item questionnaire through Internet delivery. All 26 panelists completed the fixed-alternative questionnaire portion, and 15 completed the open-ended feedback question at the end. Eleven women and 15 men completed the final round questionnaire. Sixteen identified themselves as U.S. born, 10 identified themselves as non-U.S. born (two from the United

Table A.13 Five Eliminated Items from Round 2

Adopting a "global–local" perspective	2.50	3.05
Using general communication and interpersonal relations models	2.67	4.04
Ethics-based perspective	2.44	1.50
Empathy/compassion	2.78	3.85
Bridging/synthesizing	2.74	5.17

Table A.14 Items Modified for Round 3 of the Delphi Study

Round 2 item	Modifications or additions
Effective communication	"Ability to understand another's ideas and having the other person understand your own"
Local–global perspective	"Ability to attend to both global and local consequences of one's own actions"

Table A.15 Relative to How U.S. Leaders Can Become Aware of Culture as a Factor in Conducting Business, Please Rank Each of the Items in Order of Importance

	1	2	3	4	Relative ranking	Standard deviation
Formal training/education (Higher education, academic courses, training programs)	15% (4)	12% (3)	27% (7)	46% (12)	3.04	(3.06)
Self-education (Reading, observation, research, language tapes, interviewing people)	0% (0)	12% (3)	42% (11)	46% (12)	3.35	(4.89)
Cultural immersion (Learning the language, customs, living in the culture)	65% (17)	15% (4)	15% (4)	4% (1)	1.58	(5.69)
Coach/consultant/mentor (Using the services of a person from other culture, or who has worked within another culture for some time)	19% (5)	62% (16)	15% (4)	4% (1)	2.04	(5.16)

Kingdom, two from France, two from India, one from Germany, one from Senegal, one from the Netherlands, and one from South Africa). All 26 identified their current professional activities as including aspects of intercultural specialization.

Table A.16 Relative to How U.S. Business Leaders Can Utilize the Concept of Culture in Understanding Their Own Cultural Background and Bias, Please Rank Each of the Items in Order of Importance

	1	2	3	Relative ranking	Standard deviation
Recognition (Awareness of own culture, perspectives, differences between cultures)	31% (8)	23% (6)	46% (12)	2.15	(3.63)
Engagement (Meaningfully interacting with other cultures)	42% (11)	46% (12)	12% (3)	1.69	(4.75)
Intentionality (Purposefully seeking to broaden perspective and knowledge)	27% (7)	31% (8)	42% (11)	2.15	(3.26)

Table A.17 Relative to Which Schools of Thought, Paradigms, and Tools U.S. Business Leaders Can Use to Analyze and Evaluate Intercultural Situations, Please Rank Each of the Items in Order of Importance

	1	2	Relative ranking	Standard deviation
The use of intercultural assessments and inventories	50% (13)	50% (13)	1.50	(6.17)
The use of intercultural models	50% (13)	50% (13)	1.50	(6.12)

Table A.18 Relative to Which Schools of Thought, Paradigms, and Tools U.S. Business Leaders Can Use to Negotiate and Make Decisions within Intercultural Situations, Please Rank Each of the Items in Order of Importance

	1	2	3	Relative ranking	Standard deviation
Values-based perspective	23% (6)	42% (11)	35% (9)	2.12	(3.23)
Context-based perspective	42% (11)	42% (11)	15% (4)	1.73	(4.75)
Ambiguity tolerance	35% (9)	15% (4)	50% (13)	2.15	(4.38)

Table A.19 Relative to How U.S. Business Leaders Can Motivate and Lead in Intercultural Situations, Please Rank Each of the Items in Order of Importance

	1	2	3	4	5	Relative ranking	Standard deviation
Engaging the culture and its people	35% (9)	8% (2)	19% (5)	23% (6)	15% (4)	2.77	(1.88)
"Self-other" awareness & appreciation	15% (4)	12% (3)	31% (8)	31% (8)	12% (3)	3.12	(2.42)
Global perspective	4% (1)	19% (5)	8% (2)	15% (4)	54% (14)	3.96	(4.41)
Build intercultural understanding/ sensitivity/ communication effectiveness	27% (7)	38% (10)	23% (6)	8% (2)	4% (1)	2.23	(2.97)
Culture is integrated and part of business practices (Feedback/ rewards/goal-setting)	19% (5)	23% (6)	19% (5)	23% (6)	15% (4)	2.92	(1.09)

Table A.20 Relative to How U.S. Business Leaders Can Develop Intercultural Teams, Please Rank Each of the Items in Order of Importance

	1	2	3	4	Relative ranking	Standard deviation
Shared or joint leadership	15% (4)	8% (2)	31% (8)	46% (12)	3.08	(3.44)
Cultural preparation prior to assignment	31% (8)	15% (4)	35% (9)	19% (5)	2.42	(2.66)
Select people with cultural understanding to staff the team	31% (8)	58% (15)	12% (3)	0% (0)	1.81	(5.91)
Use processes, systems, and business models that are appropriate to the culture	23% (6)	19% (5)	23% (6)	35% (9)	2.69	(2.38)

Table A.21 Relative to the Most Important Competencies That U.S. Business Leaders Need to Possess to Work within Intercultural Situations, Please Rank Each of the Items in Order of Importance (Intrapersonal Dimension)

	1	2	3	4	5	6	7	Relative ranking	Standard deviation
Self-awareness (including knowing one's biases)	46% (12)	23% (6)	15% (4)	4% (1)	8% (2)	4% (1)	0% (0)	2.15	(4.12)
Curiosity, learning	19% (5)	12% (3)	23% (6)	12% (3)	12% (3)	19% (5)	4% (1)	3.58	(1.72)
Flexibility & adaptability	19% (5)	19% (5)	23% (6)	23% (6)	12% (3)	0% (0)	4% (1)	3.04	(2.57)
Imagination/ creativity	0% (0)	12% (3)	4% (1)	8% (2)	19% (5)	12% (3)	46% (12)	5.54	(4.04)
Tolerate ambiguity	12% (3)	12% (3)	12% (3)	19% (5)	8% (2)	19% (5)	19% (5)	4.35	(1.27)
Patience	0% (0)	23% (6)	15% (4)	19% (5)	23% (6)	15% (4)	4% (1)	4.04	(2.57)
Mindfulness	4% (1)	0% (0)	8% (2)	15% (4)	19% (5)	31% (8)	23% (6)	5.31	(2.82)

Table A.22 Relative to the Most Important Competencies That U.S. Business Leaders Need to Possess to Work within Intercultural Situations, Please Rank Each of the Items in Order of Importance (Interpersonal Dimension)

	1	2	Relative ranking	Standard deviation
Perspective taking	62% (16)	38% (10)	1.38	(6.43)
Non-judgmental	38% (10)	62% (16)	1.62	(6.34)

What Intercultural Competencies Can U.S. Business Leaders Develop to Compete Globally?

Certain findings surfaced from the data analysis from Round 3 of this Delphi study. Three sets of leadership competencies were judged important by the study's expert panel. These sets of competencies appeared as intrapersonal, interpersonal, and cultural (social). Within each competency category, participants rank-ordered specific dimensions for importance.

Seven specific dimensions—identified in Round 1 of the study and then rated important in Round 2—in the intrapersonal competency area then appeared in order of importance. The top-ranked competency in the intrapersonal dimension judged by the panel was *self-awareness*, which received

Table A.23 Relative to the Most Important Competencies That U.S. Business Leaders Need to Possess to Work within Intercultural Situations, Please Rank Each of the Items in Order of Importance (Cultural Dimension)

	1	2	3	4	5	Relative ranking	Standard deviation
Sensitivity/appreciative of difference	27% (7)	31% (8)	23% (6)	15% (4)	4% (1)	2.38	(2.68)
Effective communication (Ability to understand another's ideas and having them understand yours)	31% (8)	27% (7)	23% (6)	15% (4)	4% (1)	2.35	(2.49)
Multilingual	12% (3)	12% (3)	15% (4)	12% (3)	50% (13)	3.77	(4.09)
Local–global perspective (Ability to pay attention to both global and local consequences of one's actions	15% (4)	12% (3)	31% (8)	19% (5)	23% (6)	3.23	(1.48)
Understanding of how leadership is conceptualized in other cultures	15% (4)	19% (5)	8% (2)	38% (10)	19% (5)	3.27	(2.68)

a relative ranking of 2.15. The second-highest ranked competency, receiving a score of 3.04, was *flexibility/adaptability*. The third-ranked competency dimension, *curiosity*, received a score of 3.58. The fourth and the fifth dimensions, *patience* and *ambiguity tolerance*, received 4.04 and 4.35, respectively. Rounding out the intrapersonal dimension ranked at sixth and seventh was *mindfulness* at 5.31 and *imagination* at 5.54.

At the culmination of Round 2, two competency areas were rated for importance and in Round 3, they were ranked in order of importance related to the interpersonal dimension. The two competencies, *perspective taking* and *nonjudgmental*, were rated 1.38 and 1.62, respectively.

On the social level, the cultural dimension, five competencies were rated and then ranked for importance. The top-ranked competency according to the panel was *effective communication* at 2.35, followed by *sensitivity/ appreciation of difference* at 2.38 and by *local–global perspective* at the third position at 3.23. The fourth and fifth positions were *understanding of how leadership is conceptualized in other cultures* at 3.27 and *multilingual* at 3.77.

How Can U.S. Business Leaders Recognize the Concept of Culture?

Relative to how U.S. business leaders can recognize the concept of culture in conducting business, the expert panel ranked *cultural immersion* as the top means with a score of 1.58. At the second spot, with a score of 2.04, was using the services of *consultants and mentors*. The third-ranked means was judged *formal training or education* with a score of 3.04, and coming in fourth was *self-education* with a score of 3.35.

How Can U.S. Business Leaders Utilize This Concept of Culture in Understanding Their Own Cultural Background and Bias?

The panel determined that there are three ways that U.S. business leaders can understand their own cultural bias. The first way of understanding was *engagement* with a ranked score of 1.69, narrowly ranked second was *recognition* with a score of 2.15, and at third position was *intentionality* with a ranked score of 2.15.

How Can U.S. Business Leaders Analyze and Evaluate Intercultural Situations?

Relative to analysis and evaluation, the 26 panelists first identified, and then in Round 3 ranked, two tools, or paradigms that U.S. business leaders can use to analyze and evaluate intercultural situations. The two tools, *use of intercultural assessments* and *use of intercultural models*, were ranked equally in terms of importance, with a score of 1.50.

How Can U.S. Business Leaders Negotiate and Make Decisions Within Intercultural Situations?

The panelists chose three paradigms through the early rounds related to negotiation and decision making: *values-based*, *context-based*, and *ambiguity-tolerant perspectives*. The *context-based perspective* garnered the top ranking with a score of 1.73; values-based was second at 2.12 and the *ambiguity-tolerant perspective* was third with a score of 2.15.

How Can U.S. Business Leaders Motivate and Lead in Intercultural Situations?

The study panelists ranked *building intercultural understanding* as the top priority related to leading and motivating with a score of 2.23. The second priority appeared as *engaging the culture and its people*, which had a score of 2.77. The third priority perceived by the panel was *integrating culture with business processes and practices*, which received a rank of 2.92. The fourth and fifth priorities were having a *self-other appreciation* and having a *global perspective* with scores of 3.12 and 3.96, respectively.

How Can U.S. Business Leaders Develop Intercultural Teams?

The study panelists determined that *selection of team members with intercultural savvy* is the top priority in developing intercultural teams, ranking it with a score of 1.81. In second position was *preparation prior to assignment* with a score of 2.42. Ranked third at 2.69 was *using culturally appropriate business models and processes. Shared or joint leadership* ranked fourth.

Appendix B
Geoleadership Resources

The following resources are provided for your continued education on the selected topics:

Culture and International Business

Books

*Book summaries from Amazon.com

Managing Cultural Differences: Global Leadership Strategies for the 21st Century (Harris, Moran, Moran, Butterworth-Heinemann, 2007)
This new edition of a business textbook bestseller has been completely updated. In particular, the book presents a fuller discussion of global business today. Also, issues of terrorism and state security as they affect culture and business are discussed substantially. The structure and content of the book remain the same, with thorough updating of the plentiful region and country descriptions, demographic data, graphs, and maps. This book differs from textbooks on International Management because it zeroes in on culture as the crucial dimension and educates students about the cultures around the world so they will be better prepared to work successfully for a multinational corporation or in a global context.

Culture's Consequences: Comparing Values, Behaviors, Institutions and Organizations Across Nations (Hofstede, Sage Publications, 2003)
The long-anticipated *Second Edition* of a true classic is thoroughly updated with an expanded coverage and scope. This excellent work explores the differences in thinking and social action that exist between members of more than 50 modern nations and will be the new benchmark for scholars and professionals for years to come. It argues that people carry "mental programs" which are developed in the family in early childhood and reinforced in school and organizations, and that these mental programs contain a component of national culture. They are most clearly expressed in the different values that predominate among people from different countries.

Exploring Culture: Exercises, Stories, and Synthetic Cultures (Hofstede and Pedersen, Intercultural Press, 2002)
Contains over 100 culture awareness exercises, dialogs, stories of incidents, and simulations that bring to life Geert Hofstede's five dimensions of culture. These dimensions are: power distance, collectivism versus individualism, femininity versus masculinity, uncertainly avoidance, and long-term versus short-term orientation.

World on Fire (Chua, Doubleday, 2002)
As global markets open, ethnic conflict worsens and democracy in developing nations turns ugly and violent. Examining the actual impact of economic globalization in every region of the world, from Africa to Asia to Russia and Latin America, Chua exposes an unexpected reality. In every one of these regions, free markets have concentrated disproportionate, often spectacular wealth in the hands of a resented ethnic minority. These "market dominant minorities"—Chinese in Southeast Asia, Croatians in the former Yugoslavia, whites in Latin America and South Africa, Indians in East Africa, Lebanese in West Africa, Jews in post-communist Russia—invariably become targets of violent hatred. Chua is not an anti-globalist. But she presciently warns that, far from making the world a better and safer place, democracy and capitalism—at least in the raw—unrestrained form in which they are currently being exported—are intensifying ethnic resentment and global violence, with potentially catastrophic results.

Journals

Intercultures Magazine
http://www.dfait-maeci.gc.ca/cfsi-icse/cil-cai/magazine/menu-en.asp
Intercultures Magazine is an electronic quarterly that explores international work from an intercultural perspective.

International Journal of Intercultural Relations
http://www.elsevier.com/wps/find/journaldescription.cws_home/535/description#description
IJIR is dedicated to advancing knowledge and understanding of theory, practice, and research in intergroup relations. The contents encompass theoretical developments, field-based evaluations of training techniques, empirical discussions of cultural similarities and differences, and critical descriptions of new training approaches. The *International Journal for Intercultural Relations* is now affiliated to The International Academy for Intercultural Research.

Journal of Intercultural Communication
http://www.immi.se/intercultural/
The goal of the journal is to promote research but also education and training in the area of intercultural communication. The journal is an

outgrowth of the activities of NIC—the Nordic Network for Intercultural Communication. The great interest shown in the activities of NIC have pointed to a need for more journals employing a peer review procedure within the area of intercultural communication. By starting this journal, we hope to encourage more research and to facilitate contacts between interested researchers as well as to provide better possibilities for reviewed publication.

Websites

*Website descriptions from individual websites

Background Notes

http://www.state.gov/r/pa/ei/bgn/

These publications include facts about the land, people, history, government, political conditions, economy, and foreign relations of independent states, some dependencies, and areas of special sovereignty. The Background Notes are updated/revised by the Office of Electronic Information and Publications of the Bureau of Public Affairs as they are received from the Department's regional bureaus and are added to the database of the U.S. Department of State website.

BusinessCulture.com

http://www.businessculture.com/

This site contains a series of reports on business customs, etiquette, cross-cultural communication, proper gifts, negotiating tactics, business culture, manners, business entertainment, and much more.

Business as an Agent of World Benefit

http://www.bawbglobalforum.org/

Businesses increasingly realize that corporate citizenship is not a peripheral activity but rather a core element of their business strategy. Global corporate citizenship is the future of business. Business leaders and scholars who attend this Forum are not people who need to be sold on the business case. Many, however, have more questions than answers. They want to learn how corporate citizenship can be leveraged strategically in their business. Therefore, the Forum will seek to (1) answer some of those questions and (2) more importantly create learning laboratories and action groups around the questions so that follow-up work after the Forum can be done to continuously answer those questions. The main reason scholars and business practitioners are coming together in this unique Forum is to combine the strengths of each sector to create a living, learning action network.

CIA World Factbook

https://www.cia.gov/library/publications/the-world-factbook/index.html

The World Factbook is an annual publication by the Central Intelligence Agency of the United States with basic almanac-style information about the various countries of the world. The Factbook gives a two- to three-page summary of the demographics, location, telecommunications capacity, government, industry, military capability, etc., of all US-recognized countries and territories in the world.

Country Reports
http://www.countryreports.org/

CountryReports.org was established in 1997 out of a love for international relations and culture. Entirely web-based, the site offers more than 26,000 pages of content covering a wide range of topics. Their statistical data and cultural information have proven to be valuable to students, parents, teachers, and researchers alike.

Culturegrams
http://www.culturegrams.com

CultureGrams are concise, reliable, up-to-date reports on more than 200 countries, each US state, and all 13 Canadian provinces and territories.

Delta Intercultural Academy
http://dialogin.com/

A knowledge community on culture and communication in international business.

Economist Country Briefings
http://www.economist.com/countries/

Country Reports analyze political and economic trends in nearly 200 countries and show you exactly how national, regional, and global events will affect your business in the short to medium term. Each report examines and explains the issues shaping the countries where you operate: the political scene, economic policy, domestic economy, sectoral trends, and foreign trade and payments. Every report also includes a two-year economic and political forecast.

Executive Planet
http://www.executiveplanet.com/

Executive Planet provides valuable tips on business etiquette, customs, and protocol for doing business worldwide. Printed guides are co-authored by experts in international business etiquette, who are available to answer questions on the discussion board.

Geert Hofstede
http://www.geert-hofstede.com/

Geert Hofstede's research gives us insights into other cultures so that we can be more effective when interacting with people in other countries. If understood and applied properly, this information should reduce your level of frustration, anxiety, and concern. But most important, Geert Hofstede will give you the "edge of understanding" which translates to more successful results.

Global Edge
http://globaledge.msu.edu/ibrd/ibrd.asp

A rich collection of thousands of resources selected based on content and usability. This section also includes the proprietary Market Potential Indicators and the Database of International Business Statistics.

International Chamber of Commerce
http://www.iccwbo.org/

ICC (International Chamber of Commerce) is the voice of world business championing the global economy as a force for economic growth, job creation, and prosperity. Because national economies are now so closely interwoven, government decisions have far stronger international repercussions than in the past. ICC is the world's only truly global business organization responds by being more assertive in expressing business views. ICC activities cover a broad spectrum, from arbitration and dispute resolution to making the case for open trade and the market economy system, business self-regulation, fighting corruption, or combating commercial crime.

Kwintessential Language and Culture Specialists
(http://www.kwintessential.co.uk/cross-cultural/dvd/global-teams.html)

In our global and inter-reliant economies intercultural communication is a "must." Business success is now more and more about understanding and nurturing strong relationships with international and multicultural colleagues, customers, and clients. *Cross-Cultural Communication* is paramount in a world full of differences. Kwintessential plays a key role in helping individuals, companies, and organizations acquire the necessary intercultural skills to succeed in the global marketplace.

International Trade Administration
http://trade.gov/index.asp

ITA's mission is to create prosperity by strengthening the competitiveness of US industry, promoting trade and investment, and ensuring fair trade and compliance with trade laws and agreements. Trade.gov provides you access to ITA's valuable information and services regarding US international trade policy.

Transparency International
http://transparency.org/about_us

Transparency International is a global network including more than 90 locally established national chapters and chapters-in-formation. These bodies fight corruption in the national arena in a number of ways. They bring together relevant players from government, civil society, business and the media to promote transparency in elections, in public administration, in procurement, and in business. TI's global network of chapters and contacts also use advocacy campaigns to lobby governments to implement anti-corruption reforms.

WorldBiz.com

http://www.worldbiz.com/index.php

Worldwide Business Reports offers a series of country-specific reports on international business practices, business customs and protocol, cross-cultural communication, negotiating, international etiquette, business entertainment, and much more. Worldwide Business Reports were developed by Worldwide Business Practices Report together with the leading experts in international business from around the world.

Consulting services

Center for Creative Leadership

http://www.ccl.org/leadership/solutions/index.aspx

CCL addresses individual leader development needs while establishing systematic, integrated leadership development practices within organizations. CCL applies a unique perspective—an unwavering focus on developing leaders and organizational leadership—to our clients' business challenges, strategies, cultures, and people. Much of CCL's custom work stems from collaborative relationships with CCL client organizations and involves initiatives that evolve over time. Clients often build on the experience and results of initial programs by engaging CCL in multi-phase, multi-year, intensive solutions.

GeoLeadership Group

http://www.geoleadership.com

Geoleadership Group provides proven *culture-specific* solutions that assess whether an organization is capable of executing its strategy and take actions to close Capability Gaps and strengthen the organization's execution and business results. Geoleadership also offers proven *Consulting Services* to develop leaders and managers from *client corporations* across the globe. The Geoleadership Group also hosts the Geoleadership Network which provides global managers and executive leaders the opportunity to meet online on a basis for sharing insights and problems. This frequent online community also offers resources for specific and leadership challenges and solutions. For more information, please contact: webmaster@geoleadership.com

International Association for Languages and Intercultural Communication

http://www3.unileon.es/grupos/ialic/

IALIC is a specialist forum for academics, practitioners, researchers, and students. Working within an interdisciplinary and critical framework, members share a unique concern for the theoretical and practical interplay of living languages and intercultural understanding.

Simulation Training Systems
http://stsintl.com/

STS designs, produces, delivers, and sells experiential training programs (simulations). For more than 34 years, thousands of companies, organizations, universities, and charities worldwide have used our award winning simulations to help them create profoundly memorable learning experiences. STS products include, Ba FA Ba Fa, the Power of Leadership, and Pumping the Colors.

Organizational Culture

Books

Culture, Leadership, and Organizations
(House, Hanges, Javidan, Dorfman, Gupta, Sage Publications, 2004)

Leadership, Culture and Organizations reports the results of a 10-year research program, the Global Leadership and Organizational Behavior Effectiveness research program (GLOBE). GLOBE is a long-term program designed to conceptualize, operationalize, test, and validate a cross-level integrated theory of the relationship between culture and societal, organizational, and leadership effectiveness. A team of 160 scholars worked together since 1994 to study societal culture, organizational culture, and attributes of effective leadership in 62 cultures. *Leadership, Culture, and Organizations* reports the findings of the first two phases of GLOBE. The book is primarily based on the results of the survey of over 17,000 middle managers in three industries: banking, food processing, and telecommunications, as well as archival measures of country economic prosperity and the physical and psychological well-being of the cultures studied.

Organizational Culture and Leadership
(Schein, Jossey-Bass, 2004)

In this third edition of his classic book, Edgar Schein shows how to transform the abstract concept of culture into a practical tool that managers and students can use to understand the dynamics of organizations and change. Organizational pioneer, Schein, updates his influential understanding of culture—what it is, how it is created, how it evolves, and how it can be changed. Focusing on today's business realities, Schein draws on a wide range of contemporary research to redefine culture, offers new information on the topic of occupational cultures, and demonstrates the crucial role leaders play in successfully applying the principles of culture to achieve organizational goals. He also tackles the complex question of how an existing culture can be changed—one of the toughest challenges of leadership. The result is a vital resource for understanding and practicing organizational effectiveness.

Journals

Academy of Management Executive
http://journals.aomonline.org/amp/

The mission of the new Academy of Management Perspectives (AMP) is to provide accessible articles about important issues concerning management and business. AMP articles are aimed at the non-specialist academic reader, not practicing managers, and rely on evidence as opposed to theory or opinion for their arguments. All articles are fundamentally based on research evidence, which can be quantitative or qualitative, but not on opinion. Articles focus on the phenomenon of business and management rather than theory; they do not necessarily have to advance the existing academic literature. Articles might include reviews of what we already know about particular topics, with an orientation specifically toward practical implications. Descriptive articles and those without a theoretical foundation, typically excluded from academic journals, might also be relevant if they advance our understanding of business and management practice.

Academy of Management Journal
http://www.aom.pace.edu/amjnew/

The mission of the *Academy of Management Journal* is to publish empirical research that tests, extends, or builds management theory and contributes to management practice. All empirical methods—including, but not limited to, qualitative, quantitative, field, laboratory, and combination methods—are welcome. To be published in AMJ, a manuscript must make strong empirical and theoretical contributions and highlight the significance of those contributions to the management field. Thus, preference is given to submissions that test, extend, or build strong theoretical frameworks while empirically examining issues with high importance for management theory and practice. AMJ is not tied to any particular discipline, level of analysis, or national context.

Academy of Management Review
http://www.aom.pace.edu/amr/

The mission of the *Academy of Management Review (AMR)* is to publish new theoretical insights that advance our understanding of management and organizations. *AMR* is receptive to a variety of perspectives, including those seeking to improve the effectiveness of, as well as those critical of, management and organizations. Submissions to AMR must extend theory in ways that permit the development of testable knowledge-based claims. To do this, researchers can develop new management and organization theory, significantly challenge or clarify existing theory, synthesize recent advances and ideas into fresh, if not entirely new theory, or initiate a search for new theory by identifying and delineating a novel theoretical problem. The contributions of *AMR* articles often are grounded in "normal science disciplines" of economics, psychology, sociology, or social psychology as well as non-traditional perspectives, such as the humanities. *AMR* publishes novel, insightful and carefully crafted conceptual work that challenges conventional wisdom concerning all aspects of organizations and their roles in society.

Academy of Management Learning and Education
http://journals.aomonline.org/amle/
   The *Academy of Management Learning & Education (AMLE)* advances the knowledge and practice of management learning and education. It does so by publishing theoretical models and reviews, qualitative and quantitative research, critique, exchanges, and retrospectives on any substantive topic that is conceived with, and draws implications for, how managers learn the educational process and context. AMLE is an interdisciplinary journal that broadly defines its constituents to include scholars, educators, program directors, deans, and other administrators at academic institutions, as well as consultants, policy makers, and practitioners in private or public organizations in which management learning and education are of central concern.

Culture and Organizations
http://www.tandf.co.uk/journals/titles/14759551.asp
   Culture and Organization features refereed articles that offer innovative insights and provoke discussion. It particularly offers papers which employ ethnographic, critical and interpretive approaches, as practised in such disciplines as communication, media, and cultural studies, which go beyond description and use data to advance theoretical reflection. The journal also presents papers which advance our conceptual understanding of organizational phenomena. Theoretically, *Culture and Organizations* bridges the arts and humanities and the social sciences, and welcomes papers which draw on the disciplinary practices and discourses of philosophy, the performing arts, literary and art criticism and historical analysis, for example, and applies them to the organizational and relevant social arenas.

Journal of Organizational Culture, Communications and Conflict
http://www.alliedacademies.org/Public/Journals/JournalDetails.aspx?jid=11
   The *Journal of Organizational Culture, Communications and Conflict (JOCCC)* is a double blind, refereed journal which publishes theoretical and empirical works in Organizational Communications, Conflict Resolution, Organizational Behavior, Human Resources Management or Leadership.

Authors of practical or educational papers may also submit them to the *JOCCC* for review. The primary objective is to expand the boundaries of the literature by supporting the exchange of ideas and insights which further the understanding of communication.

Journal of Organizational Behavior Management
http://www.obmnetwork.com/resources/JOBM/

The *Journal of Organizational Behavior Management*—the official journal of the OBM Network—belongs on the desk of every personnel, industrial, or managerial professional who truly believes that there are scientific principles to improve employee performance and wants to bring these principles out of the lab and into the workplace! The journal publishes research and review articles, case studies, discussions, and book reviews on the topics that are critical to today's organization development practitioners and human resource managers.

Journal of Occupational and Organizational Psychology
http://www.bps.org.uk/publications/journals/joop/joop_home.cfm?&redirectCount=0

This journal contains published empirical and conceptual papers which aim to increase understanding of people and organizations at work. Papers include: industrial, organizational, vocational, and personnel psychology, as well as behavioral aspects of industrial relations, ergonomics, human factors, and industrial sociology.

Journal of Organizational Behavior
http://www3.interscience.wiley.com/cgi-bin/jhome/4691

The *Journal of Organizational Behavior* aims to report and review the growing research in the industrial/organizational psychology and organizational behavior fields throughout the world. The journal will focus on research and theory in all the topics associated with occupational/organizational behavior including motivation, work performance, equal opportunities at work, job design, career processes, occupational stress, quality of work life, job satisfaction, personnel selection, training, organizational change, research methodology in occupational/organizational behavior, employment, job analysis, behavioral aspects of industrial relations, managerial behavior, organizational structure and climate, leadership and power.

Organization Studies
http://oss.sagepub.com/

Organization Studies (OS), published in collaboration with the European Group of Organization Studies (EGOS), aims to promote the understanding of organizations, organizing, and the organized in and between societies, through the publication of double-blind peer-reviewed, top quality theoretical and empirical research. *OS* is a multidisciplinary journal, rooted in the social sciences, inspired by diversity, comparative in its outlook, and open to paradigmatic plurality. Although a journal of European roots, it is currently global in its reach, which is reflected in its highly international and geographically dispersed editorial structure and decentralized mode of operation.

Leadership

Books

High Performance Leadership: HRD Strategies for the New Work Culture
(Harris, HRD Press, 1994)

The author explores the importance of effective leadership by supervisors, managers, and executives. His premise is that leaders have a human resource development responsibility and must engender personal growth among employees to increase the productivity, service, and quality of their organizations' human capital.

Leadership: Enhancing the Lessons of Experience
(Hughes, Ginnett, and Curphy, McGraw-Hill/Irvin, 2006)

Leadership: Enhancing the Lessons of Experience, 4e, was written for the general student to serve as a stand-alone introduction to the subject of leadership. The text consists of 13 chapters and a final section on Basic and Advanced Leadership Skills. Authors Hughes, Ginnett, and Curphy have drawn upon three different types of literature: empirical studies; interesting anecdotes, stories and findings; and leadership skills to create a text that is personally relevant, interesting, and scholarly. The authors' unique quest for a careful balancing act of leadership materials will help students apply theory and research to their real-life experiences.

Leadership in a Diverse and Multicultural Environment: Developing Awareness, Knowledge, and Skills
(Pedersen and Connerley, Sage Publications, 2005)

Leading in a Multicultural Environment is suitable for a variety of management courses, well grounded in solid research, but written in an easy to comprehend style that: provides a culturally centered leadership perspective allowing organizational leaders the opportunity to attend to the influence of culture; helps the reader find examples of how multicultural awareness can make their leadership task easier; and promotes an organizational culture that is more satisfying to both individuals and their leaders by embracing and celebrating differences.

29 Leadership Secrets from Jack Welch
(Slater, McGraw-Hill, 2003)

This is the first concise book of essential Welch-isms, abridged from the bestselling "Get Better or Get Beaten." Jack Welch built a career out of fighting waste. "29 Leadership Secrets from Jack Welch" follows in Welch's footsteps, boiling the legendary CEO's leadership successes down to 29 strategies that made GE the world's most competitive company-and Welch the world's most successful and admired CEO. This all-in-one Welch reference updates material from Robert Slater's bestselling "Get Better or Get Beaten", and is today's ultimate fast-paced, no-nonsense handbook on the ways of Jack Welch. It taps into the World of Welch's courage, innovation, and leadership success by examining simple leadership secrets that include: Managing less is managing better; Make quality the job of every employee; and Have global brains and vision.

Business Leadership
(Kouzes, Jossey-Bass, 2003)

Business Leadership contains the best thinking from the biggest names in leadership on a wide range of subjects including ethics, dealing with change, vision setting, the heroic journey, the practices of leadership, and the work of leadership. With an introduction by James M. Kouzes—coauthor of the million-copy best-seller *The Leadership Challenge*—the author list of this invaluable resource reads like the who's who of business leadership. This extraordinary collection features chapters from Joseph L. Badaracco Jr., Warren Bennis, Kenneth H. Blanchard, Lee G. Bolman, Larry Bossidy, Richard Boyatzis, Susan Mitchell Bridges, William Bridges, Marcus Buckingham, Ram Charan, Joanne B. Ciulla, Donald O. Clifton, James C. Collins, Terrence E. Deal, Max De Pree, Stephen Drotter, Peter F. Drucker, Daniel Goleman, Robert K. Greenleaf, Victoria A. Guthrie, Gary Hamel, David A. Heenan, Ronald A. Heifetz, Paul Hersey, Frances Hesselbein, John P. Kotter, James M. Kouzes, Donald L. Laurie, Morgan W. McCall Jr., Annie McKee, Burt Nanus, James Noel, James O'Toole, Jerry I. Porras, Barry Z. Posner, Robert E. Quinn, Edgar H. Schein, Gretchen M. Spreitzer, Noel M. Tichy, Ellen Van Velsor, and Margaret J. Wheatley.

Countries of the World and Their Leaders Yearbook (Thomson Gale, 2008)
www.gale.com/eBooks

Covering nearly 200 countries, this yearbook is filled with background notes reports from the US Department of State. Entries typically cover geography, history, government, and political conditions, economy, and state of relations with the United States. Also highlights detailed travel notes, including passport applications, visa requirements, regulations and duties, medical information, and national holidays, as well as international adoption regulations and annually updated comprehensive terrorism reports. This title is now available in eBook format through *Gale Virtual Reference Library*. *Gale Virtual Reference Library* is taking eBooks to the next level by delivering a wealth of reference content in a database format. This valuable new product allows libraries of any size—based on user's needs and usage patterns—to develop collections at their own pace and within their own budget.

Journals and magazines

International Journal of Cross-Cultural Management
http://ccm.sagepub.com/current.dtl

The *International Journal of Cross-Cultural Management* provides a specialized academic medium and main reference for the encouragement and dissemination of research on cross-cultural aspects of management, work, and organization.

Journal of Leadership Studies
http://www3.interscience.wiley.com/cgi-bin/jabout/114054396/Product Information.html?CRETRY=1&SRETRY=0

The mission of the *Journal of Leadership Studies* is to publish leadership research and theoretical contributions that bridge the gap between scholarship and practice and that exemplify critical inquiry into contemporary organizational issues and paradigms. The journal promotes interdisciplinary and interorganizational theory, fostering dialog that transcends industry-specific contexts and that explores leadership's role in improving organizational practices and human life. Published material in the journal will include research-based and theoretical papers that explicitly address leadership on various social, cultural, and organizational contexts.

Leadership
http://www.sagepub.co.uk/journalsProdDesc.nav?prodId=Journal201698
http://lea.sagepub.com/

Leadership is an international, peer-reviewed journal designed to provide an ongoing forum for academic researchers to exchange information, insights and knowledge based on both theoretical development and empirical research on leadership. It will publish original, high quality articles that contribute to the advancement of the study of leadership. The journal will be global in orientation and focus.

Leadership & Organization Development Journal
http://www.emeraldinsight.com/0143-7739.htm

The *Leadership & Organization Development Journal* explores behavioral and managerial issues relating to all aspects of leadership, and of individual and organization development, from a global perspective.

MIT Sloan Management Review
http://sloanreview.mit.edu/smr/leadership/

Can leadership be learned? The world's leading management thinkers have shown that those who study the art and science of leadership, and apply what they learn, do indeed become better leaders. Improve your leadership skills with a compilation of MIT Sloan Management Review's best articles from an extensive leadership archive.

Strategy and Leadership
http://www.emeraldinsight.com/info/journals/sl/sl.jsp

Each issue of *Strategy and Leadership* brings you authoritative comment from the world's leading experts in corporate strategy and strategic management. Its thoughtful, in-depth analysis looks at strategies, tools and techniques from an objective position and gives advice on where you should be going and what to avoid on your journey.

Websites

Academy of Management
http://www.aomonline.org/

The Academy of Management (the Academy; AOM) is a leading professional association for scholars dedicated to creating and disseminating knowledge about management and organizations. Founded in 1936 by two professors, the Academy of Management is the oldest and largest scholarly management association in the world.

American Society for Training & Development
http://astd.org/

ASTD (American Society for Training & Development)is the world's largest association dedicated to workplace learning and performance professionals. ASTD's members come from more than 100 countries and connect locally in almost 140 US chapters and 25 Global Networks. Members work in thousands of organizations of all sizes, in government, as independent consultants, and suppliers. ASTD started in 1944 when the organization held its first annual conference. ASTD has widened the profession's focus to link learning and performance to individual and organizational results, and is a sought-after voice on critical public policy issues.

Center for Creative Leadership
http://www.ccl.org/leadership/index.aspx

Center for Creative Leadership (CCL) is the leading non-profit institution dedicated exclusively to leadership. CCL integrates cutting-edge research with innovative training, coaching, assessment, and publishing to create proven impact for leaders and organizations around the world.

Center for Leadership and Change Management
http://leadership.wharton.upenn.edu/welcome/index.shtml

The intensifying competition for resources and demand for high performance are pressing firms to become more flexible, more results-focused, and more fast-acting. Companies are finding that such initiatives require able leadership, and the challenge for organizations and business schools alike is to help build effective leadership both in the next generation of managers and throughout the organization today. The mission of Wharton's Center for Leadership and Change Management is consequently to (1) stimulate basic research and practical application in the area of leadership and change; (2) foster an understanding of how to develop organizational leadership; and (3) support the leadership development agendas of the Wharton School and University of Pennsylvania.

Center for Servant Leadership
http://www.greenleaf.org/

The Greenleaf Center is an international, not-for-profit which seeks to help people understand the principles and practices of servant–leadership; to nurture colleagues and institutions by providing a focal point and opportunities to share thoughts and ideas on servant–leadership; to produce and publish new resources by others on servant–leadership; and to connect servant–leaders in a network of learning.

Global Leadership and Ethics
http://www.scu.edu/ethics/

The Markkula Center for Applied Ethics at Santa Clara University is one of the pre-eminent centers for research and dialog on ethical issues in critical areas of American life. The center works with faculty, staff, students, community leaders, and the public to address ethical issues more effectively in teaching, research, and action. The center's focus areas are business, health care and biotechnology, character education, government, global leadership, technology, and emerging issues in ethics. Articles, cases, briefings, and dialog in all fields of applied ethics are available on this site.

International Leadership Organization
http://www.ila-net.org/

The International Leadership Association (ILA) is the global network for all those who practice, study, and teach leadership. The ILA promotes a deeper understanding of leadership knowledge and practices for the greater good of individuals and communities worldwide.

Society for Intercultural Education, Training and Research
http://sietar.org/

SIETAR (Society for Intercultural Education, Training and Research) was founded in the United States in 1974 by a few dedicated individuals to draw together professionals engaged in various forms of intercultural learning and engagement, research and training. Originally called SITAR, the name was later changed to encompass education and the Society became SIETAR. Its goal was to provide a forum for exchanging ideas about training, theory, and research, and to learn from each other as well as to provide a place where interculturalists could strengthen their bonds with each other. They envisioned an exchange between people in different disciplines and professional activity that would strengthen the theoretical development and practice of intercultural communication. The Society rapidly grew beyond the borders of the United States attracting people from around the world who had similar concerns and interests and was named SIETAR International in 1982.

Academic Programs and Degrees

Antioch University
http://www.phd.antioch.edu/Pages/APhDWeb_Program/index

Antioch University's distinctive intensive-residency, cohort-based, geographically dispersed Ph.D. in Leadership and Change Program opened its doors in January 2002. The program is designed for working professionals who are committed to studying and leading change that improves the well-being of those they serve. The program incorporates a challenging interdisciplinary core curriculum that focuses on leading change coupled with faculty-mentored, self-paced individualized learning. The program's goal is to educate professionals from a wide range of fields and in a variety of positions to be reflective practitioners, principled leaders, and engaged scholars. The program currently has 115 inspiring and aspiring doctoral students who come from education, and the non-profit and for-profit sectors.

Capella University (Online)—Masters in Leadership
http://www.capella.edu/schools_programs/business_technology/masters/leadership.aspx

The master's degree with a leadership specialization offers an in-depth study of leading theories and best practices of leadership in today's complex global business environment. This specialization will prepare you to provide effective leadership in change management and at team and organizational levels. This online specialization is valuable for both new managers and seasoned executives in business, government, military, and non-profit organizations.

Georgetown University (Washington, DC, USA)—Masters in Leadership
http://msb.georgetown.edu/prospective/graduate/eml/

The Master's program analyzes leadership as a set of skills on three different levels of analysis: individual, interpersonal, and institutional. On the individual level of analysis, the focus is on personal leadership action plan development, critical thinking, and problem-solving skills. On the interpersonal level of analysis, the focus is on negotiation and influence skills. On the institutional level, the focus is on organizational and institution-building skills. These skill sets shape the curriculum of the Executive Master's in Leadership.

McDonough Center for Leadership and Business at Marietta College
http://mcdonough.marietta.edu/

McDonough is one of the most dynamic leadership centers in American higher education today. Our many programs, events and initiatives are designed to help students gain a deeper understanding of leadership, practice their leadership skills, and in the process grow as a leader; hence, our key themes—knowledge, action, and growth. The McDonough Center was established in 1986 through a generous $5.5 million gift from Alma McDonough and the McDonough Foundation in honor of the successful industrialist, Bernard P. McDonough (1903–1985). Through his many businesses, Mr. McDonough established a strong record of leadership and civic engagement. Today, the Center celebrates this legacy by helping generations of college students study and practice leadership, while developing their own vision of their contribution to the campus community, the local community, and even beyond.

Northeastern University School of Professional Studies
http://www.spcs.northeastern.edu/ms_leader/overview/

The traditional concept that leadership skill resides solely with a small handful of top executives has given way to contemporary collaborative models, where influence and decision-making authority are distributed throughout an organization. Today's workforce continues to diversify, and the tasks to be accomplished have become more complex. Northeastern's Master of Science in Leadership is designed to assist today's leaders and prepare emerging leaders in meeting these challenges. This program incorporates an action-learning approach that is intended to leverage the interdisciplinary backgrounds of participants to help build leadership competencies. Students in this program may apply any successfully completed SPCS graduate certificate to the overall program requirements and focus their studies on one of more than 20 areas of specialization.

Regent University
School of Global Leadership and Entrepreneurship
http://www.regent.edu/acad/global/

The School of Global Leadership and Entrepreneurship supports the advancement and dissemination of leadership research through its various online journals including the *International Journal of Leadership Studies*, *Journal of Practical Consulting*, *Journal of Biblical Perspectives in Leadership*, *Leadership Advance Online* and the *Regent Global Business Review*. The school also provides a unique platform for preparing leaders of today's enterprises with an emphasis on innovation, excellence, and values-based leadership principles. Graduate degree programs include the Master of Arts in Organizational Leadership, Master of Arts in Strategic

Foresight, Ph.D. in Organizational Leadership, Doctor of Strategic Leadership and the Master of Business Administration.

Regis University
Leadership Development Program
http://www.regis.edu/regis.asp?sctn=sr&p1=well&p2=lead

Since 1877, Regis University, a Colorado college, has been meeting the needs of students through innovative classroom-based or online programs centered in academic excellence. Regis University's commitment to the individual student is fostered through the heritage of our values-centered Jesuit education. Today more than 16,000 students call Regis University home. This Colorado-based college is comprised of three Schools—Regis College, the Rueckert-Hartman School for Health Professions, and the School for Professional Studies—and offers classes in a campus-based setting as well as online programs in a range of studies.

Thunderbird, American School of International Management
http://www.thunderbird.edu

Thunderbird's top-ranked MBA in Global Management is taught through a global lens, by Ph.D.'s from around the globe, to students from 50 different countries. The MBA-IM from Thunderbird—ranked #1 in Global Business year after year by *US News and World Report*—prepares you to take on the world.

University of British Columbia
http://www.ubc.ca/

The University of British Columbia is preparing to celebrate the centenary of the granting of its charter in 1908. In the past 100 years, UBC has grown into one of Canada's finest universities. Measured by any criterion—the intellectual caliber of its students, the quality of faculty teaching and research, the professionalism of its staff—UBC is an outstanding university, and plays a vital role in the cultural, social, and economic development of the region and Canada. In recent years UBC has seen dramatic changes. Enrollment has grown from 31,000 students in 1995–1996 to more than 45,000 today, with a corresponding expansion of UBC Vancouver's academic core, including new buildings dedicated to science and engineering, forestry, the health sciences, and the library. UBC has much to offer and underlying this wealth of offerings is their belief in several vital principles that in one way or another inform all aspects of learning and research at UBC: active engagement in civil society, the pursuit of sustainability in its social as well as its environmental forms, and commitment to global citizenship.

University of Minnesota
http://www.hhh.umn.edu/centers/cil/index.html

Center for Integrative Leadership: The Center for Integrative Leadership at the University of Minnesota is a cooperative undertaking of the Humphrey Institute of Public Affairs and the Carlson School of Management. It is dedicated to examining and advancing a new vision for cross-sector leadership so that it can be understood, taught, and deployed to help solve some of the most challenging issues of our time. To accomplish this, the center convenes thought leaders and practitioners from diverse disciplines to consider and propose new models and methods for dealing with such complex issues as world hunger, global warming, health care, free trade, disease prevention, equitable distribution of wealth, and international terrorism.

University of Richmond

Jepson School of Leadership Studies

http://jepson.richman.edu/

The Jepson School of Leadership Studies was founded to fill a significant void in higher education. All too often, institutions focus on imparting career skills, or talk about preparing future leaders, without developing a true understanding of leadership—the knowledge, ability, and conviction to drive change and positively impact the world. In bridging this critical gap, Jepson established itself as a pioneer in the field of leadership studies and a respected center for scholarship and education. A Jepson education investigates leadership as a process and a relationship among people. It is based in a rigorous academic curriculum and plentiful hands-on opportunities. It is directed toward intellectual development, professional and personal service, responsibility, and civic engagement. It is informed by the human condition and grounded in global understanding.

University of South Carolina

International MBA Program

http://mooreschool.sc.edu/moore/imba/prospective/

The International Master of Business Administration (International MBA) program at the Moore School of Business is proud to offer a cutting-edge graduate international business education that prepares students for today's global environment. Unlike many schools where international implications often are discussed only at the end of the semester, global issues and experience permeate the business classes in the International MBA program. Students are exposed to international business issues from the first day of class.

Appendix C
Power of Leadership
Training Tool

Below is a review of a recommend leadership training tool, *The Power of Leadership*, by Simulation Training Systems:

The Power of Leadership is a business simulation that helps participants understand the challenges they face when they are given power to accomplish a task. Even though power is a taboo topic for many people, it is what sets the leader apart from others in the organization. Studies show that effective leaders understand and have a need to have power. More important they know how to use it to accomplish their goals. However, using power effectively is not an easy task. There are many challenges that, if not met, will create disastrous results for individuals and the organization.

This simulation teaches leaders how to use power to resolve conflicts, communicate effectively, solve problems, and manage positive change in the corporate culture. It helps participants understand why the decisions, behavior, and attitudes of leaders are often misperceived by their followers. It helps participants who are power averse understand what they must do to improve their effectiveness and helps those who are power prone understand what discipline they must employ to use their power effectively.

The Power of Leadership brings reality and context into the teaching of leadership. It is easy to tell a group that a leader should do this or do that. What is hard is leading under the types of pressure every leader faces. For example, how do you lead people when individuals or groups are jealously competing for scarce resources? How can leaders deal with followers who are resisting changes designed to make the organization more effective? How can a leader cope with individuals or groups are forming unhealthy coalitions based on self-interest and emotion without considering the needs of the organization? The Power of Leadership highlights these issues as well as situations in which followers do not trust the leaders to use their power to make the best decisions for them or the organization and are unable to see the organization as a system.

The Power of Leadership is ideal for new managers and supervisors, as well as technical people who have been promoted into leadership positions without managerial training. Managers who have lost their motivation to be effective leaders

(Continued)

and any person who needs to know how to resolve conflicts, develop higher order thinking skills, develop one's personal leadership style, understand which behavior and attitudes toward power make him or her more or less effective can be helped by *The Power of Leadership*. The product can also be useful in dealing with participants who are power averse and need to understand what behavior changes are necessary to use power effectively. If there are participants who are power prone and need to understand the pitfalls of using power and, more important, how to use power effectively, *The Power of Leadership* will be extremely valuable. Finally, participants who need to understand that leadership requires much more than just being nice to people or working hard to achieve personal goals will find *The Power of Leadership* to be an integral tool.

The Power of Leadership works by showcasing a simulation that is conducted in rounds and is governed by two types of rules: inherited rules and rules of nature. At the end of each round, participants have a chance to change the inherited rules if they desire. The rules of nature are the permanent rules that govern the simulation and cannot be changed by the group.

To accomplish the tasks in the simulation, participants must earn individual and group points by trading. Based on the points they earned during trading, they are divided into three groups: Top Performers, Midders, and Greemers. Participants meet in groups and make plans for the rule-making session and then conduct the rule-making session. To accomplish these tasks successfully they must use power effectively, develop trust under difficult circumstances, resolve conflicts between individuals and groups, negotiate for resources, communicate, and establish roles and goals. Participants must also use higher order thinking to develop strategies and analyze the organization as a system, use super-ordinate goals to reorder priorities, establish a vision for the organization, and understand how power affects the perception of a leader's message.

What happens as a result of these activities? Conflict develops between the Midders, Greemers, and the Top Performers over scarce resources and the rules governing the simulation. Midders and Greemers discover that the Top Performers have the power to make the rules for the simulation. The Midders and Greemers must decide how or whether they are going to participate Top Performers realize that they can't progress without the cooperation of the Midders and the Greemers, so they often try to give the power away, that is, escape the responsibility of being leaders, or become patronizing and tell the Midders and Greemers, "We're going to give this to you. Aren't you happy?" Eventually all of the participants understand, "We're all in this together." They then identify the things they cannot change and try to change the things they can. They are then challenged to change the organization in ways that create a healthy productive work culture.

As a result of the simulation, managers and employees learn how to use super-ordinate goals to overcome conflict among groups. Participants also come to realize how to communicate a vision of the organization that will make it possible for all groups to work effectively together toward a common goal and how the power prone can develop a participative style of management. Another lesson learned is how those who are power averse can use power effectively. How leaders can use higher order thinking skills to analyze and fix their organization is highlighted and shows the impact that a top-down management style has

(Continued)

on the morale, effectiveness, and productivity of everyone in the organization. Participants will understand the way groups in the organization respond to and view the "same" situation differently and the importance of developing the special communication skills required of a leader.

The Power of Leadership further shows the importance of knowing how to effectively deal with the complaints and concerns of the people they are leading and how the structure and practices of the organization affect the employees both positively and negatively. In essence, participants see how important it is for a leader to constantly be evaluating the practices of the work culture and seeking ways to improve them and the importance of viewing the leaders' behavior through the eyes of the various stakeholders. In the end, participants will learn the skills they need to develop to become a more effective leader.

Logistically, a three winged board is used to simulate an office environment. It is a board that sits on a six-foot round table. The three wings create three separate areas similar to cubicle walls. The Top Performers sit behind one set of barriers, the Midders behind another, and the Greemers behind another. They cannot communicate with one another except by written messages passed through a hole in the barrier. The board is meant to represent the barriers to communication that exist in an organization. The simulation takes three to four hours to run, including the debrief. *The Power of Leadership* is designed for groups of 10 to 25 participants.

Gregory D. Metzler, President of Group Performance Associates, LLC, highly praises *The Power of Leadership* in leadership development training. His firm uses the product in the context of much broader initiative regarding leadership with many components and a number of different tools. He believes that *The Power of Leadership* is a very important component. The leaders that experience this simulation come away with several new perspectives, including seeing that leadership involves more than orchestrating tasks. There is a shift in their focus of authority and responsibility and a realization that many of the limitations they face are self-imposed or in fact do not exist. There is a greater ability to align objectives, goals, and activities with the outcomes desired and a more integrated understanding of what "win-win" really means in behavioral terms. In addition, participants feel a greater sensitivity to their sources and uses of power and how quickly they may resort to cruder, coercive forms as well as a valuable assessment of their relative reliance and ability to employ their instrumental, interpersonal, imagined, and systems skills. *The Power of Leaderships* displays an enhanced understanding of trust in behavioral terms, a practical understanding of creating value for multiple stakeholders, and more integrated understanding that other people may view things differently.

The Power of Leadership is a product that is very robust and extremely versatile. Metzler has used it as a component in leadership development, value proposition development, and strategic alliance development. His firm has used the product primarily (but not exclusively) with international groups. Some groups have been intact teams and others not. Metzler has also used it with multi-client groups, including one interesting group of 27 people representing 22 different nationalities. Since Metzler's work with a great deal of behavioral focus, he finds it very useful as a means to highlight individual differences. This of course applies to multicultural groups in the same way.

(Continued)

There is definitely a need for Metzler's client firms to understand leadership from an intercultural perspective, but with some caveats. He believes that intercultural understanding is a "two-edged sword." On the one hand, it is vitally important to understand not only the different perspectives but also where they originated. On the other, he finds that it often leads to dangerous generalizations and stereotypes. Some experts culture as "different solutions to common problems." Metzler finds this definition to be very useful because it addresses culture as a broad problem-solving and learning methodology.

Metzler also does a lot of work in Norway—population approximately 4.5 million. Even within this small country, there are no less than five distinct sub-cultures. Metzler is also doing work within Asia and of course, there are huge differences between Japanese, Korean and Chinese cultures that are often lumped into the "Asian culture." He believes that it is dangerous to begin to broadly apply the conclusions and do not consider cultural shift. Sushi is no longer just Japanese.

Metzler is also working with one firm of nearly 23,000 employees, working in 393 offices in 70 countries around the globe. He is working toward building an organizational culture that is unique to this organization and the value that it creates and that harmonizes and is built upon the best qualities and characteristics of all representative cultures. As enterprise shrinks the globe and possibly represents the best hope for global harmony and a higher global standard of living, Metzler believes that the organizational cultures become vitally important. To have this occur it is vitally important to understand the geo-political-socio-economic cultural differences.

For more information on The Power of Leadership, please visit: stsintl.com/business/pol.html

About the Author

Dr. E.S. Wibbeke currently heads the Geoleadership Group. Dr. Wibbeke spent 20 years in business leadership roles for Fortune 500 firms with 10 years spent living and working in Silicon Valley.

In addition, as an international consultant and professor of leadership and management, Dr. Wibbeke teaches in the business departments in several leading international universities, including the University of Liverpool.

After earning a Bachelor of Arts degree in European Studies from Loyola Marmount University, Dr. Wibbeke completed an MBA from the American Graduate School of International Management-Thunderbird, and went on to earn a Doctorate in Management and Organizational Leadership. Dr. Wibbeke was the founder of the Web of Culture, the leading source of intercultural information on the Internet. Previously, Dr. Wibbeke was the long-time program coordinator for the Los Angeles World Affairs Council.

Fluent in English and Spanish and with a working knowledge of German, Italian, Japanese, Dr. Wibbeke has studied in Costa Rica, Nicaragua, and Spain, lastly having studied at the Universidad de Salamanca. Dr. Wibbeke holds dual citizenship from the United States and the Republic of Ireland.

Dr. Wibbeke resides in Southern California. To contact Dr. Wibbeke by e-mail, please use the following address: docwibbeke@gmail.com.

Notes

1. Treverton, G. F. and Bikson, T. K. (2003). *New Challenges for International Leadership: Positioning the United States for the 21st Century*. Santa Monica, CA: Rand.
2. Michaels, E., Handfield-Jones, H. and Axelrod, B. (2001). *The War for Talent*. Boston: Harvard Business School Press; Suutari, V. (2002). Global leader development: An emerging research agenda. *Career Development International*, 7(4); Treverton and Bikson (2003).
3. The International Labor Organization (2004).
4. Treverton and Bikson (2003).
5. Harris, Moran and Moran (2007). *Managing Cultural Differences: Global Leadership Strategies for the 21st Century*. Elsevier; Michaels, Handfield-Jones and Axelrod (2001).
6. Sheridan (2005). *Intercultural Competencies for US Business Leaders in the New Millennium*. Unpublished dissertation.
7. Anonymous.
8. Brown, P. and Levinson, S. C. (1987). *Politeness: Some Universals in Language Use*. Cambridge University Press, Cambridge, UK.
9. Gregersen, H. B. Morrison, A. J. and Black, J. S. (1998). Developing leaders for the global frontier. *Sloan Management Review*, 40, 21–32.
10. Loubier (2006). Unpublished manuscript.
11. Michaels, Handfield-Jones and Axelrod (2001).
12. Sheridan (2005).
13. Suutari (2002); Treverton and Bikson (2003).
14. Dohn, A. (2000). Gauging the labor force effects of retiring baby-boomers. *Monthly Labor Review On-line*, July, 123–130; Perrin, T. (2001). The Towers Perrin talent report 2001: New realities in today's workforce; Scott, G. (2003). *Learning Principals: Leadership*

Capability and Learning Research in the New South Wales Department of Education and Training. Sydney, Australia: University of Technology Sydney Quality Development Unit.

15. US News and World Report, America's Best Graduate Schools (2005).
16. Sheridan (2005).
17. Barner, R. (2000). *Executive Resource Management: Building and Retaining an Exceptional Leadership Team.* Palo Alto, CA: Davies-Black Publishing.
18. Perrin (2001).
19. Gregersen, Morrison and Black (1998).
20. Jack Welch Interview (2005).
21. Loubier (2006).
22. Loubier, 2006.
23. Gregersen, Morrison and Black (1998).
24. Sheridan (2005).
25. Offermann, L. R. and Phau, L. U. (2002). Culturally intelligent leadership for a diverse world. In Riggio, R. E., Murphy, S. E. and Pirozzolo, J. (eds), *Multiple Intelligences and Leadership.* Erlbaum Mahwah, NJ pp. 187–214.
26. Earley, P. C. and Ang, S. (2003). *Cultural Intelligence: Individual Interactions Across Cultures.* Stanford University Press, Stanford, CA.
27. Pedersen, P. and Connerley, M. (2005). *Leadership in a Diverse and Multicultural Environment: Developing Awareness, Knowledge, and Skills.* Thousand Oaks, CA: Sage.
28. Hofstede, G. (2001). *Culture's Consequences.* Thousand Oaks, CA: Sage.
29. Hall, E. T. (1976). *Beyond Culture.* Garden City, NY: Anchor.
30. United Nations Human Development Report Office (2004).
31. Sheridan (2005).
32. bbc.co.uk, January 25, Google move "Black day for China".
33. http://news.bbc.co.uk/2/hi/technology/4645596.stm.
34. Sheridan (2005).
35. Loubier (2006).
36. Ibid.
37. Ibid.
38. Ibid.
39. Newsweek (2005).
40. Loubier (2006).
41. Hoovers (2006). Retrieved from Internet.
42. *Harvard Business Review* (2003); In search of intercultural leaders, August issue.
43. *The Economist*, September 16, 2006.
44. Center for Creative Leadership, Managerial Effectiveness in a Global Context.

45. Loubier (2006).
46. Loubier (2006); Sheridan (2005).
47. Sheridan (2005).
48. Javidan, M. and House, R. J. (2001). Cultural acumen for the global manager: Lessons from Project GLOBE. *Organizational Dynamics*, (29) 289–305; *CCL study* (2006); Sheridan (2005).
49. WorldLingo (2006).
50. Ibid.
51. Ibid.
52. Interview with Dr. Magdy Hussein (2006).
53. Sheridan (2005).
54. Ibid.
55. Ibid.
56. Ibid.
57. Ibid.
58. Ibid.
59. Ibid.
60. Ibid.
61. Ibid.
62. Javidan and House (2001).
63. Loubier (2006).
64. Pedersen and Connerley (2005).
65. Hofstede (2001, p. 4).
66. Harris, Moran and Moran (2006).
67. Hall (1976).
68. Kroeber, A. and Kluckholn, C. (1985). *Culture: A Critical Review of Concepts and Definitions* New York: Random House.
69. Javidan and House (2001); Schein, E. H. (1992). *Organizational Culture and Leadership* 2nd ed. San Francisco: Jossey-Bass; Schwartz, S. H. (1992). Universals in the content and structure of values: Theoretical advances and empirical tests in 20 countries. In Zanna, M. (ed.), *Advances in Experimental Social Psychology* (Vol. 25, pp. 1–65). New York: Academic Press; Spencer-Oatey, H. (2000). *Culturally Speaking: Managing Rapport Through Talk Across Cultures*. London: Continuum; Trompenaars, F. and Hampden-Turner, C. (1998). *Riding the Waves of Culture*. New York: McGraw-Hill.
70. Samovar, L. A. and Porter, R. E. (eds). (2001). *Communication Between Cultures* 4th edn. Belmont, CA: Wadsworth; House, R. J., Wright, N. S. and Aditya, R. N. (1997). Cross-cultural research on organizational leadership: A critical analysis and a proposed theory. In Earley, P. C. and Erez, M. (eds), *New Perspectives on International Industrial/Organizational Psychology* San Francisco: New Lexington, pp. 535–625.

71. Triandis, H. C. (1993). *The Contingency Model in Cross-Cultural Perspective*. San Diego, CA: Academic Press.

72. Schein (1992).

73. Pedersen and Connerley (2005).

74. Hall (1976); Hampden-Turner and Trompenaars (2000); Hofstede (1980); Kluckhohn and Strodtbeck (1961).

75. Hofstede (2004).

76. Ibid.

77. Hofstede (2004, p. 71).

78. Hofstede (2004).

79. Ibid.

80. Ibid.

81. Pedersen and Connerley (2005).

82. Hofstede, 2004 p. 113.

83. Hofstede (2004).

84. Sheridan (2005).

85. Hofstede and Hofstede (2004).

86. Stuart, R. B. (2004). Twelve practical suggestions for achieving multi-cultural competence. *Professional Psychology: Research and Practice*, (35), 3–9.

87. Pedersen and Connerley (2005).

88. Sheridan (2005).

89. House *et al.* (1997).

90. Berry, J. W., Poortinga, Y. H., Segall, M. H. and Dasen, P. R. (2002). *Cross-Cultural Psychology: Research and Applications*. Cambridge, UK: Cambridge University Press.

91. Hofstede, G. and Hofstede, G. J. (2004). *Cultures and Organizations: Software of the Mind* 2nd edn. New York: McGraw-Hill.

92. Yukl, G. (2002). *Leadership in Organizations* 5th edn. Upper Saddle River, NJ: Prentice Hall.

93. Harris *et al.* (2004).

94. Sheridan (2005).

95. Ibid.

96. Ibid.

97. Loubier (2006).

98. Kohs, S. and Irle, K. (1920). Prophesying army promotion. *Journal of Applied Psychology*, 4, 73–87; Bernard. L. (1926). *An Introduction to Social Psychology*. New York: Holt; Kilbourne, C. (1935). The elements of leadership. *Journal of Coast Artillary*, 78, 437–439; Levinson, H. (1972). *Organizational Diagnosis*. Cambridge, MA: Harvard University Press; Kets de Vries, M. (1993), Alexithymia in organizational life: the organization man revisited. In Hirschhorn, L. and Barnett, C. K. (eds), *The Pychodynamics of Organizations*,

Philadelphia, PA: Temple University Press, pp. 203–18; McGregor, D. (1957). *The Human Side of the Enterprise*. New York: McGraw-Hill; Blake, R. and Mouton, J. (1964). *The Managerial Grid*. Houston, TX: Gulf Publishing; Hersey, P. and Blanchard, K. (1996). Great ideas revisited: Life-cycle theory of leadership. *Training & Development*, 50(1), 42–47.

99. Barker (2002); Grint (1997); Ensari and Murphy (2003); Offerman and Phan (2002); Tierney (1998); Jones M. O. (1988); Smircich, L. and Morgan, G. (1982). Leadership: The management of meaning. *Journal of Applied Behavioral Studies*, 18, 257–273.

100. Ellis, B. (2001). *Scientific Essentialism*. England: Cambridge Studies in Philosophy.

101. Hemphill, J. K. (1949). The leader and his group. *Journal of Educational Research*, 28, 225–229.

102. Likert, R. (1961). *New Patterns of Management*. New York: MacGraw-Hill.

103. Blake, R. R. and Mouton, J. S. (1964). *The Managerial Grid*. Houston, TX: Gulf.

104. Fiedler, F. E. (1967). *A Theory of Leadership Effectiveness*. New York: McGraw-Hill.

105. French, J. and Raven, B. H. (1959). The bases of social power. In Cartwright, D. (ed.), *Studies of Social Power*. Ann Arbor, MI: Institute of Social Research.

106. Burns, J. M. (1978). *Leadership*. New York: Harper & Row.

107. Ibid.

108. Ibid.

109. Bensimon, E., Neumann, A. and Birnbaum, R. (1989). *Making Sense of Administrative Leadership: The "L" Word In Higher Education*. Washington DC: George Washington University Press.

110. Fuchs, S. (2001). *Against Essentialism: A Theory of Culture*. Cambridge, MA: Harvard University Press; Jones, M. O. (1996). *Studying Organizational Symbolism*. Newbury Park, CA: Sage.

111. Astin, H. and Leland, C. (1991). *Women of Influence, Women of Vision*. San Francisco: Jossey-Bass; Ayman, R. (1993). Leadership perception: The role of gender and culture. In Chemers, M. and Ayman, R. (eds), *Leadership Theory and Research: Perspectives and Directions*, San Diego: Academic Press, pp. 137–166; Bensimon, E. (1989). A feminist reinterpretation of president's definitions of Leadership. *Peabody Journal of Education*; Rhodes, K. (2001). *The Servant Leader: Does Gender Make a Difference?* www.eresusltants. com/powerofservantleadership.html.

112. Antonakis, J., Avolio, B. and Sivasubramaniam, N. (2003). Context and leadership: An examination of the nine-factor full-range leadership

theory using the multifactor leadership questionnaire. *The Leadership Quarterly*, 14(3), 261–295.

113. Bolman, L. G. and Deal, T. E. (1995). *Leading with Soul*. San Francisco: Jossey-Bass; Dawson, S. (1992). *Analyzing Organizations* 2nd edn. London: Sage; Kezar, A. (2002). Reconstructing static images of leadership: An application of positionality theory. *Journal of Leadership Studies*, 8, 94–109; Osborn, R. N., Hunt, J. G. and Jauch, L. R. (2002). Toward a contextual theory of leadership. *Leadership Quarterly*, 13, 797–837; Tierney, W. (1988). *The Web of Leadership*. Greenwich, CT: JAI Press; Calas, M. and Smircich, L. (1991). Voicing seduction to silence leadership. *Organization Studies*, 12, 567–602.

114. Ashcroft, B., Griffiths G. and Tiffin, H. (1995). General introduction. In Ashcroft, B., Griffiths, G. and Tiffin, H. (eds), *The Post-Colonial Studies Reader*. New York: Routledge, pp. 1–4.

115. Calas and Smircich (1991).

116. Grint, K. (1997). *Leadership: Classical, Contemporary, and Critical Approaches*. New York: Oxford University Press; Pearce, C. L. and Conger, J. A. (2003). *Shared Leadership: Reframing the Hows and Whys of Leadership*. Thousand Oaks: Sage; Weick, K. E. and Roberts, K. H. (1993). Collective mind in organizations: Heedful interrelating on flight decks. *Administrative Science Quarterly*, 38(3), 357–381; Gronn, P. (2002). Distributed leadership as a unit of analysis. *Leadership Quarterly*, 13, pp. 423–451.

117. Bensimon, Neumann and Birnbaum (1989).

118. Bolman, L. G. and Deal, T. E. (1984). *Modern Approaches to Understanding and Managing Organizations*. San Francisco: Jossey-Bass Publishers.

119. McCormick, M. (2001). Self-efficacy and leadership effectiveness: Applying social cognitive theory to leadership. *Journal of Leadership Studies*, (8).

120. Astin, H. and Carol Leland (1991). *Women of Influence, Women of Vision*. San Francisco: Jossey-Bass; Cantor, D. and Bernay, T. (1992). *Women in Power*. New York: Houghton Mifflin; Ferguson, K. (1984). *The Feminist Case Against Bureaucracy*. Philadelphia: Temple University Press; Helgesen, S. (1990). *Women's Way of Leading*. New York: Doubleday; Kezar, S. (2002). Reconstructing static images of leadership an application of positionality theory. *Journal of Leadership Studies*, 8(3), 94 Academic One; Rosener, J. (1990). Ways women lead. *Harvard Business Review*, 119–125; Statham, A. (1987). The gender model revisited: Differences in the management styles of men and women. *Sex Roles*, 16(7/8), 409–428.

121. Ayman, R. (1993). Leadership perception: The role of gender and culture. In Chemers, M. and Ayman, R. (eds), *Leadership Theory and Research: Perspectives and Directions*. San Diego: Academic Press, pp. 137–166; Morrison, A. (1991). *The New Leaders: Guidelines on Leadership Diversity in America*. San Francisco: Jossey-Bass; Tierney, W. (1993). *Building Communities of Difference: Higher Education in the 21st Century*. Granby, MA: Bergin and Garvey.

122. Astin and Leland (1991); Bensimon and Neumann (1993).

123. Astin and Leland (1991); Cantor and Bernay (1993); Ferguson (1984); Helegesen (1990); Rosener (1990); Statham (1987).

124. Astin and Leland (1991); Cantor and Bernay (1993); Helegesen (1990).

125. Ayman (1993); Morrison (1991); Tierney (1993).

126. Dickson, M. W., Den Hartog, D. N. and Mitchelson, J. (2003). Research on leadership in a cross-cultural context: Making progress, and raising new questions. *Leadership Quarterly*, 14(6), 729–768; Dorfman, P. W. (2004). International and cross-cultural leadership. In Punnett, B. J. & Shenkar, O. (eds), *Handbook for International Management Research* 2nd edn. Ann Arbor: University of Michigan Press, pp. 265–355; House, R. J., Wright, N. S. and Aditya, R. N. (1997). Cross-cultural research on organizational leadership: A critical analysis and a proposed theory. In Earley, P. C. and Erez, M. (eds), *New Perspectives on International Industrial/Organizational Psychology*. San Francisco: New Lexington, pp. 535–625.

127. Dickson, Den Hartog and Mitchelson (2003).

128. Ayman (1993); Cox, Jr., T. (1993). *Cultural Diversity in Organizations*. San Francisco: Berrett-Koehler; Ensari, N. and Murphy, S. E. (2003). Cross-cultural variations in leadership perceptions and attribution of charisma to the leader. *Organizational Behavior and Human Decision Processes*, 92(1–2), 52–66.

129. Chong, L. M. A. and Thomas, D. C. (1997). Leadership perceptions in cross-cultural context: Pakeha and Pacific Islanders in New Zealand. *Leadership Quarterly*. 8(3), 275–293; Ensari and Murphy (2003); Hofstede (1991); Offerman, L. R. and P. S. Hellman (1997). Culture's consequences for leadership behavior: National values in action. *Journal of Cross-Cultural Psychology*, 28(3), 342–351; Offerman and Phan (2002). Culturally intelligent leadership for a diverse world. In Sternberg, R. (ed.), *Multiple Intelligences and Leadership*. New York: Basic Books, pp. 187–210.

130. Parry, O. (1997). Schooling is fooling: Why do Jamaican boys underachieve in school? *Gender and Education*, 9(2), 223–31; Pettigrew, A. (1997). What is a processual analysis? *Scandinavian Journal of*

Management, 13(4), 337–348; Pettigrew, A., Woodman, R. and Cameron, K. (2001). Study of organizational change and development: Challenges for future research. *Academy of Management Journal*, 44(4), 697–713.

131. Osborn, R., Hunt, J. and Jauch, L. (2002). Toward a contextual theory of leadership. *The Leadership Quarterly*, 13(6), 797–837.

132. Chaffee, E. and Tierney, W. (1988). *Collegiate Cultures and Leadership Strategies*. New York: Ace-Oryx Press; Pettigrew (1997).

133. Jones, M. O. (1998). *Inside Organizations*. Sage Publications.

134. Chaffey and Tierney (1988).

135. Dawson (1994).

136. Hazy, J. K. (2004). A Leadership and Capabilities Framework for Organizational Change: Simulating the Emergence of Leadership as an Organizational Meta-Capability, unpublished dissertation, Washington, DC: The George Washington University; Lichtenstein, B., Uhl-Bien, M., Marion, R., Seers, A., Orton, J. D. and Schreiber, C. (2006). Complexity Leadership Theory: An Interactive Perspective on Leading in Complex Adaptive Systems.

137. Javidan and House (2001).

138. Bass, B. M. (1990). *Bass & Stogdill's Handbook of Leadership: Theory, Research, & Managerial Applications* 3rd edn. New York: The Free Press; Javidan & House (2001); Sheridan (2005).

139. Javidan and House (2001).

140. Triandis (1993).

141. Dorfman (2004).

142. Sanchez, J., Spector, P. and Cooper, C. (2000). Adapting to a boundaryless world: A developmental expatriate model. *Academy of Management Executive*, 14(2), 96–106.

143. Moro Bueno, C. and Tubbs, S. L. (2004). Testing a global leadership competencies (GLC) model. *The Business Review*, Cambridge, 1(2), 11–15.

144. Chin, C., Gu, J. and Tubbs, S. (2001). Developing global leadership competencies. *Journal of Leadership Studies*, 7(3), 20–31.

145. Mendenhall, M. E. (1999). On the need for paradigmatic integration in international human resource management. *Management International Review*, 39(2), 1–23.

146. Rosen, R. and Digh, P. (2001). Developing globally literate leaders. *Training and Development*, 55(5), 70–81.

147. Ibid.

148. Karim, A. (2003). A developmental progression model for intercultural consciousness: A leadership imperative. *Journal of Education for Business*, 79, 34–40; Adler, N. J. (2002). *International Dimensions*

of Organizational Behavior 4th edn. Cincinnati, OH: South-Western College Publishing.

149. Goleman, D., Boyatzis, R. and McKee, A. (2002). *Primal Leadership: Realizing the Power of Emotional Intelligence.* Boston: Harvard Business School Press; McCall, Jr., M. W. and Hollenbeck, G. P. (2002). *Developing Global Executives.* Boston: Harvard Business School.

150. Kouzes, J. M. and Posner, B. Z. (2002). *The Leadership Challenge* 3rd edn. San Francisco: Jossey-Bass.

151. Moro Bueno and Tubbs (2004).

152. Sue, D. W., Arredondo, P. and McDavis, R. J. (1992). Multicultural counseling competencies and standards: A call to the profession. *Journal of Counseling and Development*, 70, 477–486.

153. Pedersen, P. and Connerley, M. (2005). *Leadership in a Diverse and Multicultural Environment: Developing Awareness, Knowledge, and Skills.* Thousand Oaks, CA: Sage.

154. Ibid.

155. Sue *et al.* (1992).

156. Sheridan (2005).

157. Simons, G. and Berardo, K. (2004). What's hot and what's not? Targeting needs and leads in intercultural interventions. Paper presented at the SIETAR USA Conference, Bloomington, IN.

158. Hofstede and Hofstede (2004); Sue *et al.* (1992); Sheridan (2005).

159. McNamara, C. (2002). Overview of Leadership in Organizations. Retrieved August 19, 2002, from Retrieved August 19, 2001, from UOP Online Library Research web site: http://www.uophx.edu.

160. Dawson (2003); Sheridan (2005).

161. Ibid.

162. Ibid.

163. Javidan and House (2001).

164. Ibid., pp. 242–253.

165. Freeman (1984). *Strategic Management: A Stakeholder Approach.* Boston, Pittman/Ballinger.

166. Ibid.

167. Post, J. E., Preston, L. E. and Sach, S. (2002). Managing the extended enterprise: The new stakeholder view. *California Management Review*, 45, 5–28.

168. Smith, H. J. (2003). The shareholders versus stakeholders debate. *MIT Sloan Management Review* 44(4), 85–91; Jones, T. M. and Wicks, A. C. (1999). The current state of stakeholder theory research. *Academy of Management Review*, 24, 206–222.

169. Hill, C. W. L. and Jones, T. M. (1992). Stakeholder-agency theory. *Journal of Management Studies*, 29(2), 131–154.

170. Friedman, A. L. and Miles, S. (2002). Developing stakeholder theory. *Journal of Management Studies*, 39(1), 1–22.
171. Kluckhohn, F. and Strodtbeck, F. K. (1961). *Variations in Value Orientation*. Evanston, IL: Row, Petersen.
172. House *et al.* (1999).
173. Sue *et al.* (1992).
174. Shafritz, J. M. and Ott, J. S. (2001). *Classics of Organization Theory* 5th edn. San Antonio, TX: Harcourt College.
175. Sheridan (2005).
176. Sheridan (2005).
177. Kouzes and Posner (2002).
178. Moro-Bueno and Tubbs (2003).
179. Javidan and House (2001).
180. Sheridan (2005).
181. Adler (2002).
182. Moro Bueno and Tubbs (2003).
183. Simons and Berardo (2004).
184. Checkland, P. and Scholes, J. (1999). *Soft Systems Methodology in Action*. New York: Wiley.
185. Pedersen and Connerley (2004).
186. Goleman (1995).
187. Spitzberg, B. H. (2000).A model of intercultural communication competence. In Samovar, L. and Porter, R. (eds), *Intercultural Communication: A Reader* 9th edn. Belmont, CA: Wadsworth, pp. 375–387.
188. Nishizaka, A. (1995). *The Interactive Constitution of Interculturality: How to be Japanese with Words*. The Netherlands: Klugar Academics.
189. Sheridan (2005).
190. Sanchez *et al.* (2000).
191. Paige (1993).
192. Hampden-Turner and Trompenaars (2000).
193. Gudykunst, W. B. (1994). *Bridging Differences: Effective Intergroup Communication* 2nd edn. London: Sage.
194. Pedersen and Connerley (2005).
195. Daniel Goleman (1995).
196. Taylor, S. (2006). *Toward a Theory of Leader Self-awareness*. Case Western Reserve University.
197. Sheridan (2005).
198. Bennis, W. (2003). *On Becoming a Leader*. (Revised). Perseus: NY.
199. Leslie, J. B. Dalton, M., Ernst, C. and Deal, J. (2002). *Managerial Effectiveness in a Global Context*. Center for Creative Leadership.
200. O'Reilly, C. and Pfeffer, J. (2000). *Hidden Power*. Harvard: Harvard Business School Press.

201. Barkema, H. G., Bell, J. H., and Pennings, M. (1996). Foreign entry, cultural barriers, and learning. *Siniiegic MKIIII. Journal*, 17, 151–166; Kogut, B. and Singh, H. (1988). The effect of national culture on the choice of entry mode. *Journal of International Business Studies*, 19, 411–432; Li, J. T. and Guisinger, S. (1992). The globalization of service multinationals in the triad regions: Japan, Western Europe and North America. *Journal of International Business Studies*, 23, 675–696.

202. Hofstede (2001).

203. Ibid.

204. Barley, S. R. and Tolbert, P. (1997). Institutionalization and structuration: Studying the links between action and institution. *Organization Studies*, 18, 93–117.

205. Hofstede (2001).

206. Dowling, P. and Schuler, R. (1994). *International Dimensions of Human Resource Management* 2nd edn. Belmont, CA: Wadsworth; Kirkman, B. L. and Shapiro, D. L. (1997). The impact of cultural values on employee resistance to teams. *Academy of Mgmt. Review*, 22, 730–757; Stohl, C. and Cheney, G. (2001). Participatory processes/paradoxical practices. *Management Communication Quarterly*, 14, 349–407.

207. Tegar, A. (1980). *Too Much Invested to Quit*. New York: Pergamon Press; Zaltman, G., Duncan, R. and Holbok, J. (1973). *Innovations and Organizations*. New York: John Wiley & Sons.

208. The Aga Khan, Spirit & Life: Masterpieces of Islamic Art from the Aga Khan Museum Collection (2007).

209. *Oxford Dictionary* (2004).

210. *Encarta Dictionary* (North America, 2007).

211. Argyris, C. and Schön, D. (1996). *Organizational Learning II: Theory, Method and Practice*. Reading, Mass: Addison Wesley.

212. Shafritz and Ott (2001).

213. Grouzet, Kasser, Ahuvia, Dols, Kim, Lau, Ryan, Saunders, Schmuck and Sheldon (2005). The structure of goal contents across 15 cultures. *Journal of Personality and Social Psychology*, 89(5), 800–816.

214. Gundling, E. (2003). Working GlobeSmart: 12 People Skills for Doing Business Across Borders. Palo Alto, CA: Davies-Black, p. 331.

215. Linstone, H. A. and Turoff, M. (2002). *The Delphi Method: Techniques and Applications*. Retrieved December 1, 2004, from http://www.is.njit.edu/pubs/delphibook/.

216. Dajani, J. S., Sincoff, M. Z. and Talley, W. K. (1979). Stability and agreement criteria for the termination of Delphi studies. *Technological Forecasting and Social Change*, 13, 83–90.

217. Turoff, M. and Hiltz, S. R. (1996). *Computer Based Delphi Process*. Retrieved December 1, 2004, from http://eies.njit.edu/~turoff/Papers/delphi3.html#Introduction.

218. Delbecq, A. L., Van de Ven, A. H. and Gustafson, D. H. (1975). *Group Techniques for Program Planning: A Guide to Nominal Group and Delphi Processes*. Glenview, IL: Scott, Foresman.

219. McCoy, R. (2001). Computer competencies for the 21st century information systems educator. *Information Technology, Learning, and Performance Journal*, 19, 21–35.

220. Thach, E. C. and Murphy, K. L. (1995). Competencies for distance education professionals. *Educational Technology Research and Development*, 43, 57–79.

221. Satterlee, B. (1999). The acquisition of key executive skills and attitudes required for international business in the third millennium, ERIC.

Index